Inspired by Nature

DAVID TRAPNELL

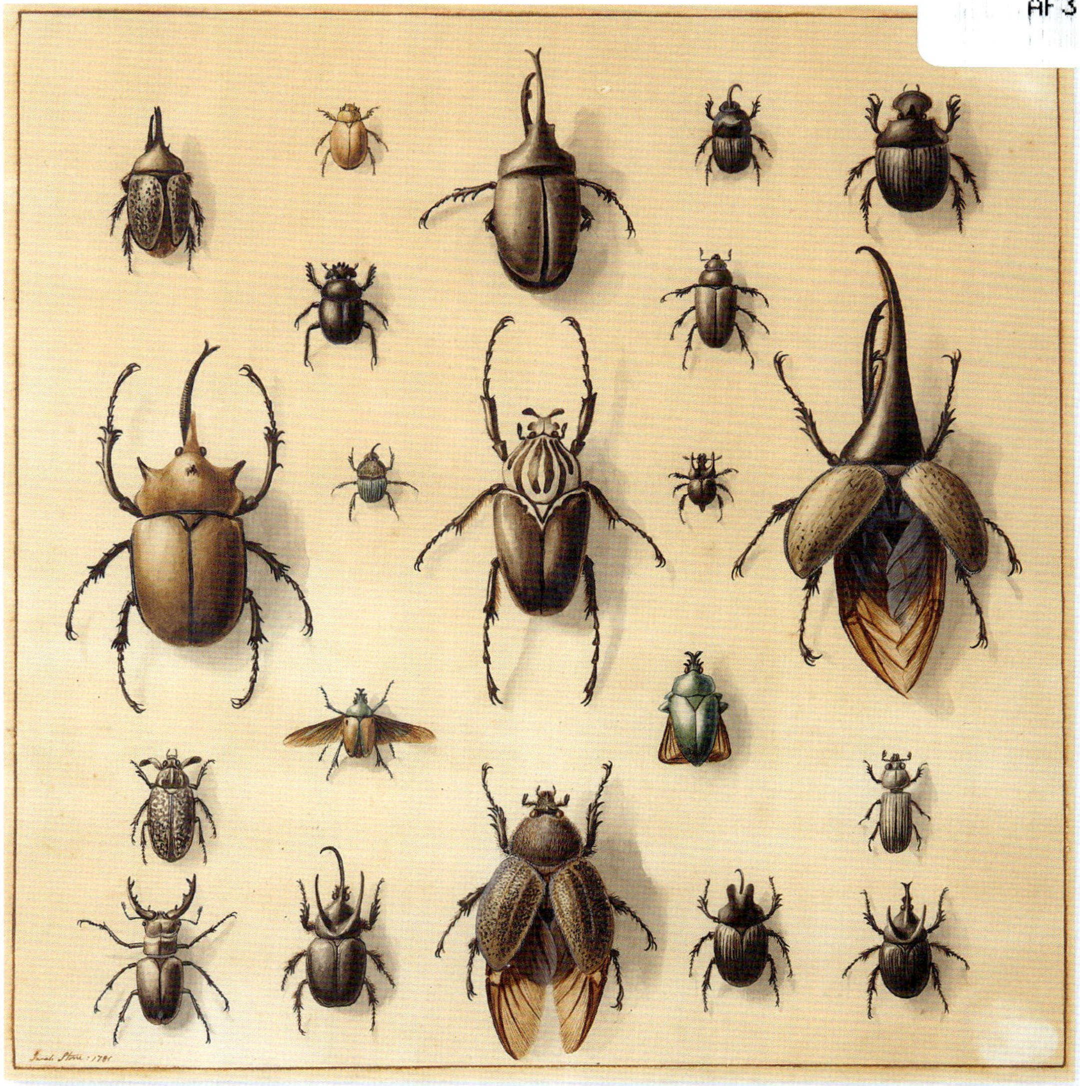

*Sarah Stone (1760 –1844), UK. **Beetles**. Watercolour on paper, 45cm x 43.5cm. Signed and dated 1781.
Later known as Sarah Smith, she was a natural history illustrator (as here) and painter.*

Published in Great Britain in 2018 by Mascot Media, Norfolk.

Mascot Media Ltd, Granary Barn, Mill Road, Sutton, Norfolk NR12 9RZ.

Tel: 01692 582811

Email: mascot_media@btinternet.com   www.mascotmedia.co.uk

© Mascot Media

A CIP catalogue record for this book is available from the British Library.

ISBN: 978-1-9998457-2-8

All the works in this book are held in the permanent collection of Nature in Art. We are very grateful to those artists who have given permission for their work to be reproduced in this book. In spite of exhaustive searches, we have been unable to find the copyright owners of the works of some artists. For the few whose permission we have been unable to obtain, we gratefully acknowledge their work.

Design and layout by Alan Marshall.
Edited by Alan Marshall and Marion Scott Marshall.

Printed by Swallowtail Print, Drayton Industrial Park, Taverham Road, Drayton, Norwich, Norfolk NR8 6RL.
Email: contact@swallowtailprint.co.uk   www.swallowtailprint.co.uk

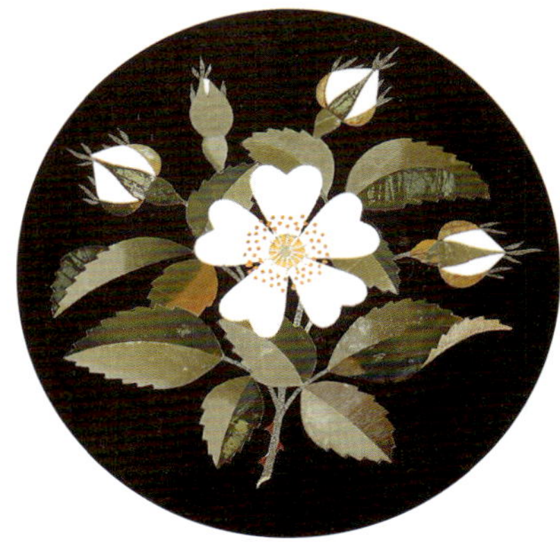

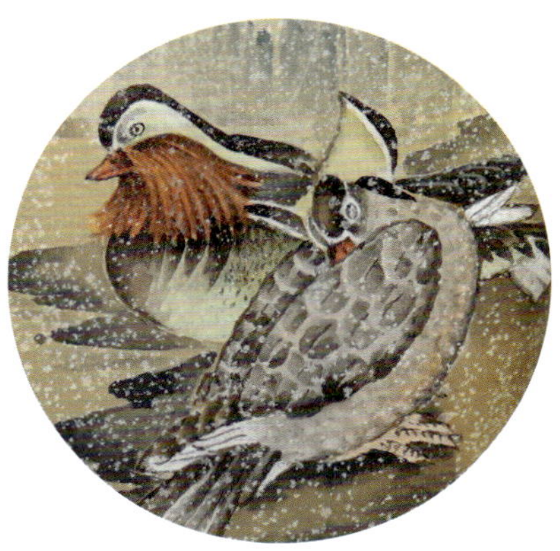

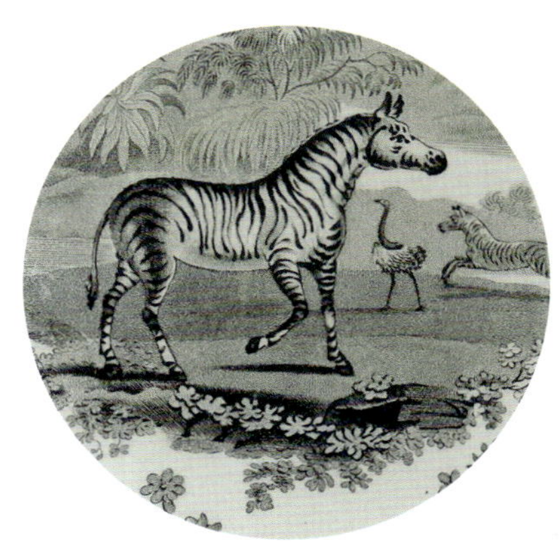

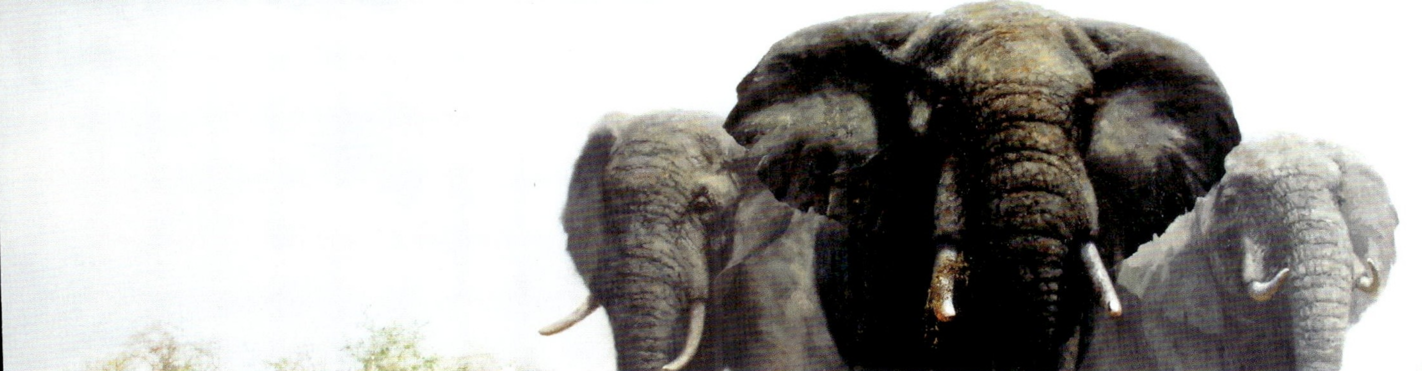

Museums today provide opportunities for inspiration, learning and, perhaps most importantly, discovery. Nature in Art appears to have plugged a gap in the public collections, for the first time, by focusing exclusively on fine examples of art inspired by nature.

Man has always been a creative being. As early as 25,000BC the subjects of his first paintings were animals. Small wonder that some would say that the heritage of art inspired by nature is richer and deeper rooted than any other. Today, boosted by the growth globally of a sense of public and individual responsibility for conservation of the environment and our heritage in nature, there is a new awareness of the value of top-quality examples of works of nature-inspired art from around the world.

With such a broad subject and international base, it is inevitable that Nature in Art, and probably this book, will include the unexpected as well as wonderful examples of the more familiar. That is deliberate! The joy of discovery, of receiving surprises and making new connections is part of having a fulfilled life.

This is not a temporary catalogue, but a timeless celebration of excellence and a glimpse of items added to Nature in Art's permanent collection that people will be able to enjoy for years to come. Personally selected by the museum's founder, they are a fraction of the individual building blocks of a collection that is constantly growing.

These diverse examples of skilful endeavour, and the many others in the collection, can resonate with every generation. With Nature in Art's help, their creative voices will speak for centuries to come and will be louder than ever in this increasingly virtual world where our natural environment is under ever-growing threat.

Simon H Trapnell
Director, Nature in Art

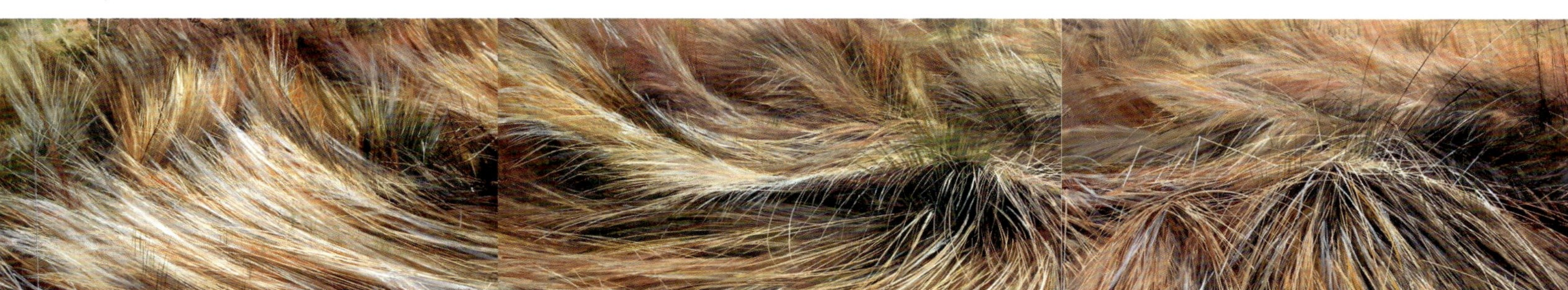

PAINTINGS

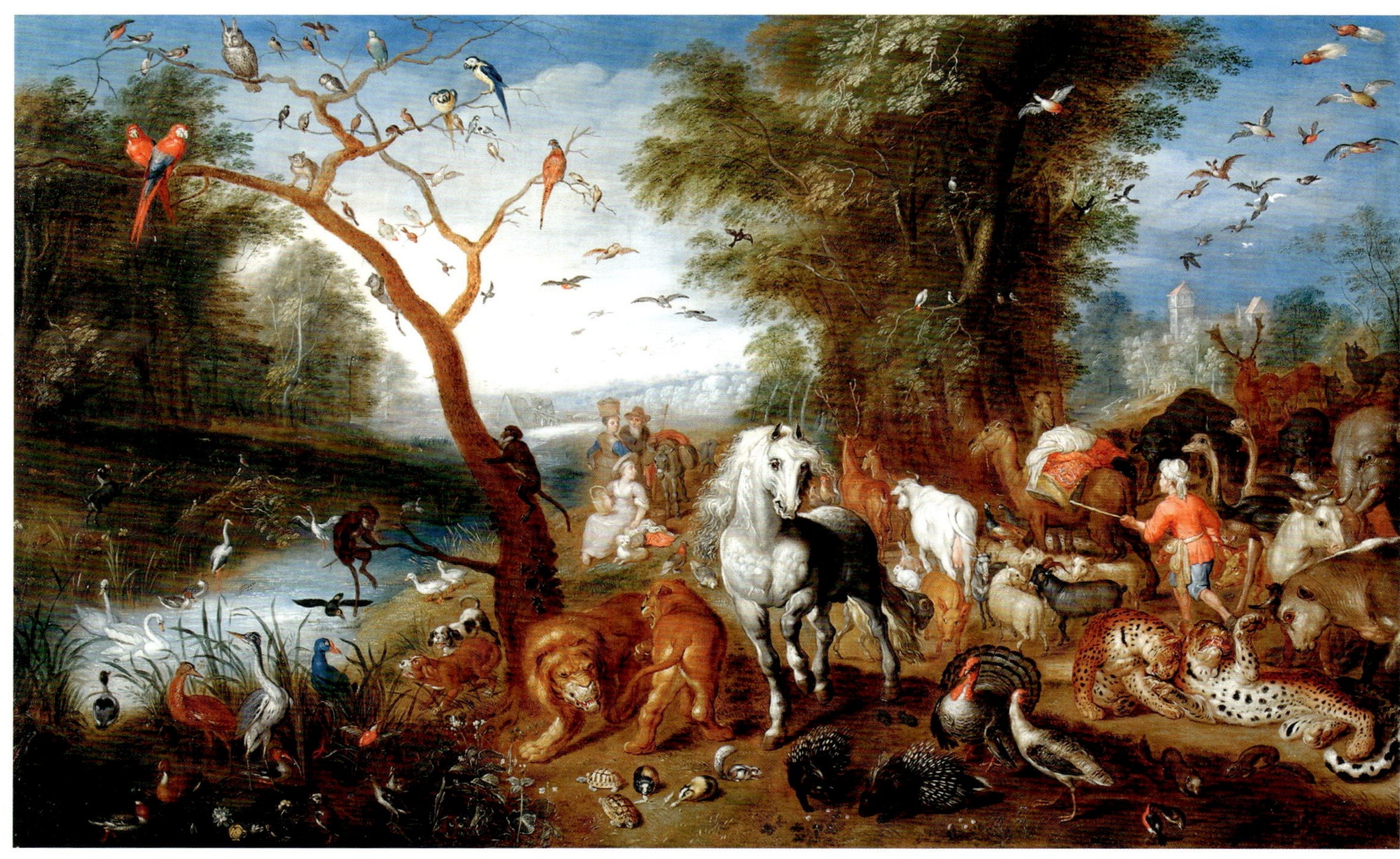

Above: Attributed to Jan van Kessel the Younger (1654-1708), The Netherlands.
Noah Entering the Ark. *Oil on oak panel, 55.5cm x 88.9cm.*
Not signed or dated. Bought with the assistance of the Victoria & Albert Museum (V&A) Purchase Grant Fund and The Art Fund.

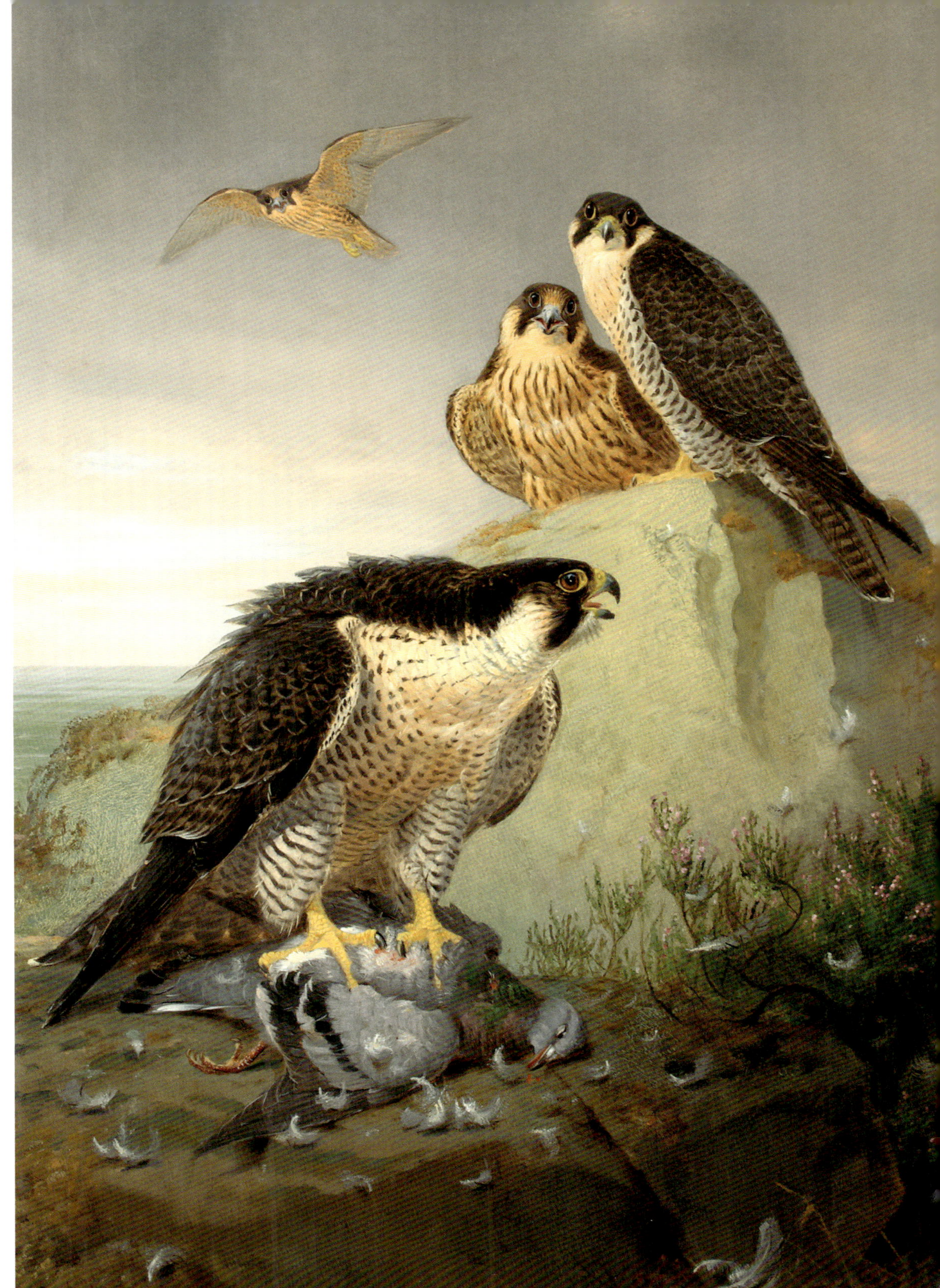

*Right: Joseph Wolf (1820-1899), UK. **Peregrines**. Oil on canvas, 88cm x 62cm. Signed and dated 1866. Born in Germany, he worked in the UK – in London and later in the Highlands of Scotland.*

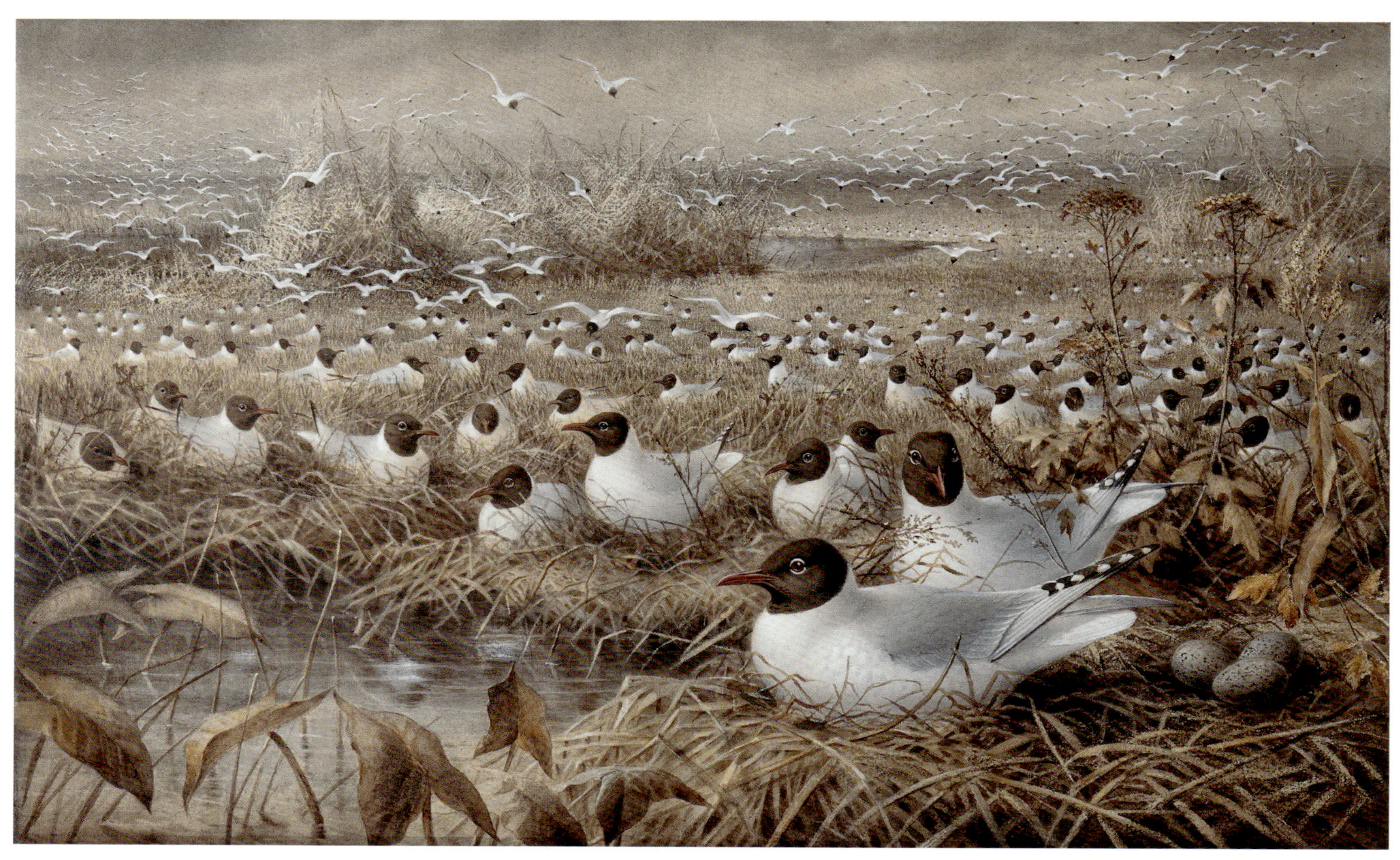

*John Gerrard Keulemans (1842-1912), The Netherlands; worked in the UK. **Black-headed Gull Colony**.*
Watercolour and gouache on paper, 59.5cm x 95.8cm. Not signed or dated (c.1880s).
This was one of his few commissioned (large) works. He was known for his small works.
More than 5,400 of his illustrations were published in books and academic journals.

David M. Reid-Henry
(1919-1977), UK.
Golden Eagle.
Oil on canvas, 70cm x 57cm.
Signed. Although painted
100 years after Wolf's
'Peregrines' on page 5, the
style is similarly formal.

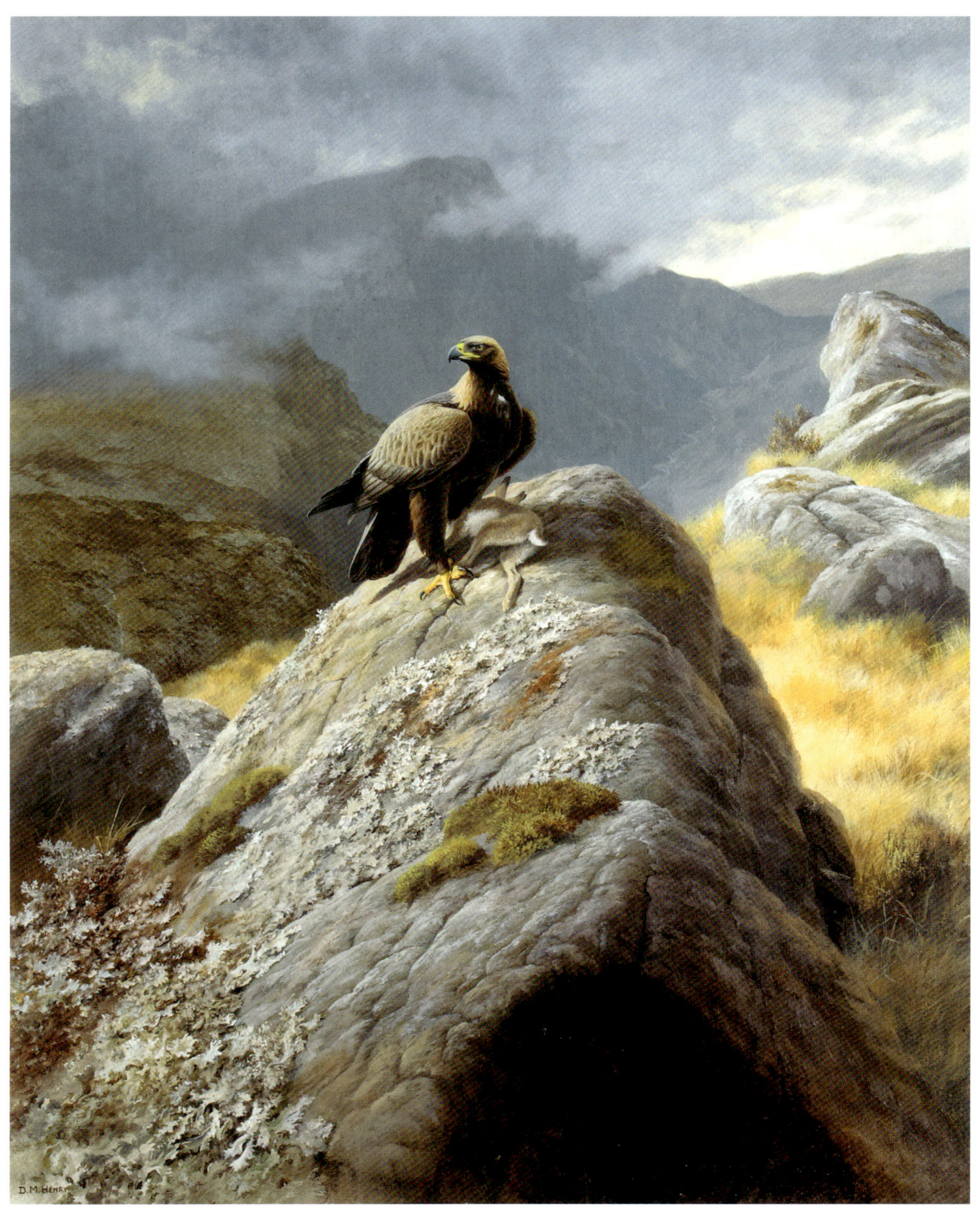

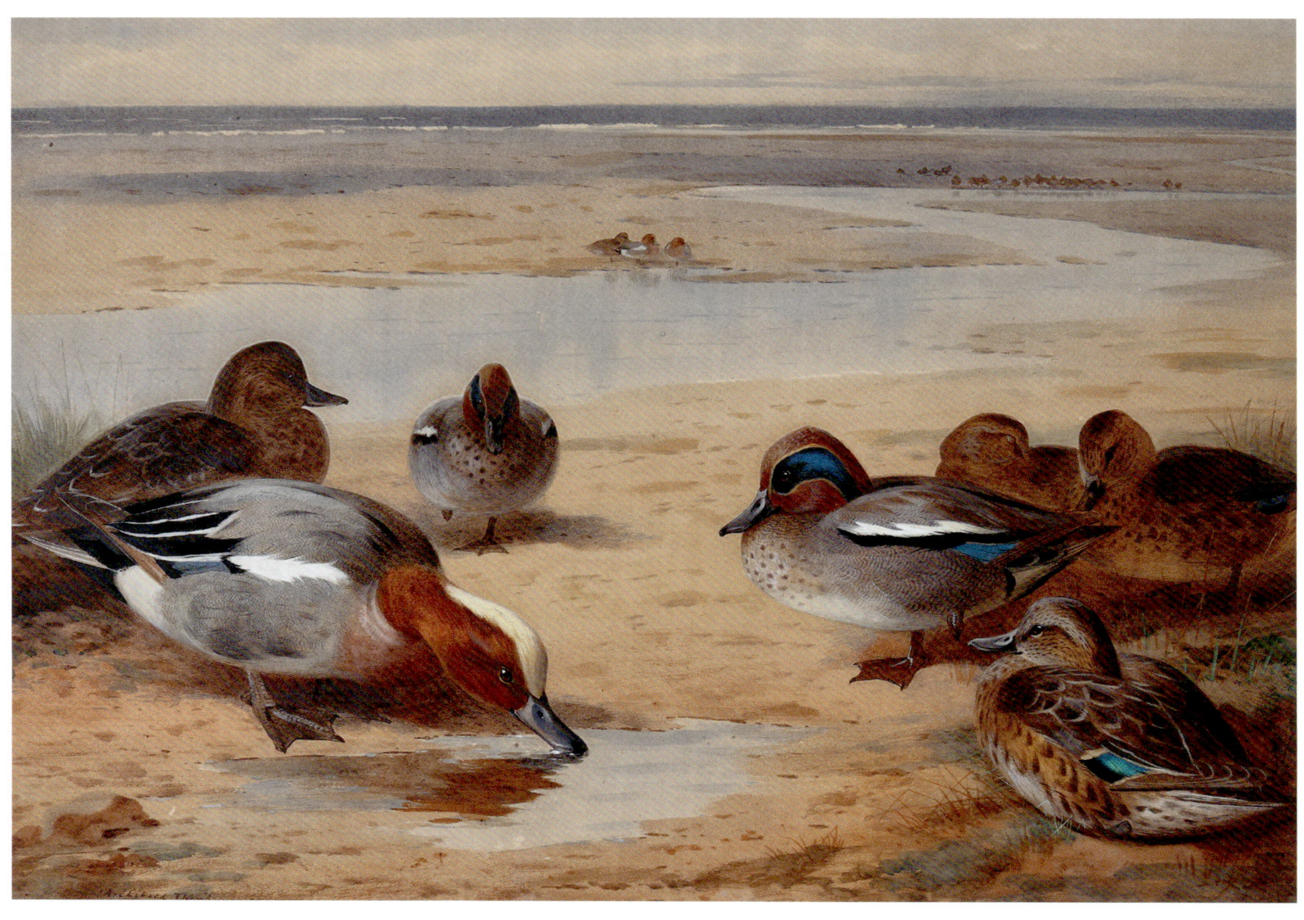

Archibald Thorburn (1860–1935), UK. **Widgeon and Teal**. *Watercolour on paper, 53cm x 73.5cm. Signed and dated 1902,*
This is one of the scarce large watercolours made by Thorburn to private commission.

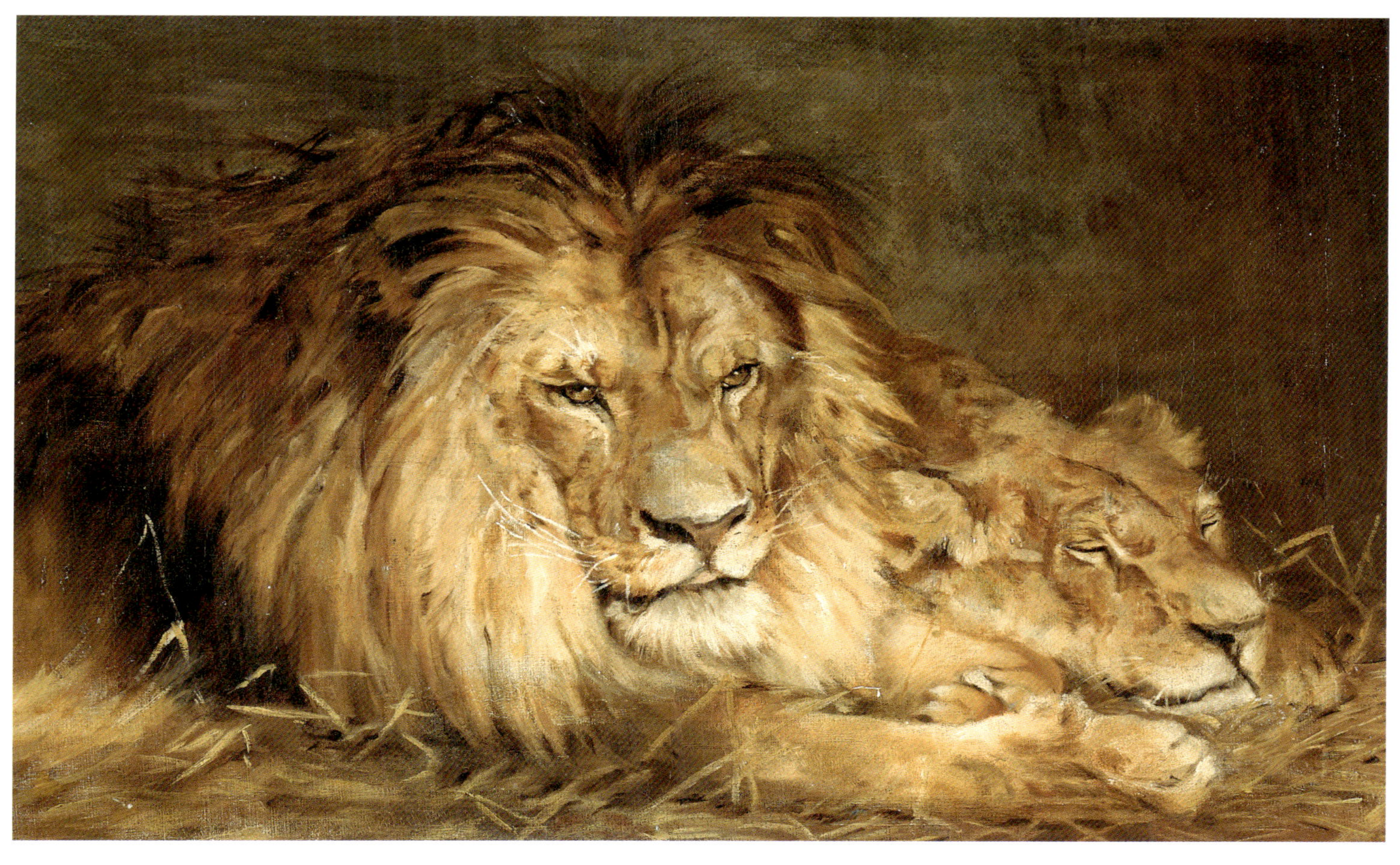

*After Géza Vastagh (1866-1919), Hungary. **Lion and Lioness**. Oil on canvas, 52cm x 75cm. Not signed or dated. This may be a preparatory study for the much larger final work that is signed.*

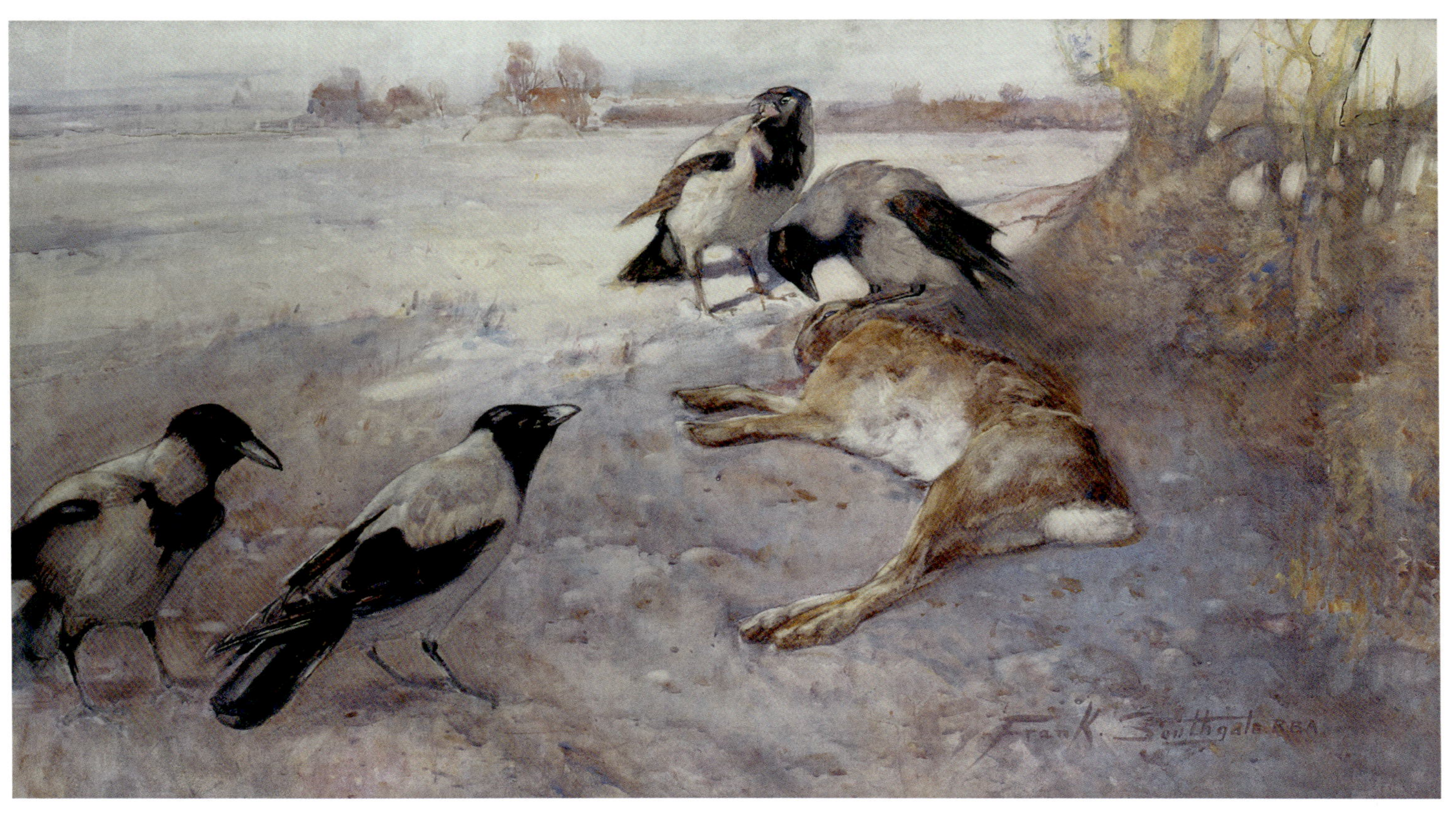

Frank Southgate (1872-1916), UK. **Hooded Crows and Dead Hare**. *Watercolour and gouache on paper, 62cm x 111cm. Signed.*
Nature is kind and economical in its recycling. The hare is dead but, on this winter's day, his corpse gives the crows their lunch.
The artist's handling of watercolour is masterly.

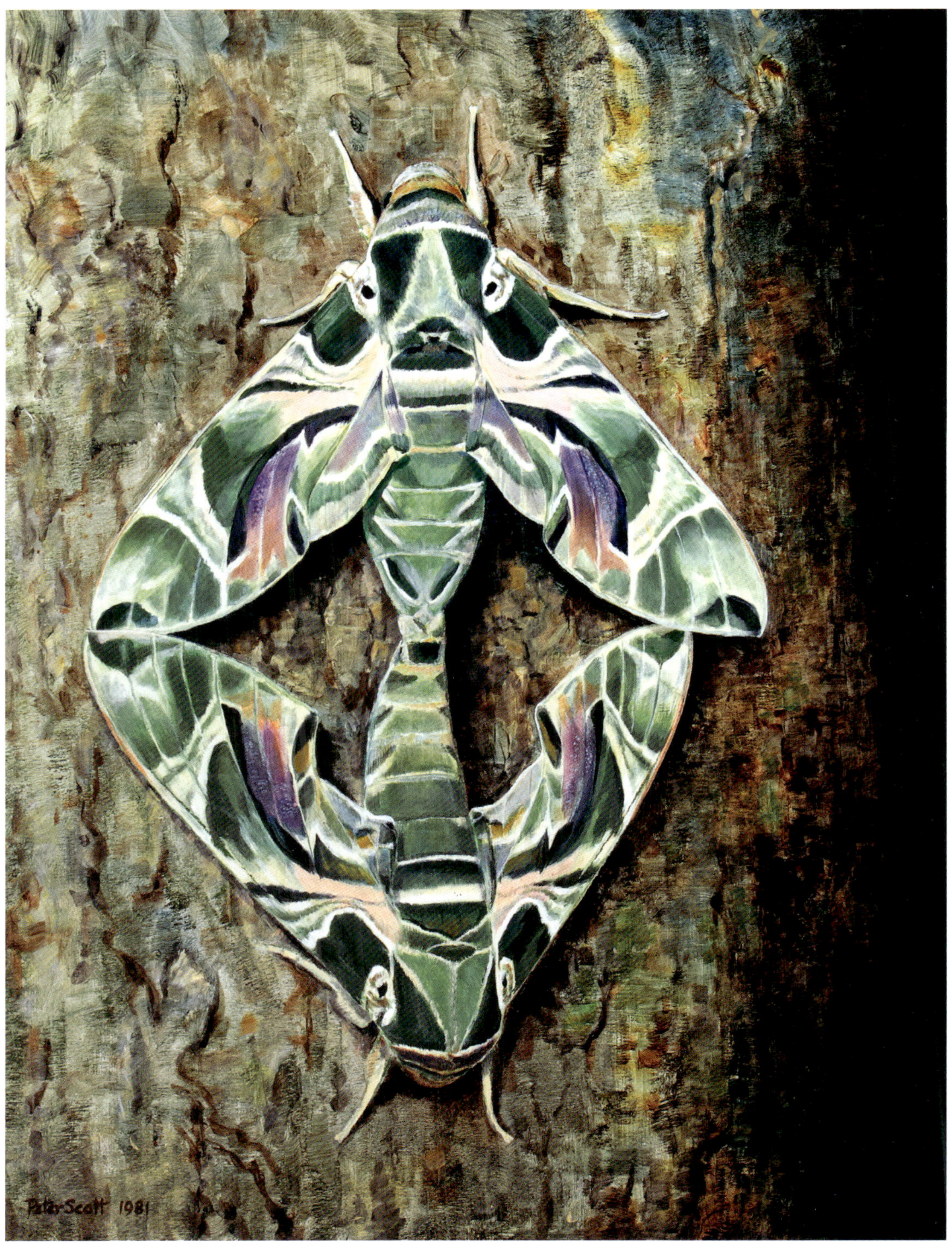

Peter Scott (1909–1989), UK.
Oleander Hawk Moths Mating*.*
Oil on canvas, 50cm x 40.5cm.
Signed and dated 1981.
The artist thought that this was
his best-ever work.

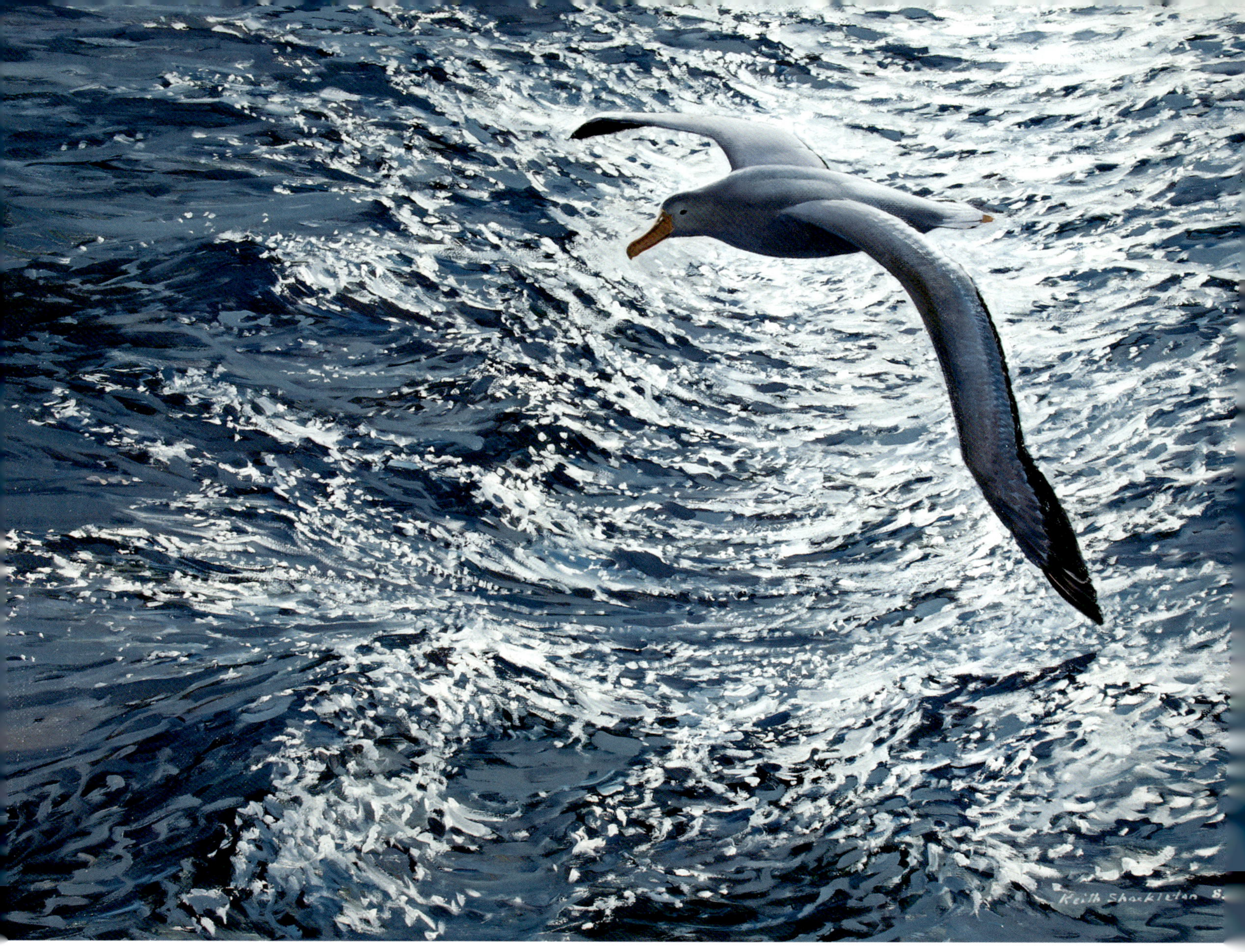

*Keith Shackleton (1923-2015), UK. **Albatross Escort**. Oil on canvas, 76cm x 101.5cm. Signed and dated 1985.*

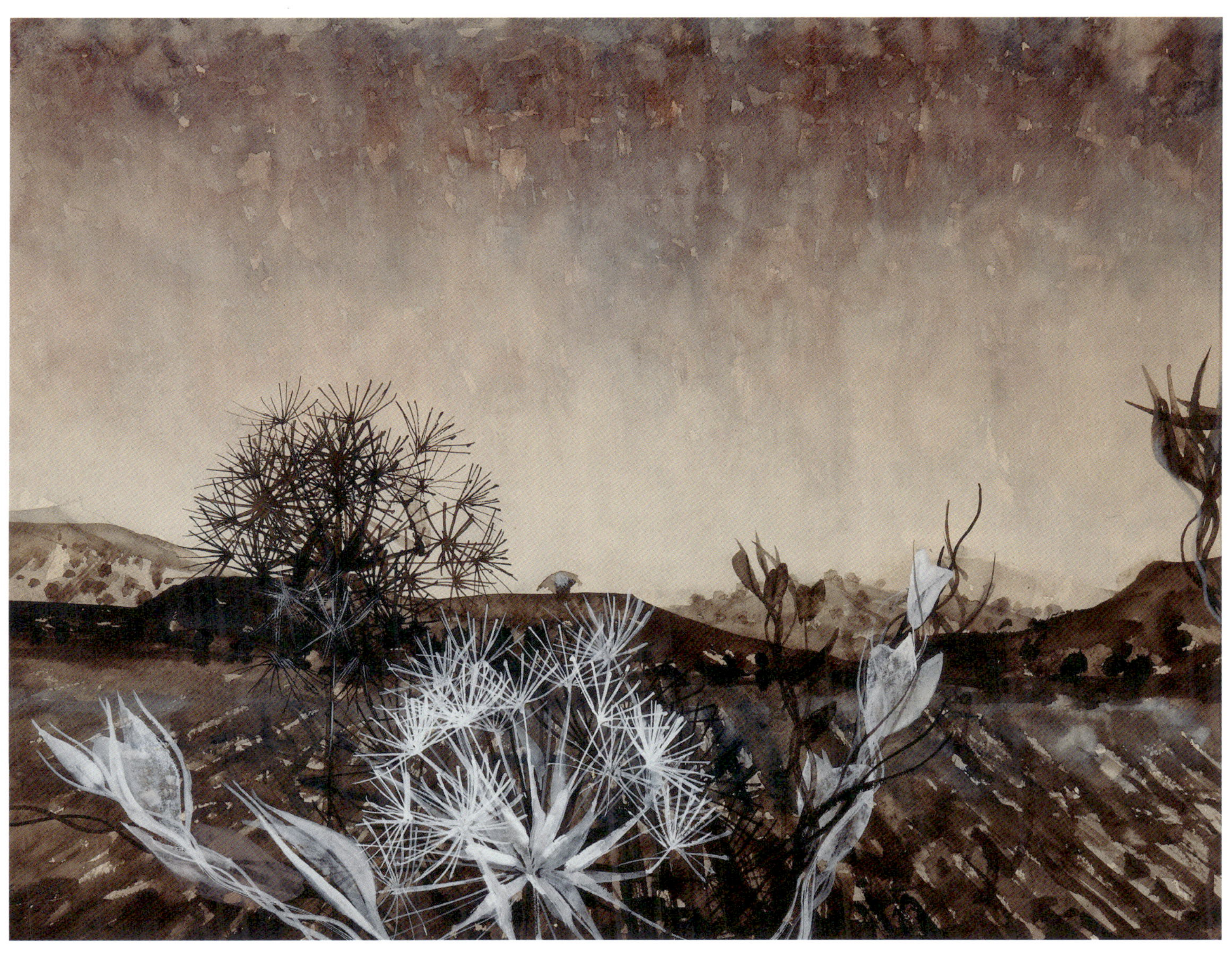

*Alan Reynolds (1926-2014), UK. **An Evening**. Watercolour and gouache on paper, 33cm x 43cm. Signed, not dated.*

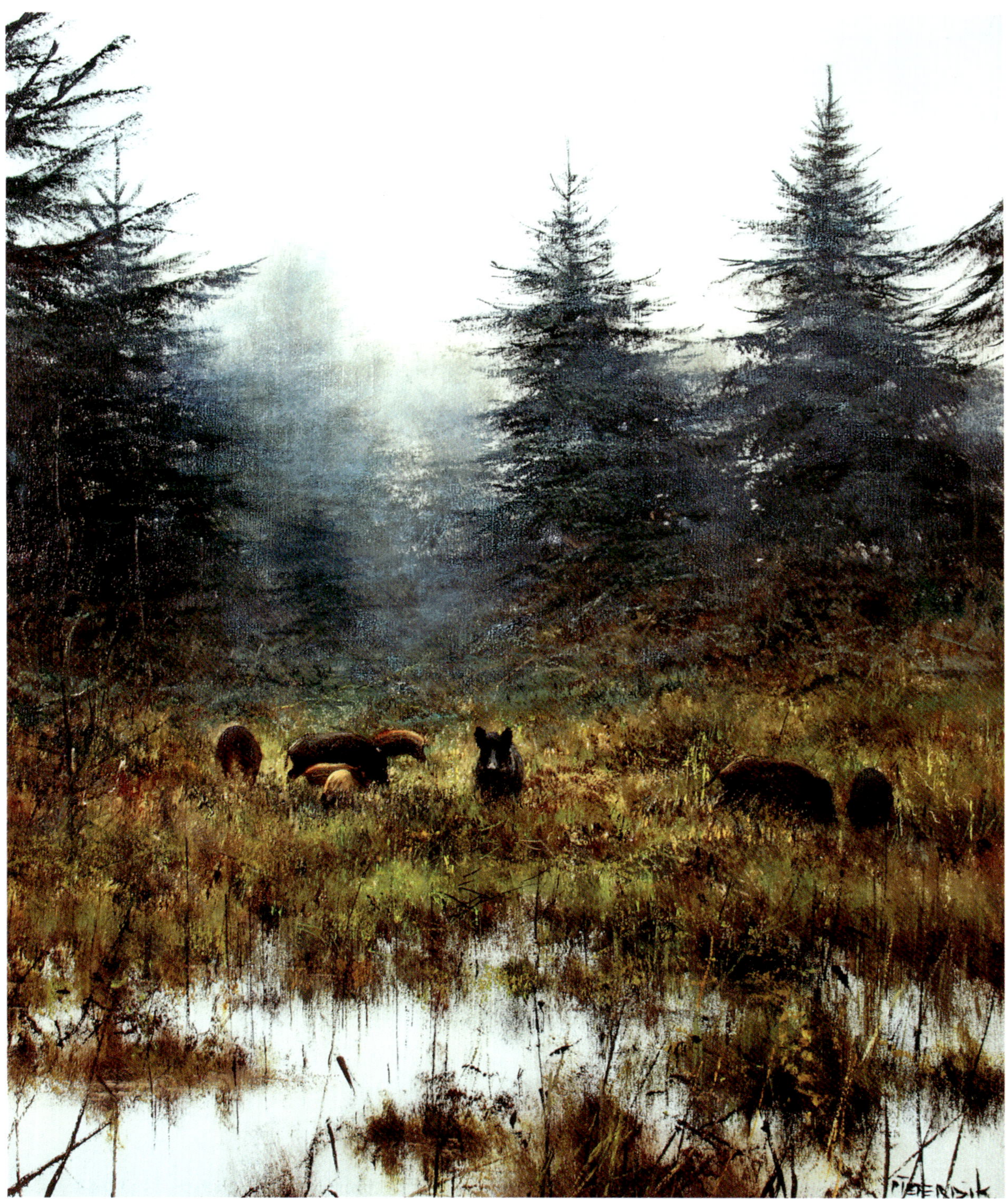

*Left: Pieter Dik
(1943-1984),
The Netherlands.*
**The Sounder –
Wild Boar**.
*Oil on canvas,
83cm x 68cm. Signed.
By priming the whole
canvas with pale blue
paint he has, in effect,
already painted about
a third of the picture,
the foreground pool
reflecting the sky.*

*Facing page:
Lennart Sand
(1946 –), Sweden.*
Golden Eagle.
*Oil on canvas,
200cm x 230cm.
Signed and dated 1982.*

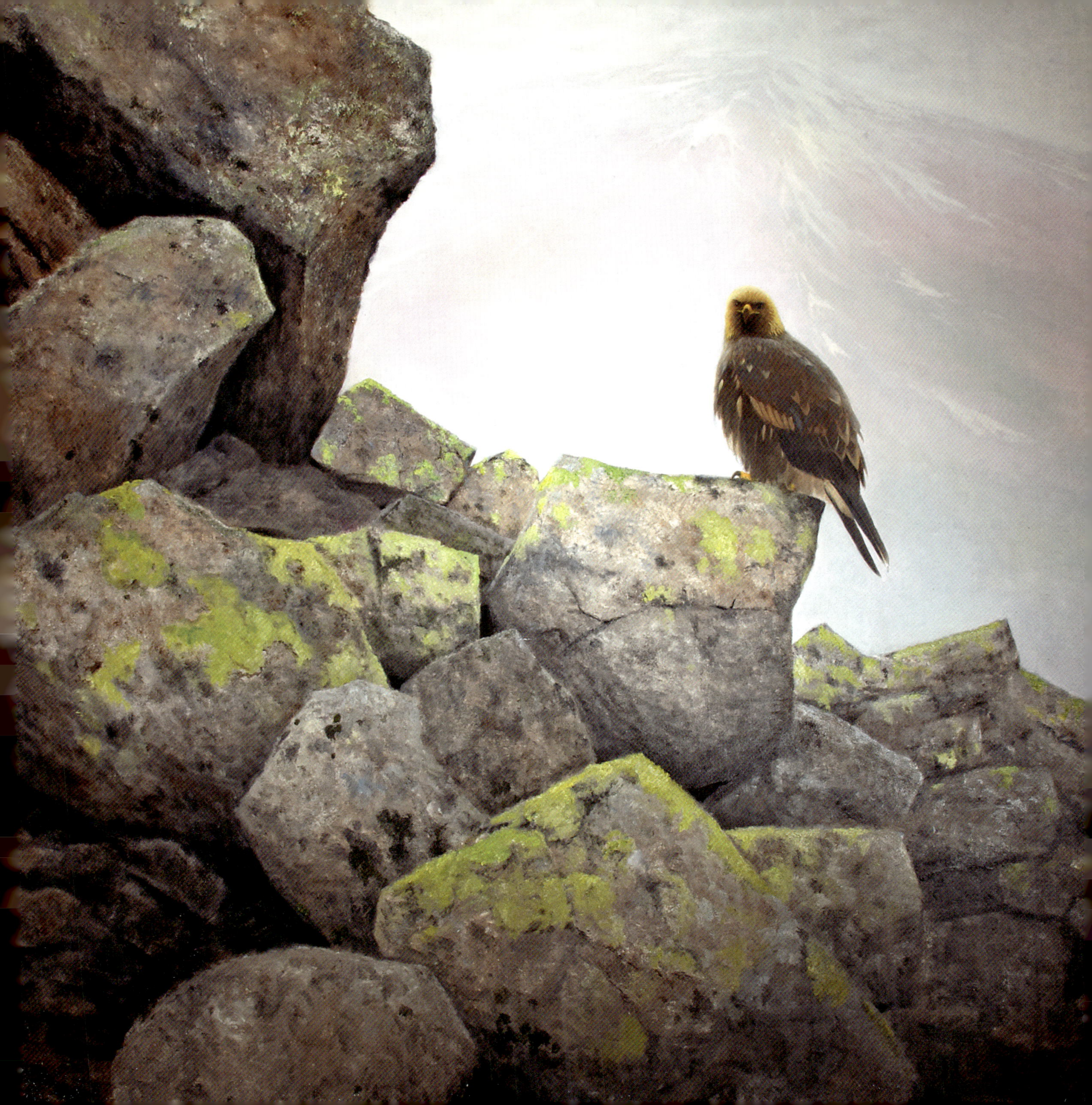

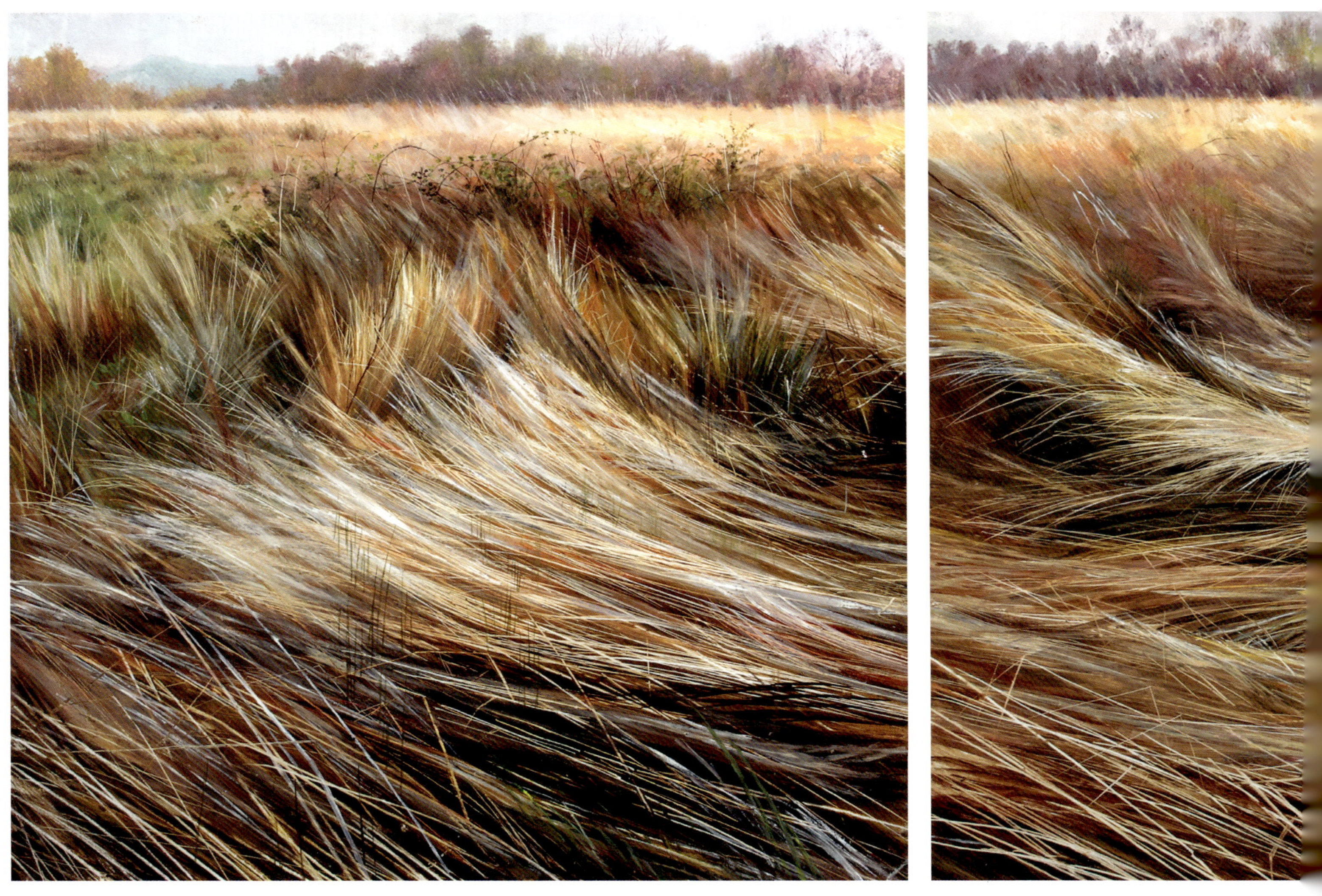

*Meg Stevens (1931-2012), Wales, UK. **Sea of Grasses – Molinia** (purple moor grass). Triptych, oil on board, each 60cm x 60cm.
Here the artist draws our attention to a part of nature that most of us would never notice.*

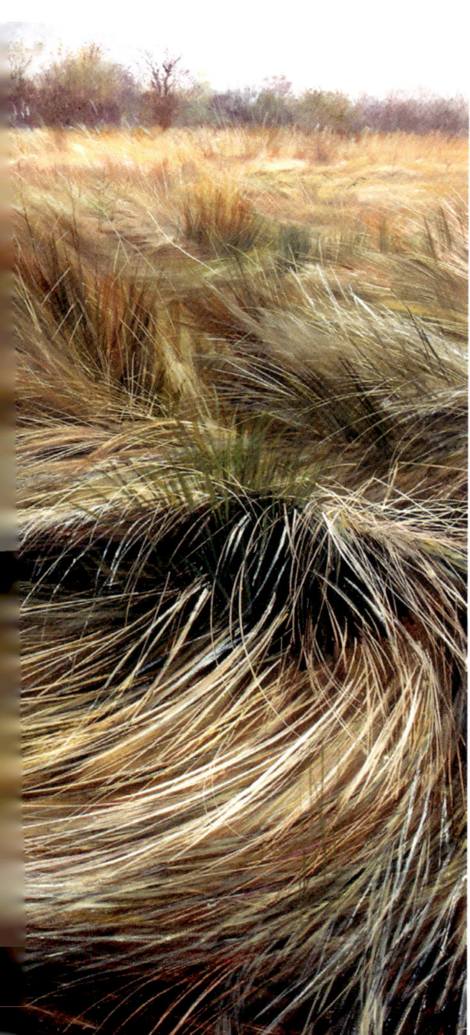

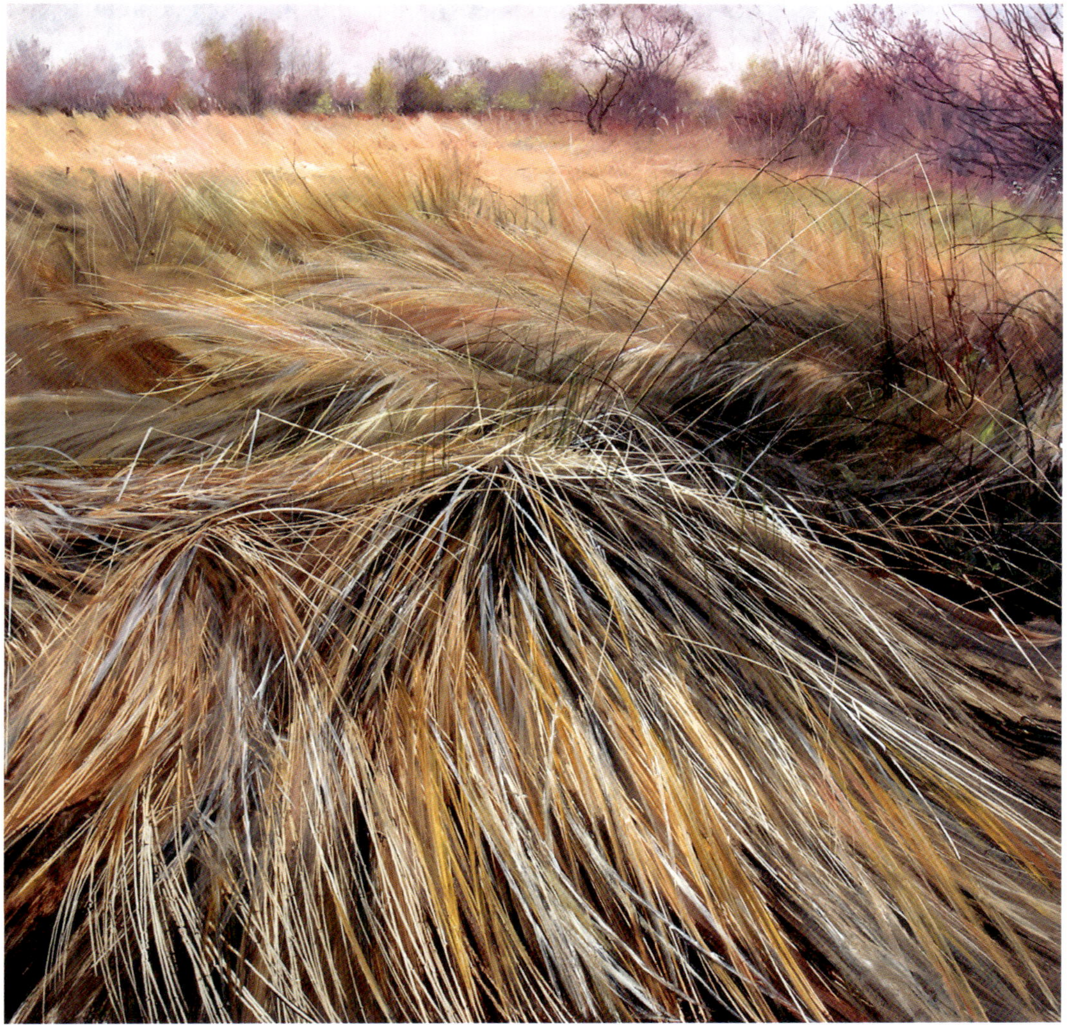

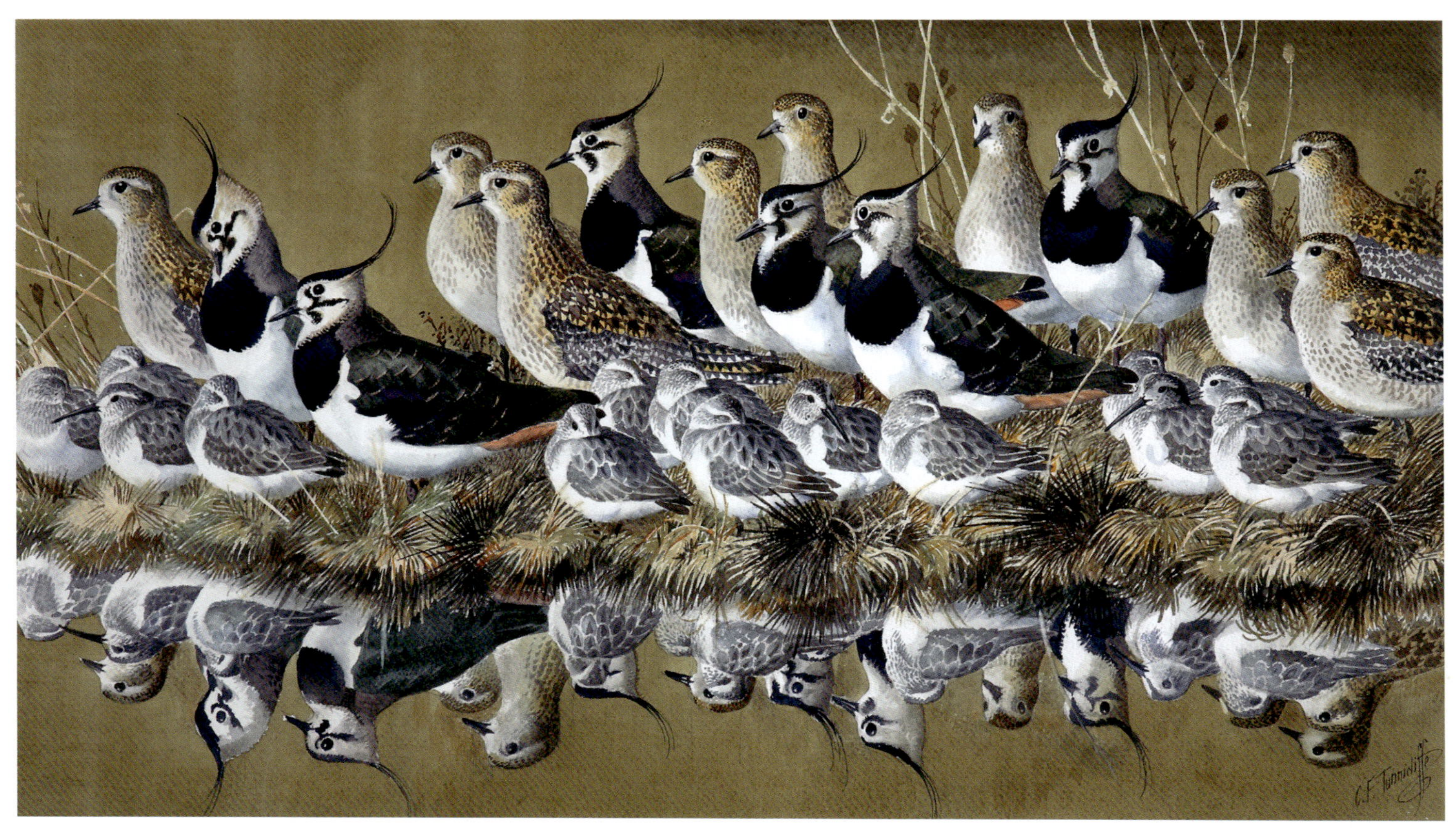

Charles Frederick Tunnicliffe, RA (1901–1979), UK. **Green, Gold and Dun** (Golden Plover, Green Plover and Sanderling).
Watercolour on paper, 42cm x 72cm. Signed.
Bought with the assistance of the Victoria & Albert Museum (V&A) Purchase Grant Fund and The Art Fund.

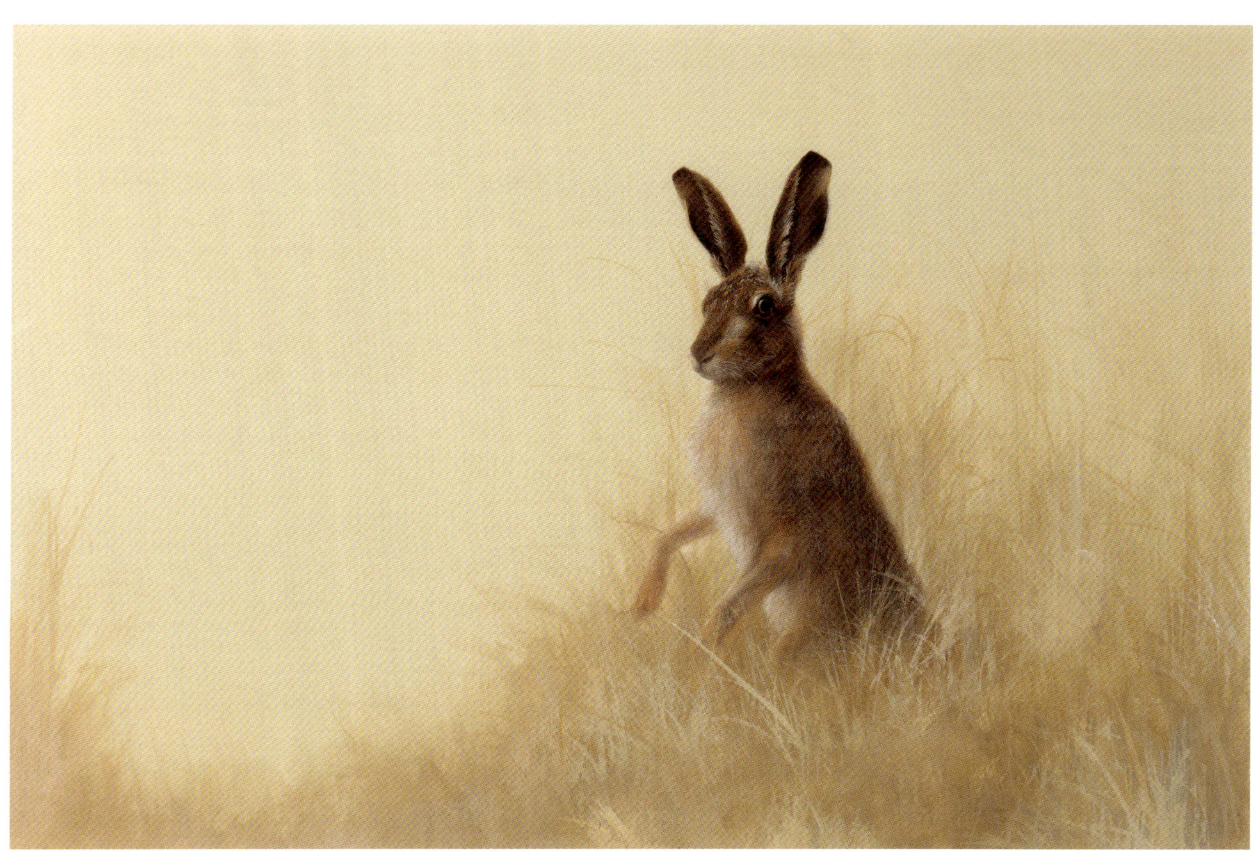

*John Wilder (1946 –), UK. **Hare Alert**. Watercolour on paper, 19cm x 26cm. Not signed or dated.*
This artist knew that detail is not needed in every part of a picture to achieve 'realism'.

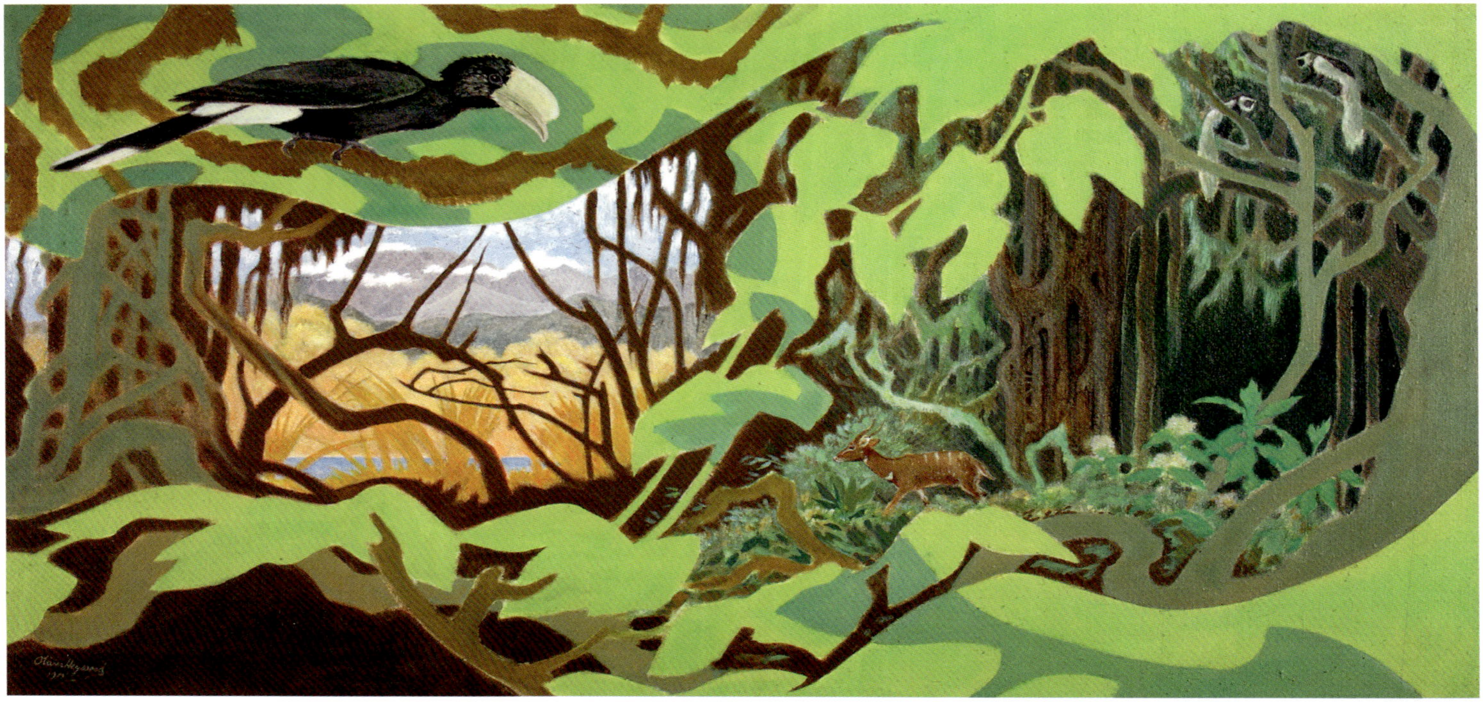

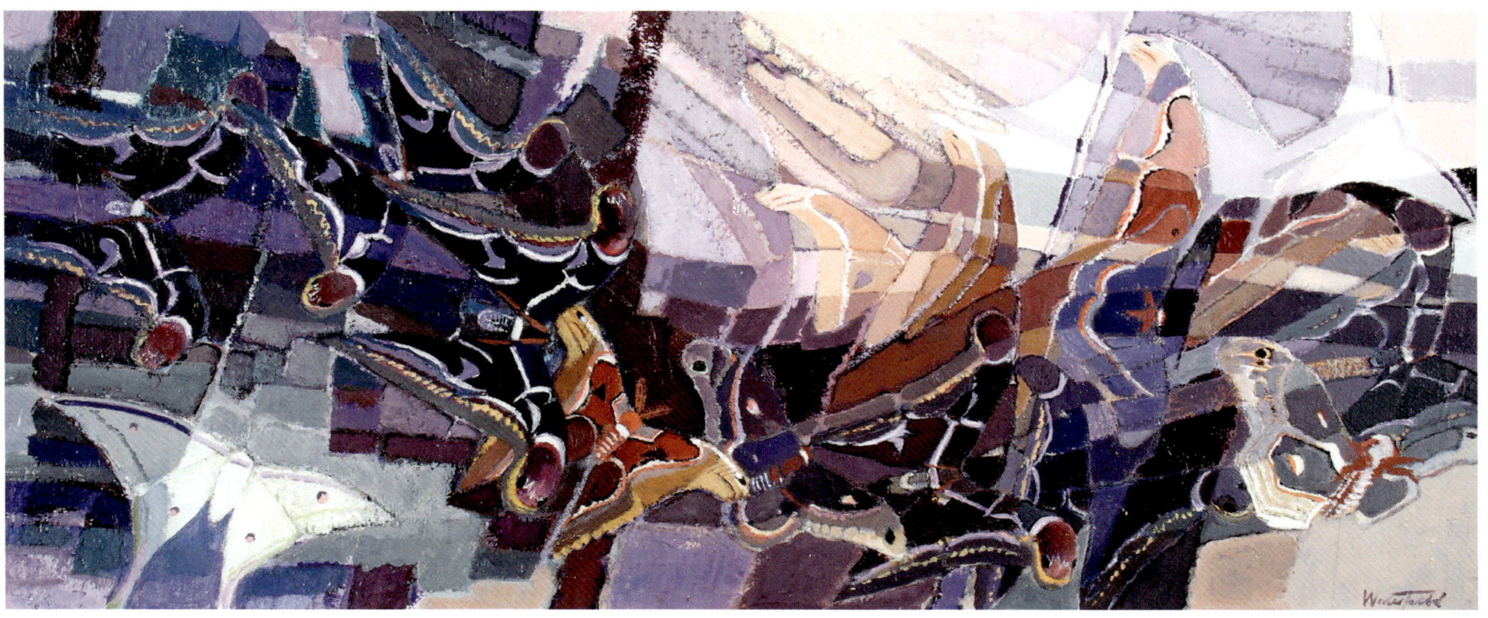

Above: (Sir) Oliver Heywood (1920-1992), UK. **Hornbill, Bushbuck and Colobus**. *Oil on canvas, 49.2cm x 118.5cm. Signed and dated 1975.*

Below: Ken Waterfield (1927 –), UK. **Nine-day Wonders** *(seven species of exotic moth). Oil on canvas, 49.2cm x 118.5cm. Signed. Nature in Art holds the artist's diagram identifying each species.*

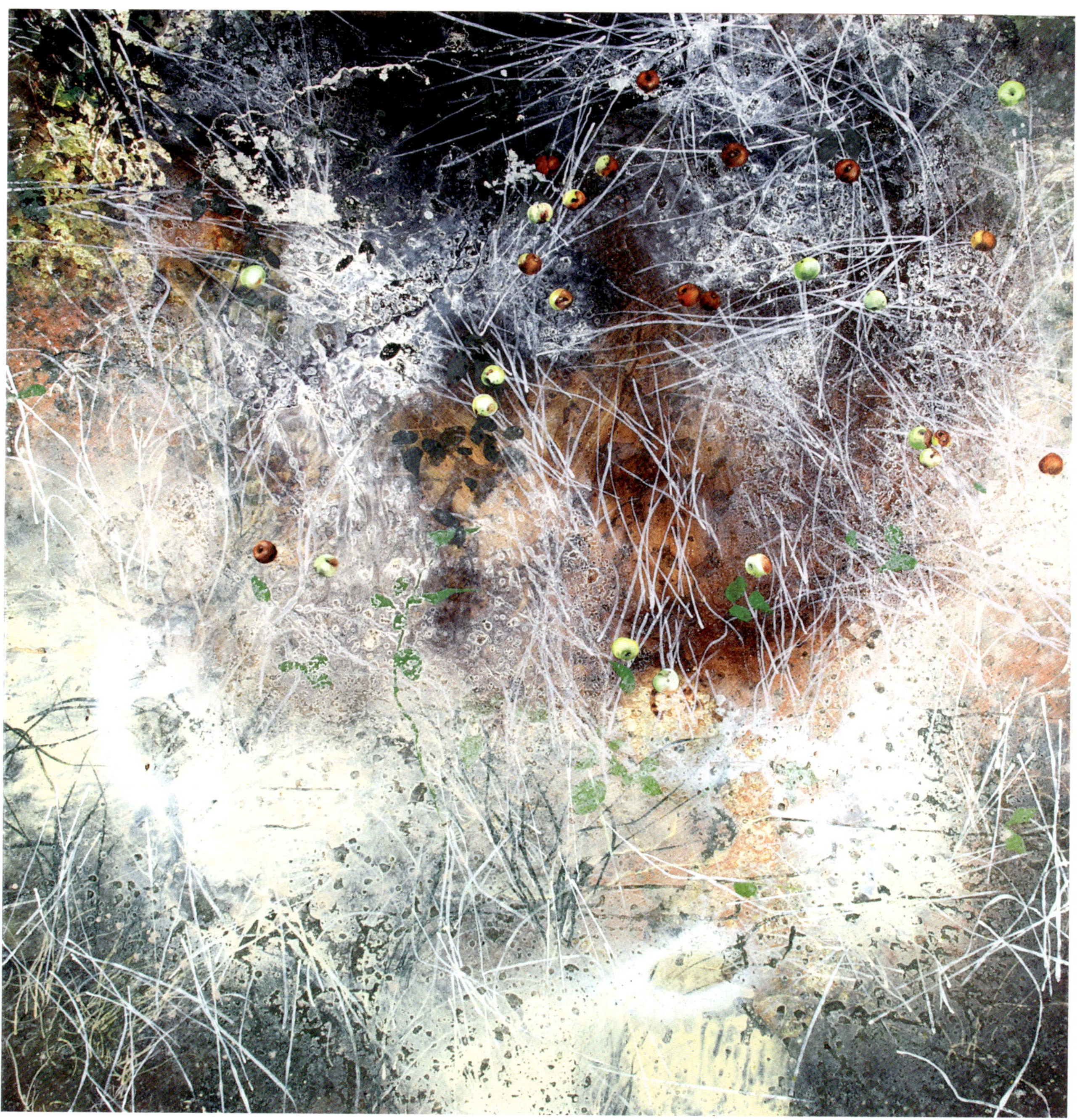

*Michael Porter (1948 –), UK. **The Road to Issel**. Mixed media and PVA on canvas, 120cm x 110cm. Signed on reverse, 2006.*
Purchased with the assistance of the MGC V&A Purchase Grant Fund and the Art Fund.
While most pictures 'look' out horizontally or upward, this 'looks' at the ground. Even so, the artist says he is a "landscape
artist". The background is entirely abstract, but some life-like crab apples are shown against it.

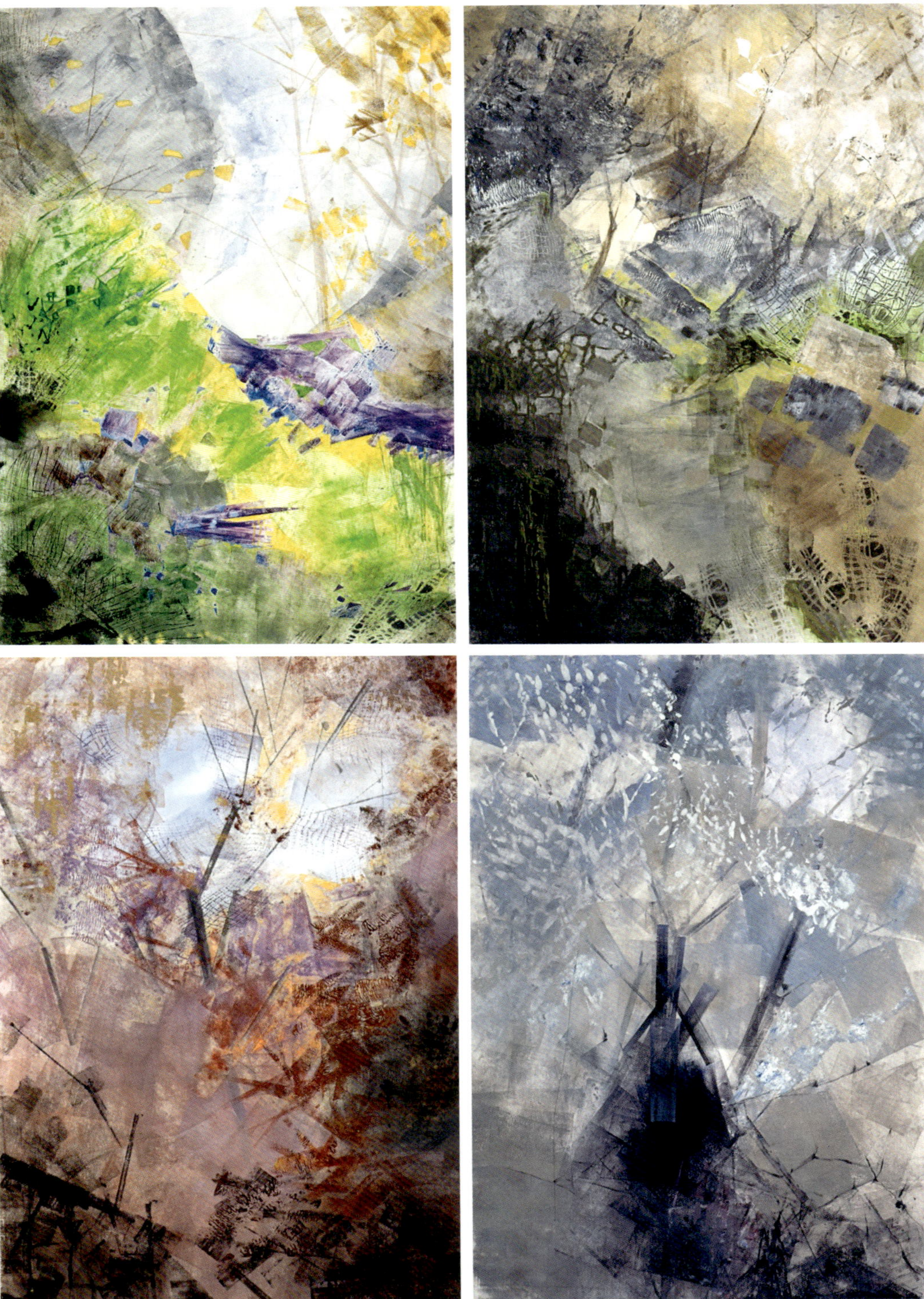

Ben Venuto (1928 –), UK.
The Four Seasons.
*Gouache and acrylic on paper,
each 109cm x 76.5cm.
Signed and dated 1991.
The paintings were made entirely
with different-sized printmaker's
rollers and scrim.*

Jill Confavreux (1940 –), UK.
In The Forest.
Mixed media on board,
91cm x 44.7cm. Signed, not dated.
This work was made in the artist's studio
at Nature in Art. Included in it are are
leaves, burnt paper, bubble-wrap
and many other media.

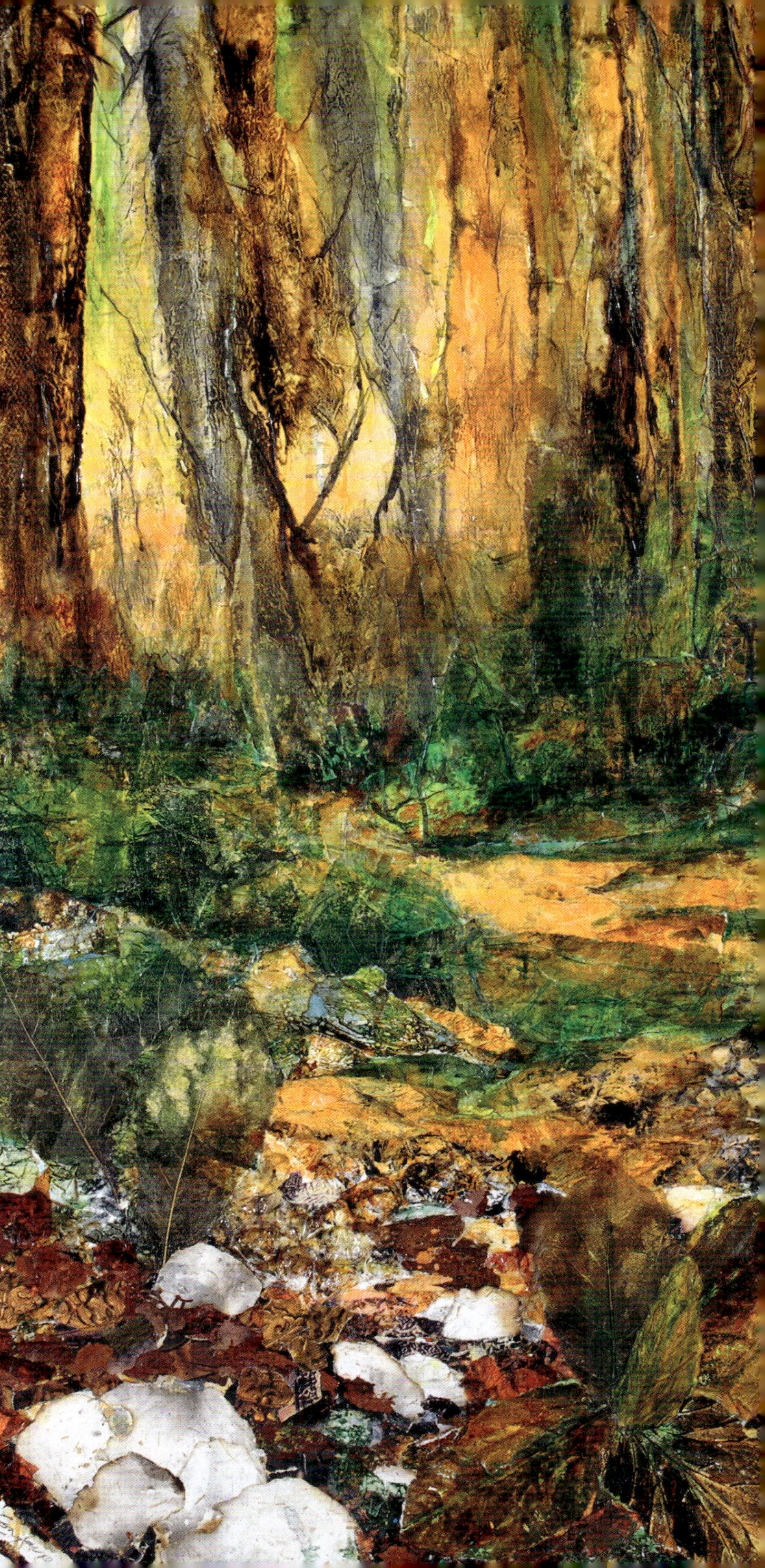

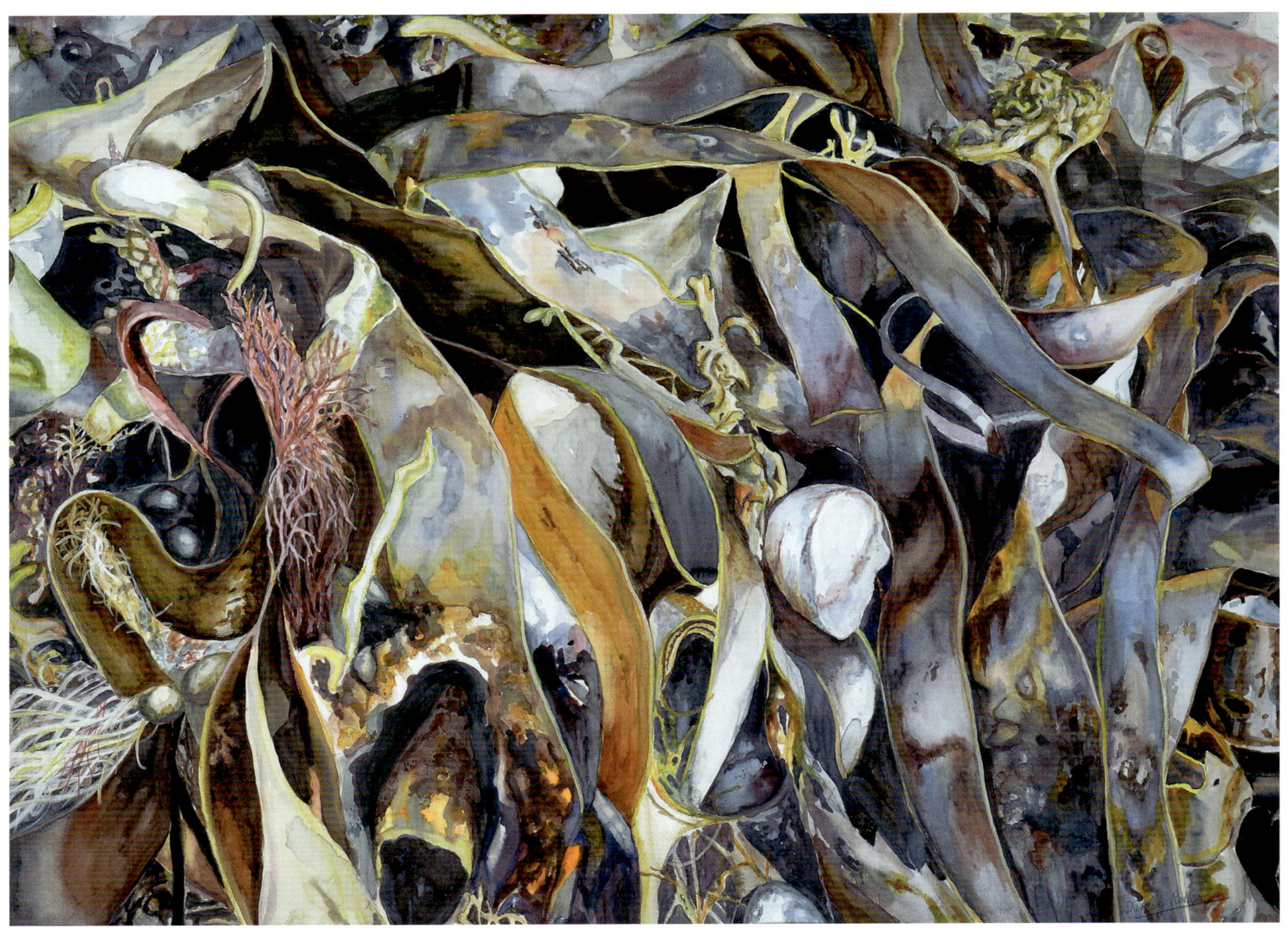

Shirley Robson (died 2003), UK. *Nature's Spectrum*.
Watercolour on paper, 54cm x 73.5cm. Not signed or dated.
This is both an accurate depiction of dead seaweed on the high-tide line and, at the same time,
an abstract image of nature's harmonious colours – a theme that fascinated the artist.

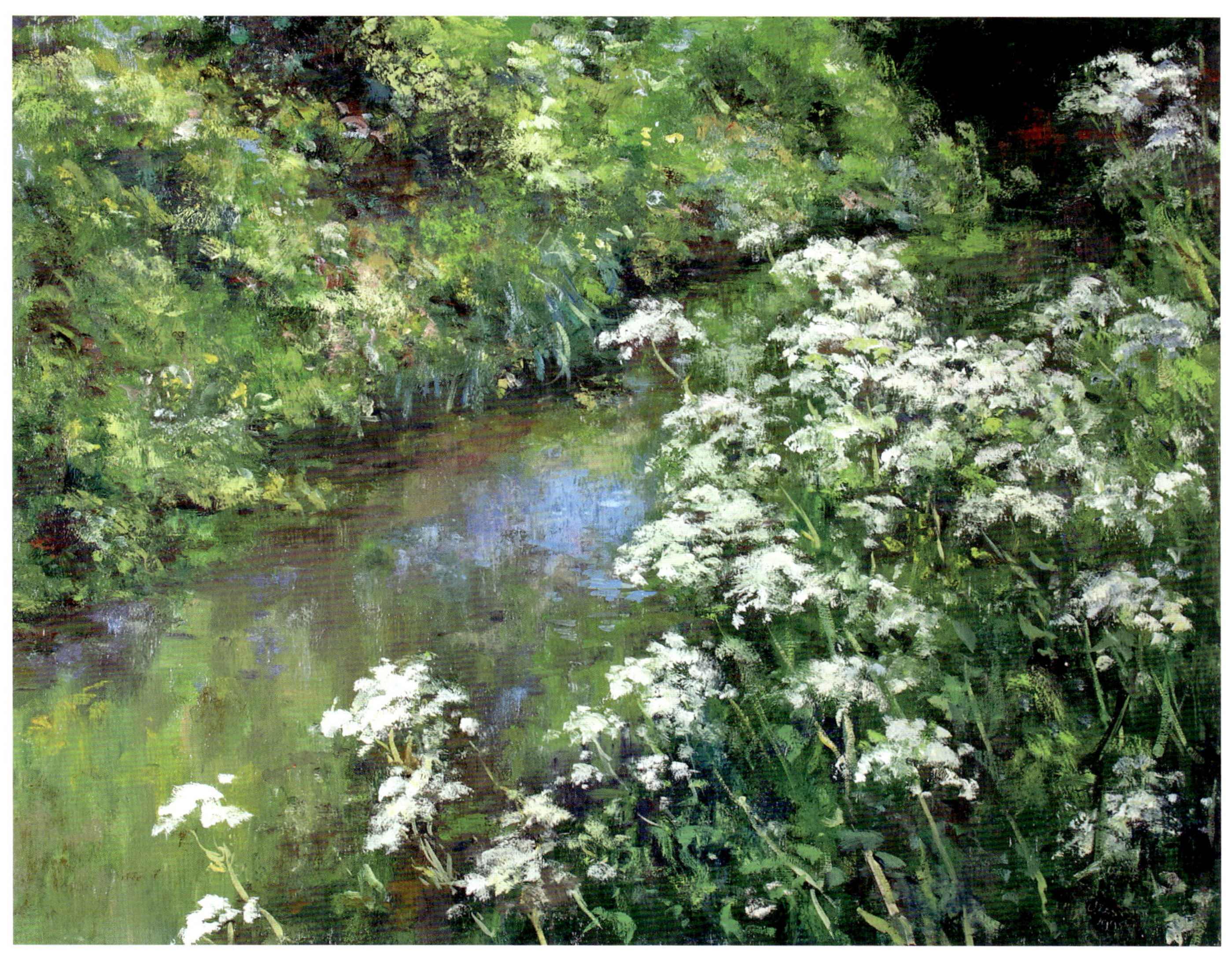

Hermann van Zeggeren (1916-1996), The Netherlands. **Hogweed by the Stream**. *Oil on canvas, 78.5cm x 99cm. Not signed or dated.*

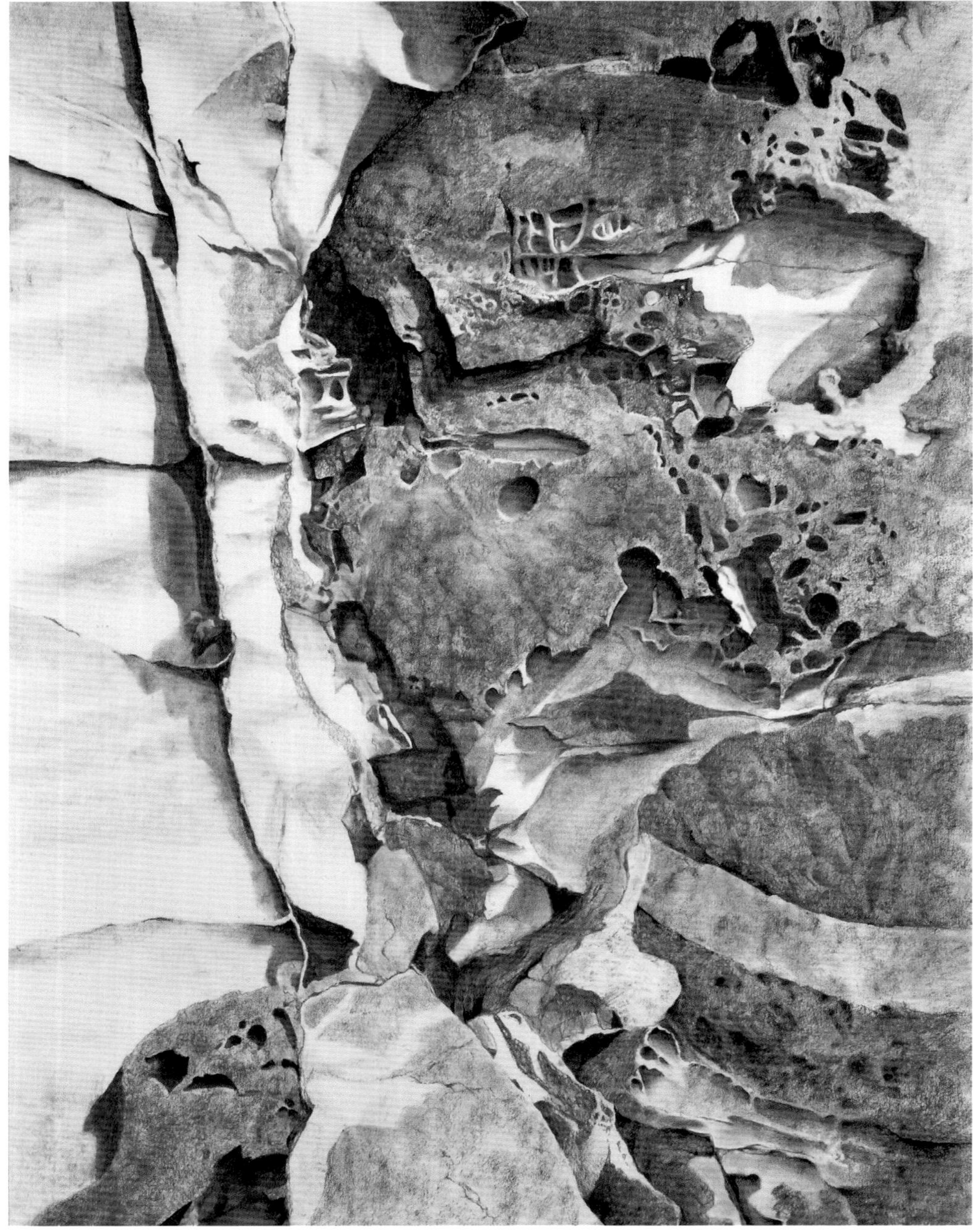

Ben Venuto (1928 –), UK.
Wind-blown Cliff, Newgale Bay.
Charcoal on paper, 81cm x 61cm.
Signed and dated 1992.
This image is at once an accurate
drawing and an abstract picture.

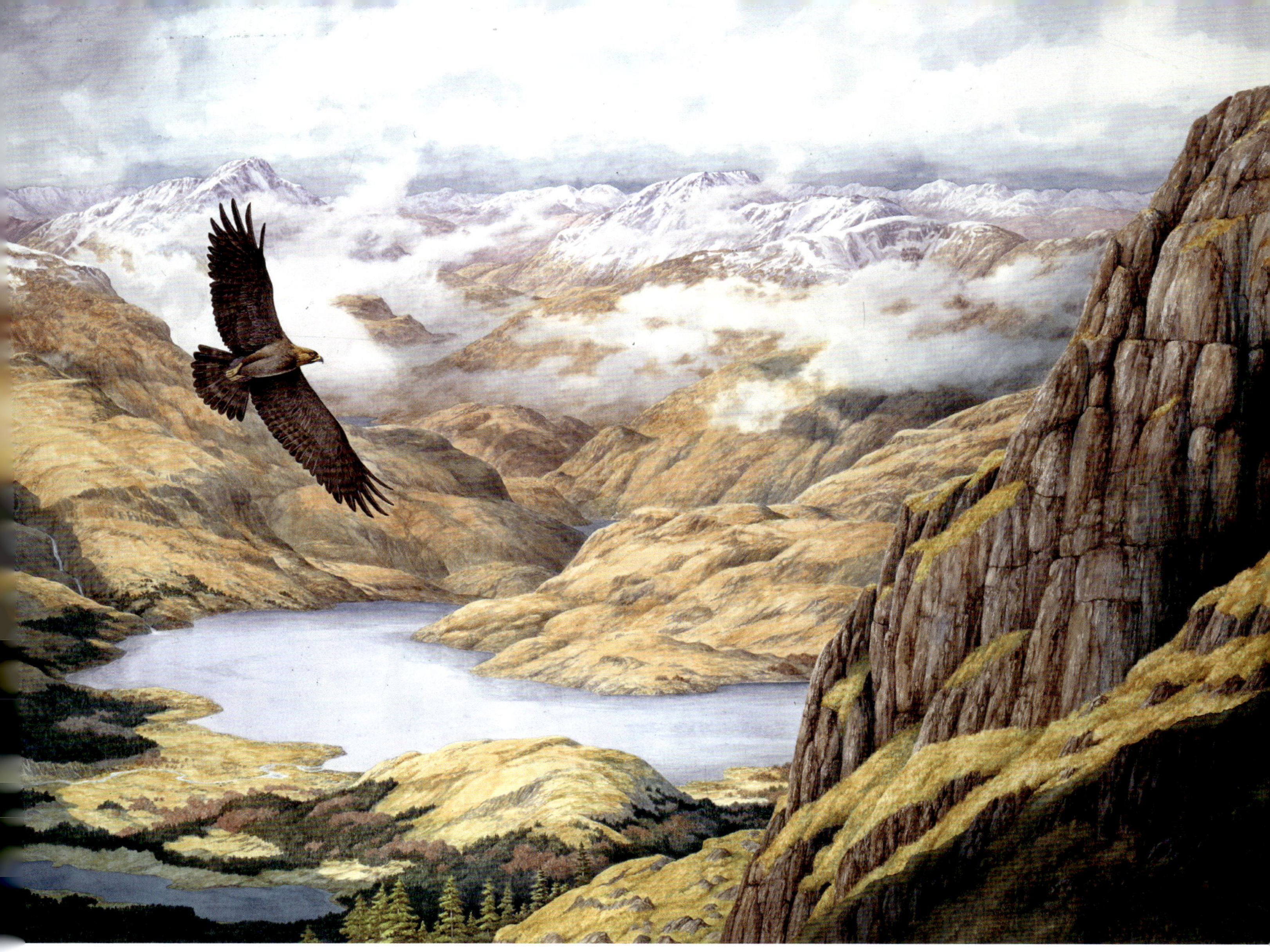

Elizabeth Gray (1928 –), UK. Signed, 1985. *Golden Eagle*.
Watercolour on paper, 106.5cm x 145.5cm.
This is an unusually large watercolour, perhaps partly because of the difficulty of finding paper of this size and quality.
It was too big to stretch in the traditional way, so the artist painted the sky first and rolled the paper over the top of her easel.
The eagle was painted after the imaginary landscape was completed.

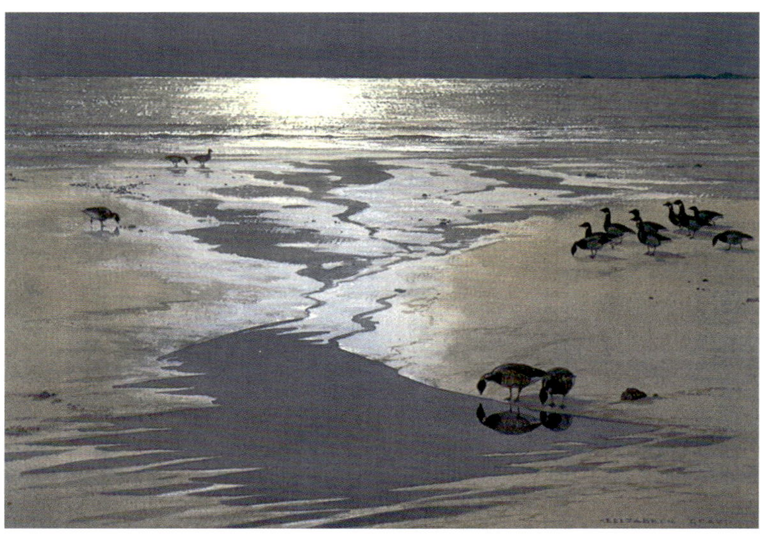

*Elizabeth Gray (1928 –), UK. **Brent Geese by Moonlight**.*
Watercolour on paper, 36cm x 53cm. Signed, 1979.
Although most visitors are not familiar with the Dark-bellied Brent Geese
that winter in the UK, or the mud-flats where they feed, this is a very
popular picture. The colours are restrained and harmonious.

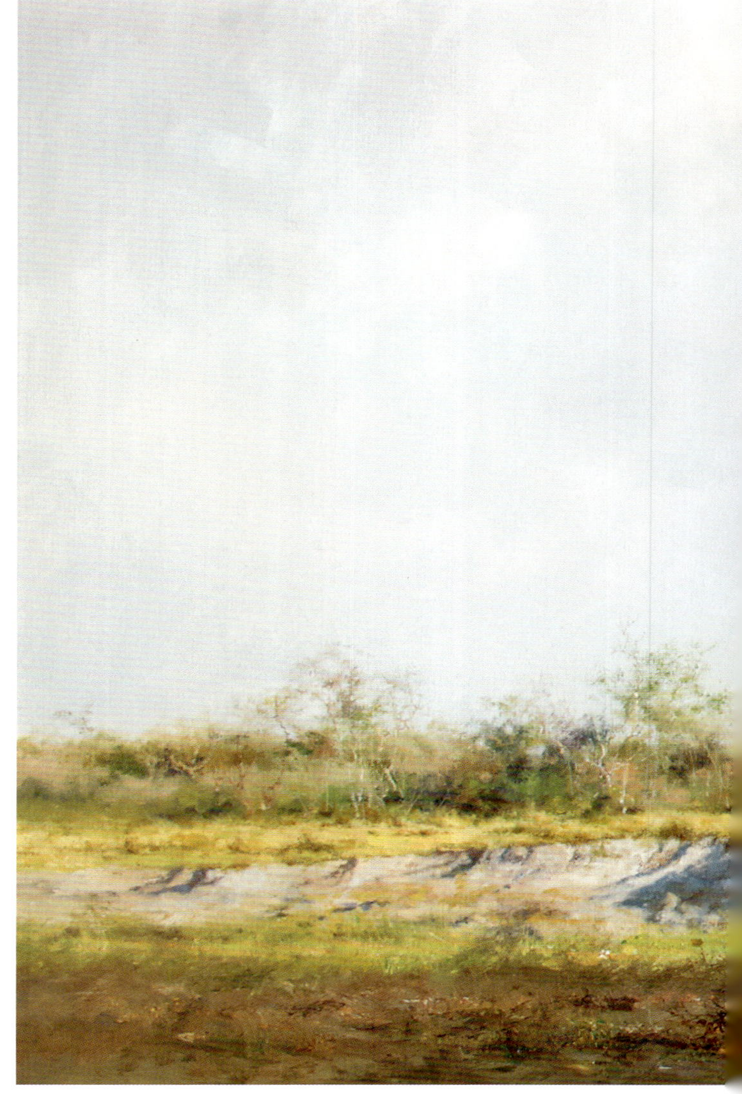

David Shepherd (1931-2017), UK.
***Three Old Gentlemen of Savuti**.*
Oil on canvas, 71cm x 155cm. Signed and dated January 1990.
As with Wilder's 'Hare Alert' on page 19, the artist has put detail only
where it is essential. More would have spoilt the picture.

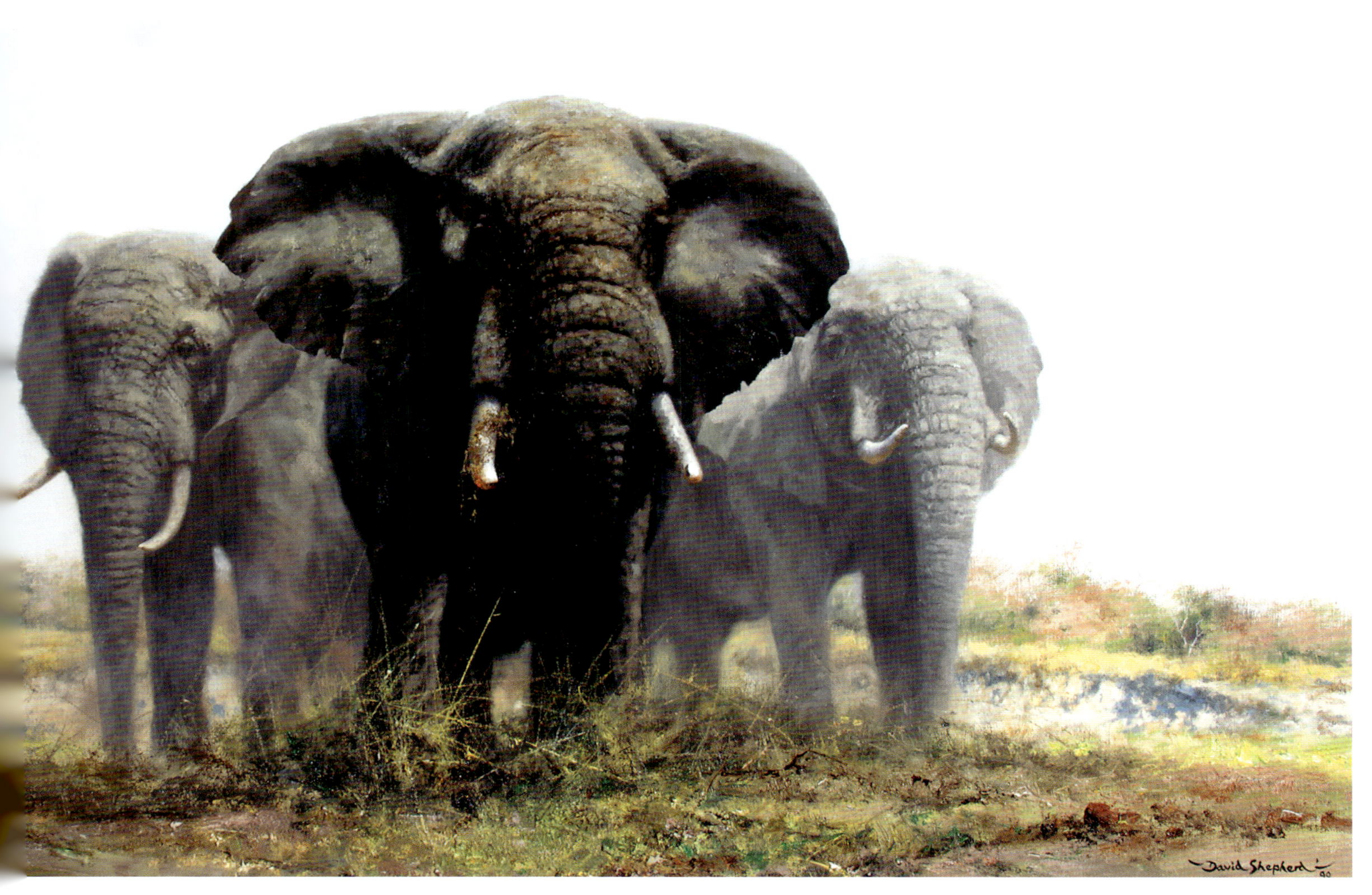

PRINTS

Artists' prints are not reproductions. They are hand-made, often by applying ink to blocks of wood, linoleum or metal (and the like) that have had the design cut into them. Paper is then pressed on to the inked plate or block (or, sometimes, the other way round) so that the mirror-image appears when it is seen on the paper.

To make an engraving, a sharp tool is used to make grooves directly into the metal or wood that will hold the ink. Alternatively, the metal may be covered in a layer of wax (often blackened by a candle flame to make the cuts more obvious). This is then cut into in a similar way to allow strong acid to 'bite' into the metal plate where it is exposed (to make an etching).

Another method of printmaking is to cut the wood, linoleum, etc, away and apply ink to the exposed (uncut) surface with a rigid roller so that no ink goes into the cut parts of the block – to make so-called intaglio prints (wood block print, linocut, etc).

The first prints, from the sixteenth to nineteenth centuries, were made primarily as illustrations for books. The pictures were printed using black ink. Some (more expensive) books had their illustrations coloured by teams of people (usually ladies) by hand. Even so, many such despised and dismissed "mere illustrations", whether coloured or not, were actually works of art and should be respected and valued as such.

After mechanisation had replaced the labour-intensive work of earlier centuries, printmakers continued to use the old techniques, and variations of them, to make their works of art.

Because the blocks had ink applied to them and were compressed time and time again in the printing press, gradually the sharpness of the block was lost by wear and tear. So museums, galleries and private collectors alike take care, if they can, to acquire prints of the very best quality and condition.

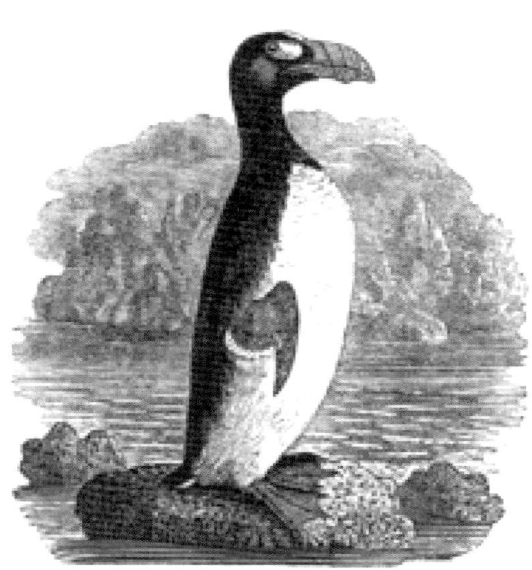

*Thomas Bewick (1753-1828), UK. **Great Auk**.*
Wood engraving, 8.3cm x 8.1cm. From the artist's famous book 'British Birds', 1797-1804.
Because the bird could not fly, ruthless hunters and greedy egg collectors made the Great Auk extinct by the mid-nineteenth century.

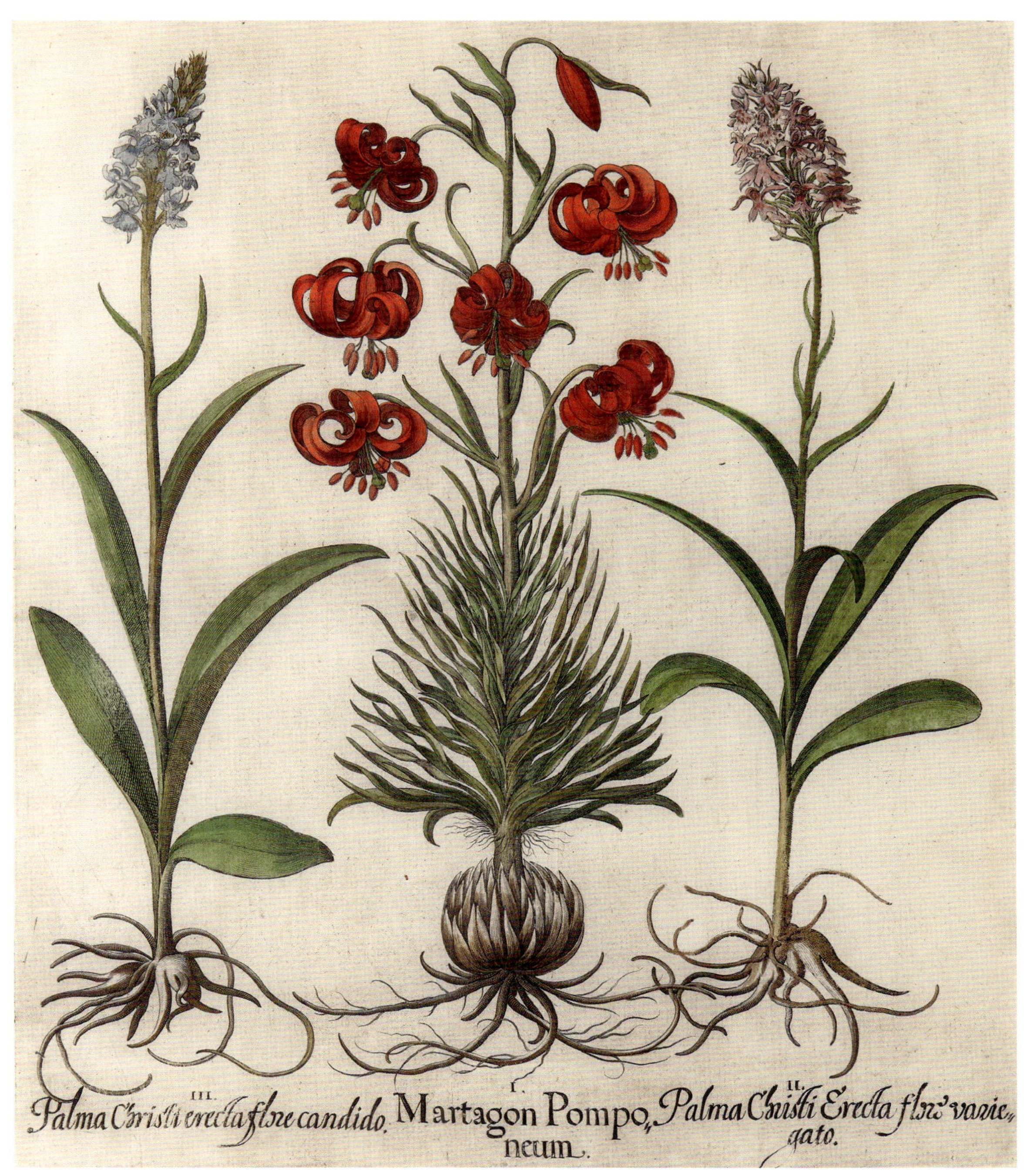

Basilius Besler (1561–1629), Germany. **Martagon Pomponeum** *(Turk's Head Lily).*
Hand-coloured engraving, 47.5cm x 40cm. From the first edition of his two-volume 'Hortus Eystettensis',
published in 1613, said to be the first book in the world to show plants as objects of beauty.

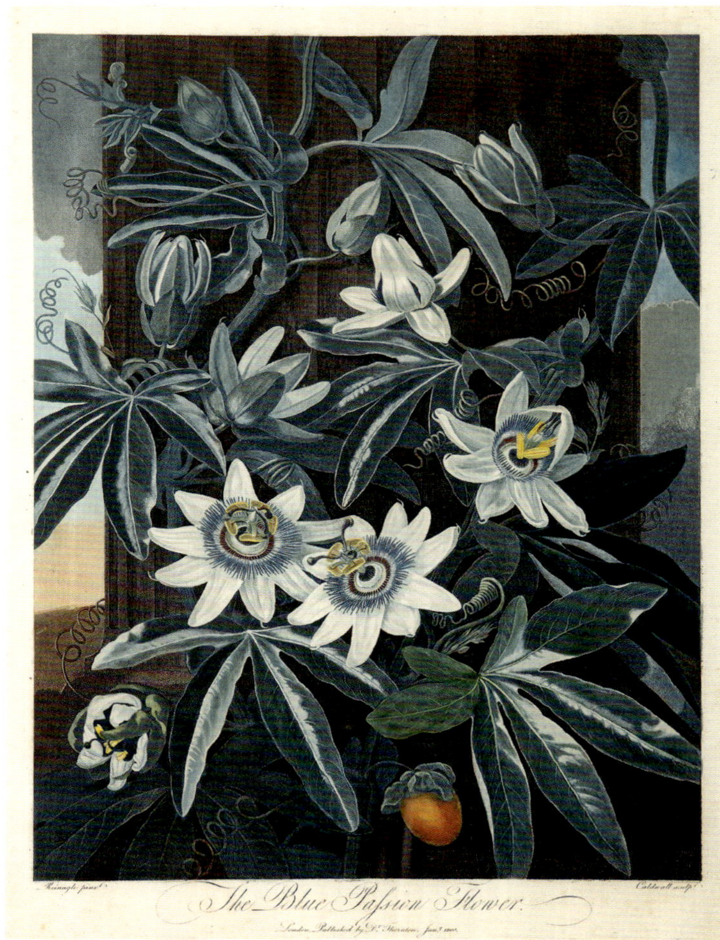

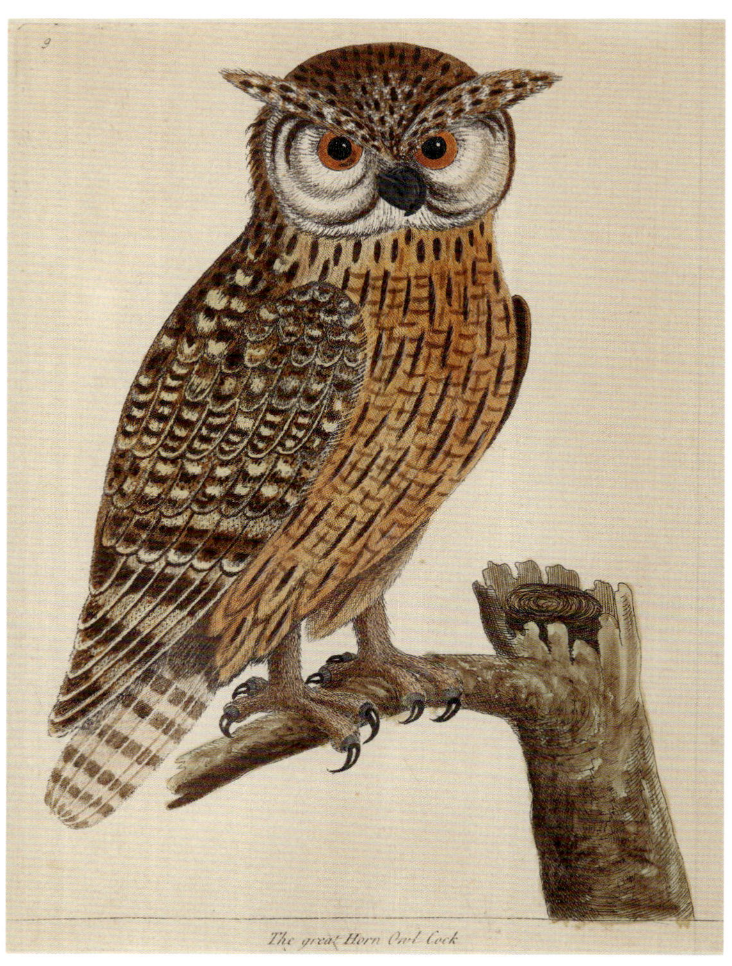

Above left: Philip Reinagle (1749-1833), UK. **The Blue Passion Flower.**
Hand-coloured engraving on paper, 31.5cm x 23.5cm. Dated 1811.

Above right: Eleazar Albin (died 1741/2), UK. **The Great Horn Owl Cock.**
Hand-coloured copper plate etching, 25.5cm x 20.5cm. Not signed or dated.

Right: George Edwards (1694-1773), UK. **Blue Jay**.
Hand-coloured copper plate etching, 24.5cm x 19.5cm.
The size of the bird in relation to the tree on which it perched
could be misleading. So the artist has drawn a diagram of
the head and beak, lower right, labelled "Bigness of life".
Edwards was one of very few artists who recorded on the plate the exact
date that the work was finished – here, 29th September 1759.

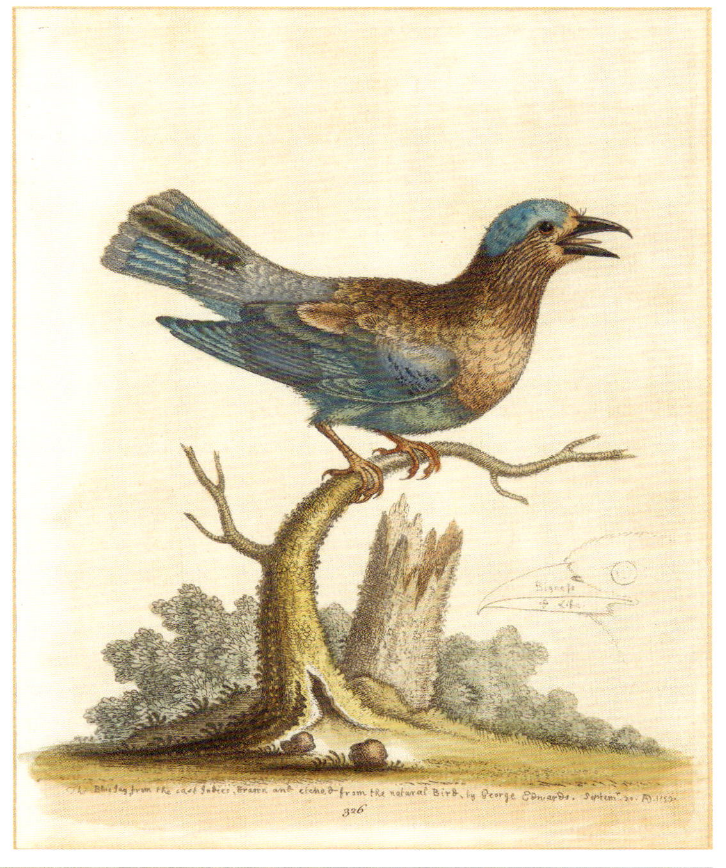

Right: Herbert Dicksee (1862-1942), UK.
Raiders – Lion and Lioness.
Hand-coloured etching, 38cm x 66cm.
Inscribed 1898.
Typical of the drama so popular then.

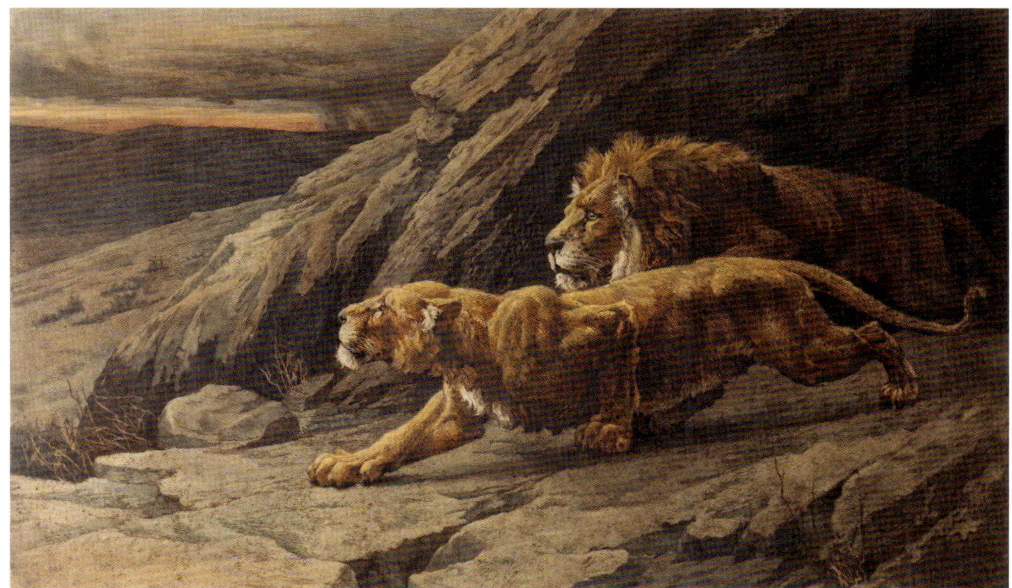

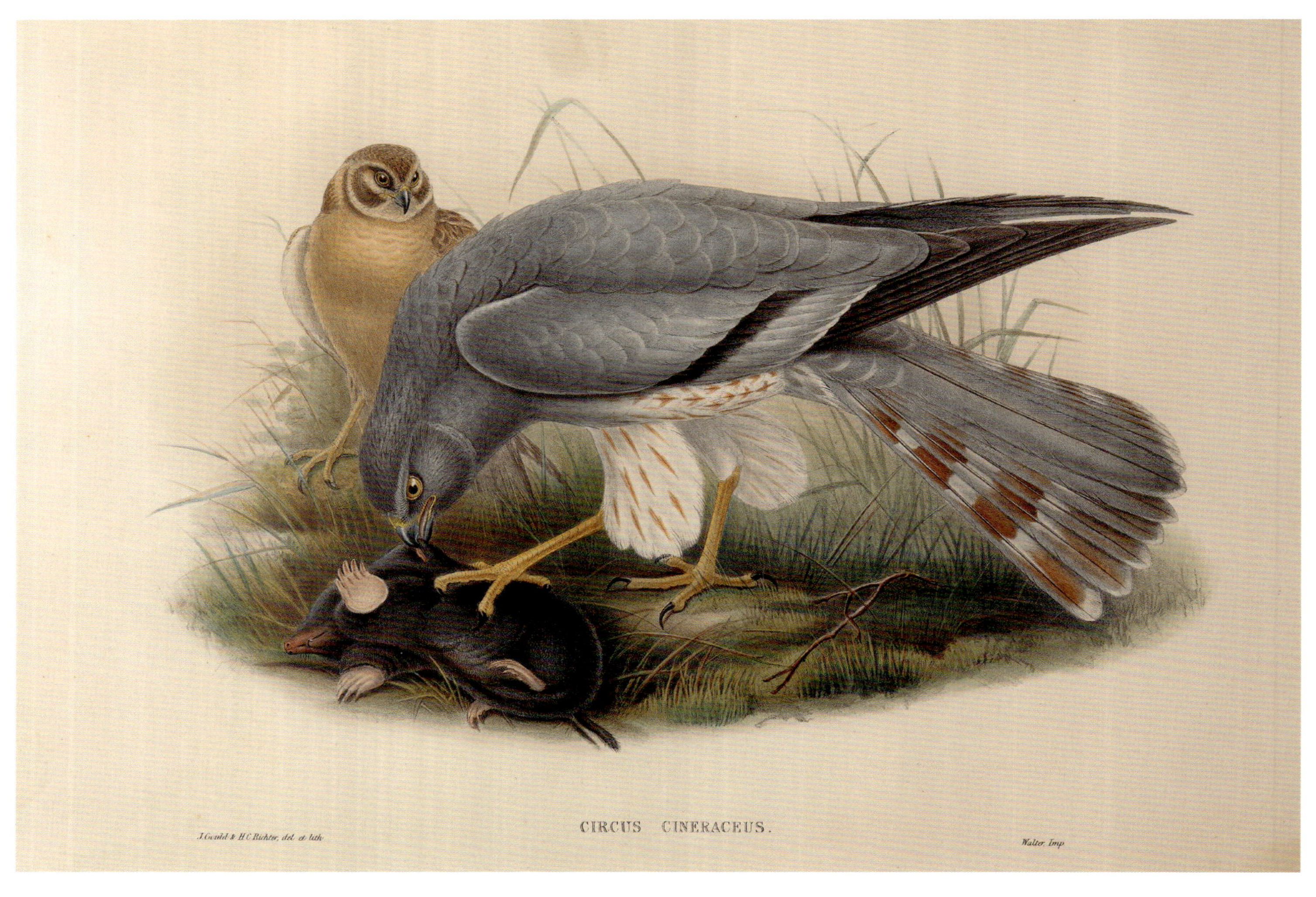

After John Gould (1804-1881), UK.
Montague's Harrier. Hand-coloured lithograph, 35cm x 53cm, Henry Constantine Richter (1821–1902), UK.

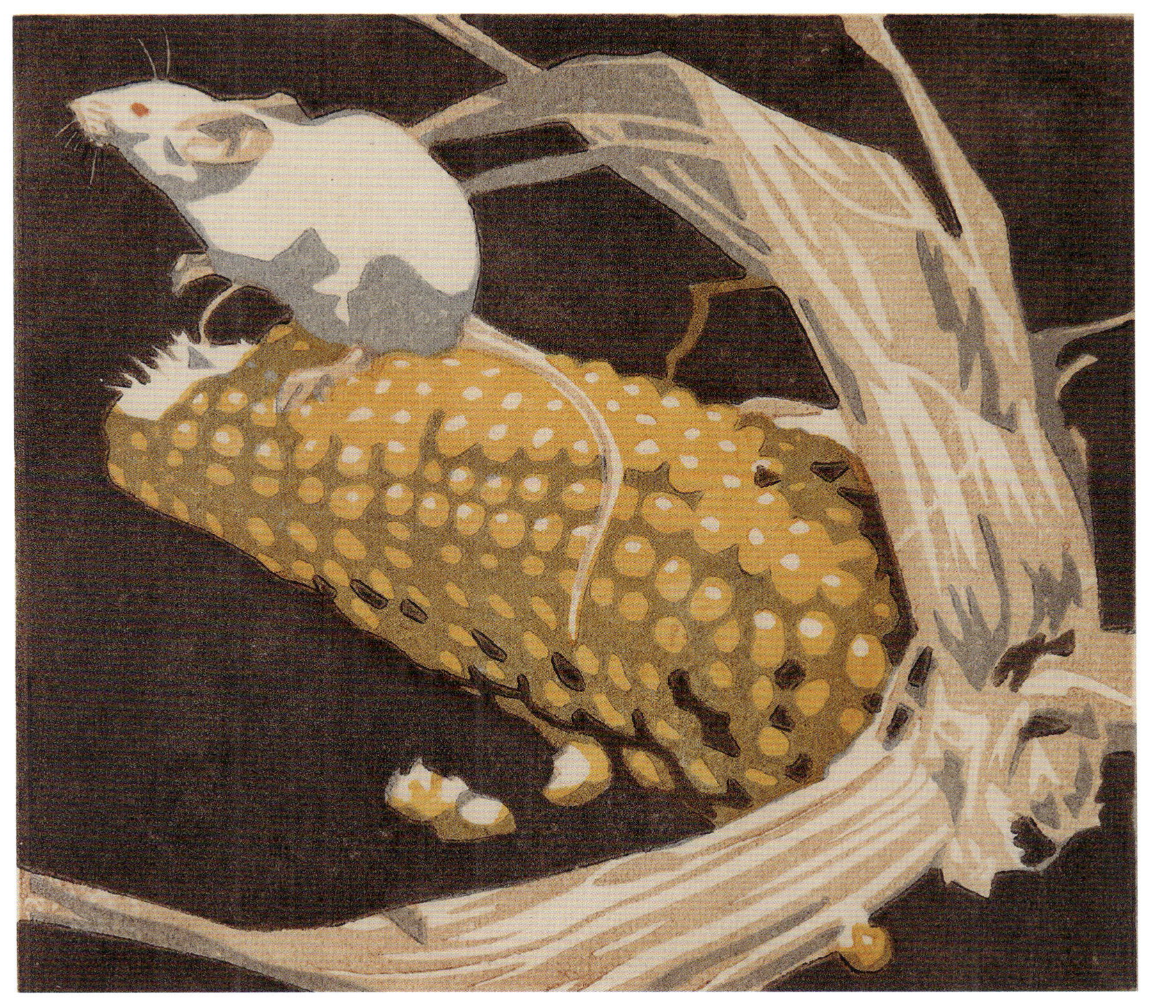

Norbertine von Bresslern-Roth (1891-1987), Austria. **Mouse on Maize**.
Woodblock print in four colours on paper, 13cm x 14cm. Inscribed, not dated.

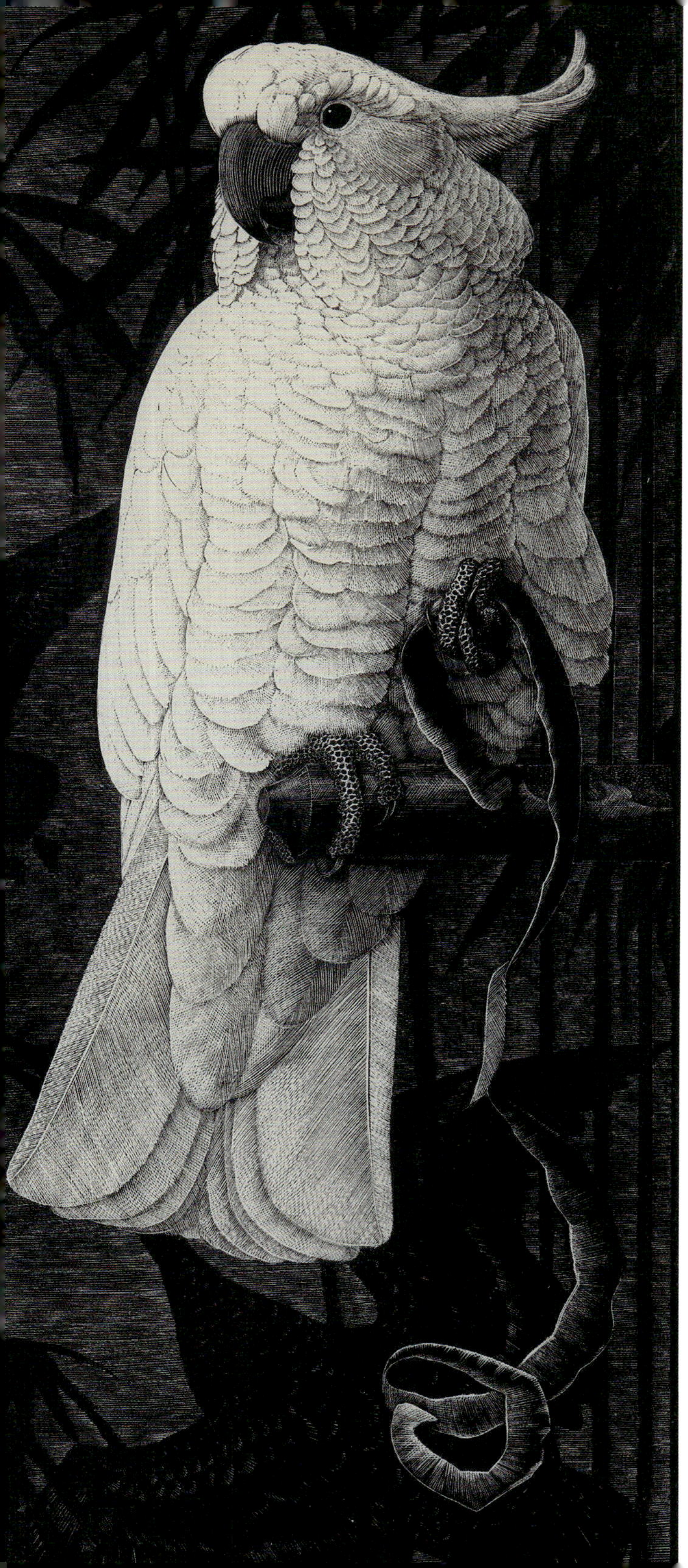

Left: Charles F. Tunnicliffe, R.A. (1901-1979), UK.
Cockatoo. Wood engraving, 42cm x 18cm.
Inscribed, not dated.
Masterly wood engraving by a painter.

Below: Robert Hainard (1906 – 1999), Switzerland.
Bouquetins, troupe de mâles dans la neige
(troupe of Alpine Ibex in the snow).
Woodblock print on toned paper, 29.5cm x 37.5cm.
Numbered "13/62". Signed and dated 1944.

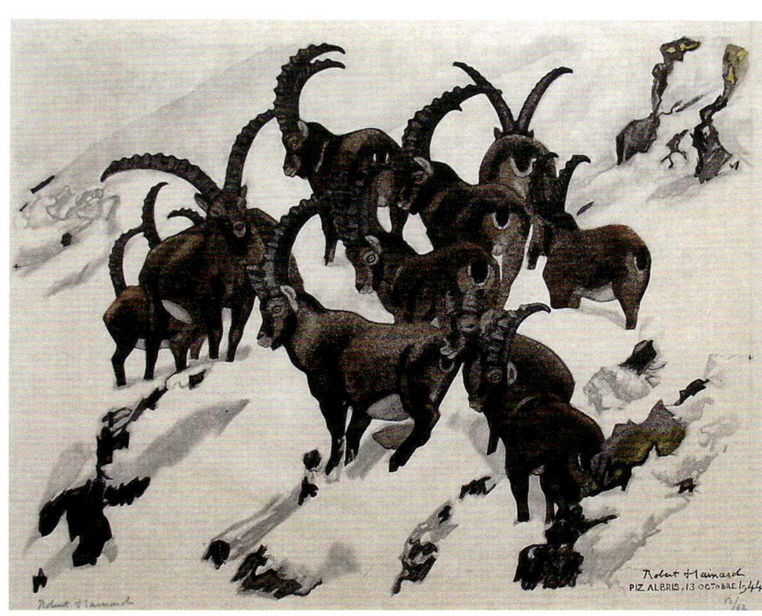

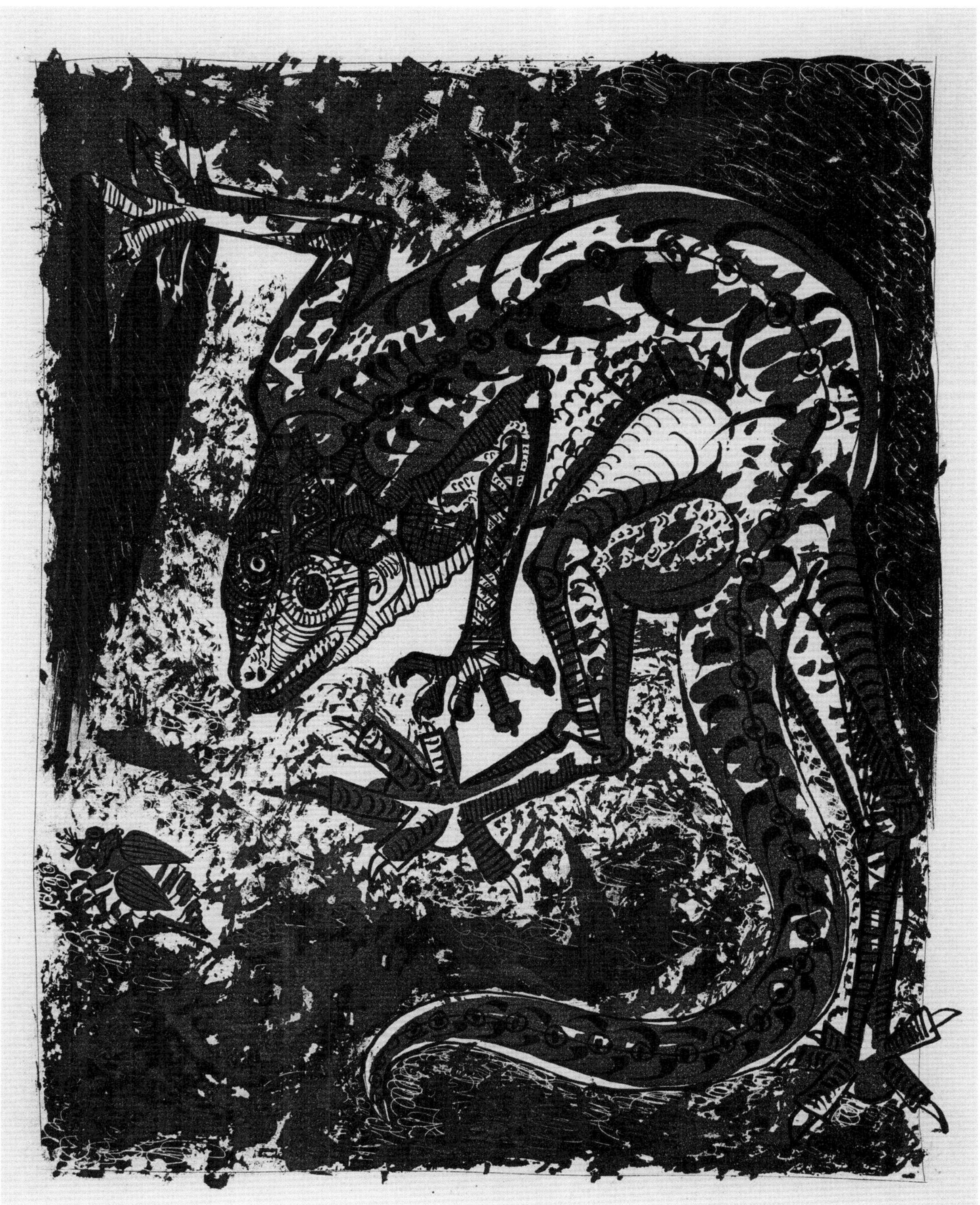

*Pablo Picasso
(1881-1973), Spain.
Le Lézard (The Lizard).
Aquatint with drypoint
from his Buffon Suite
(printed 1947, published
in an unsigned edition
of 226 in 1942),
27cm x 22cm.*

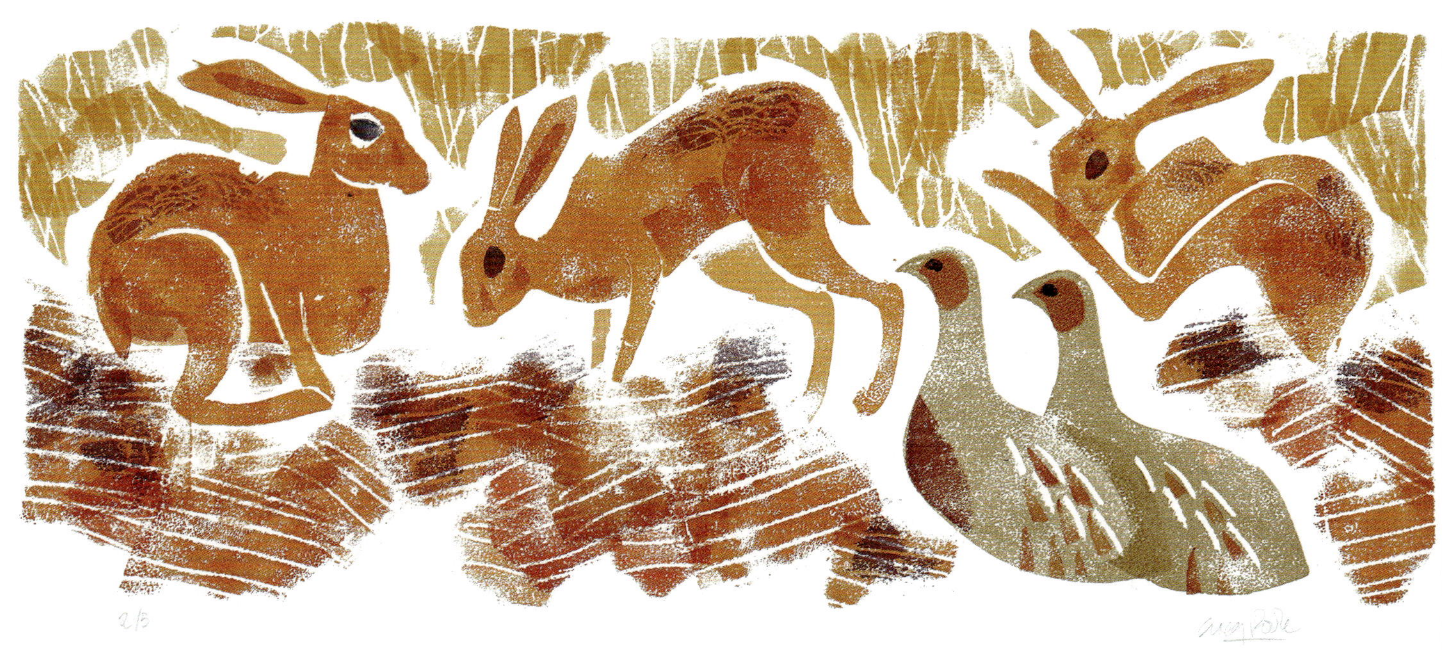

Above: Greg Poole (1960 –), UK.
Hares and Partridge. *Polystyrene print, 30.5cm x 65cm. Inscribed and numbered 2/5.*
This print was made by cutting out pieces of recycled polystyrene (hot food containers) and inking them with a roller,
then applying them to the paper separately.

Facing page: Nik Pollard (1960 –), UK.
Hare and Redshank. *Monoprint, 68cm x 89cm. Signed and dated 2003.*

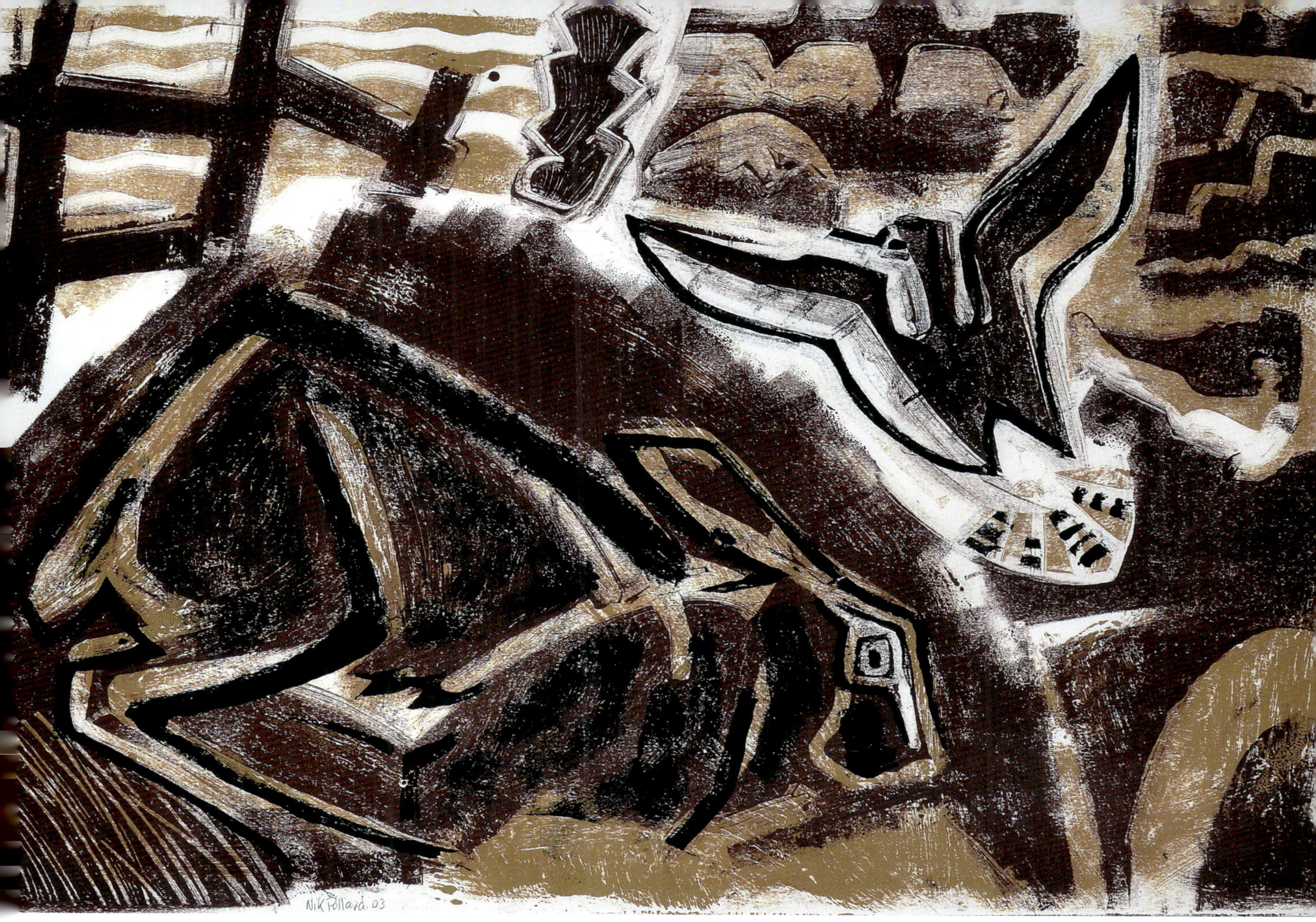

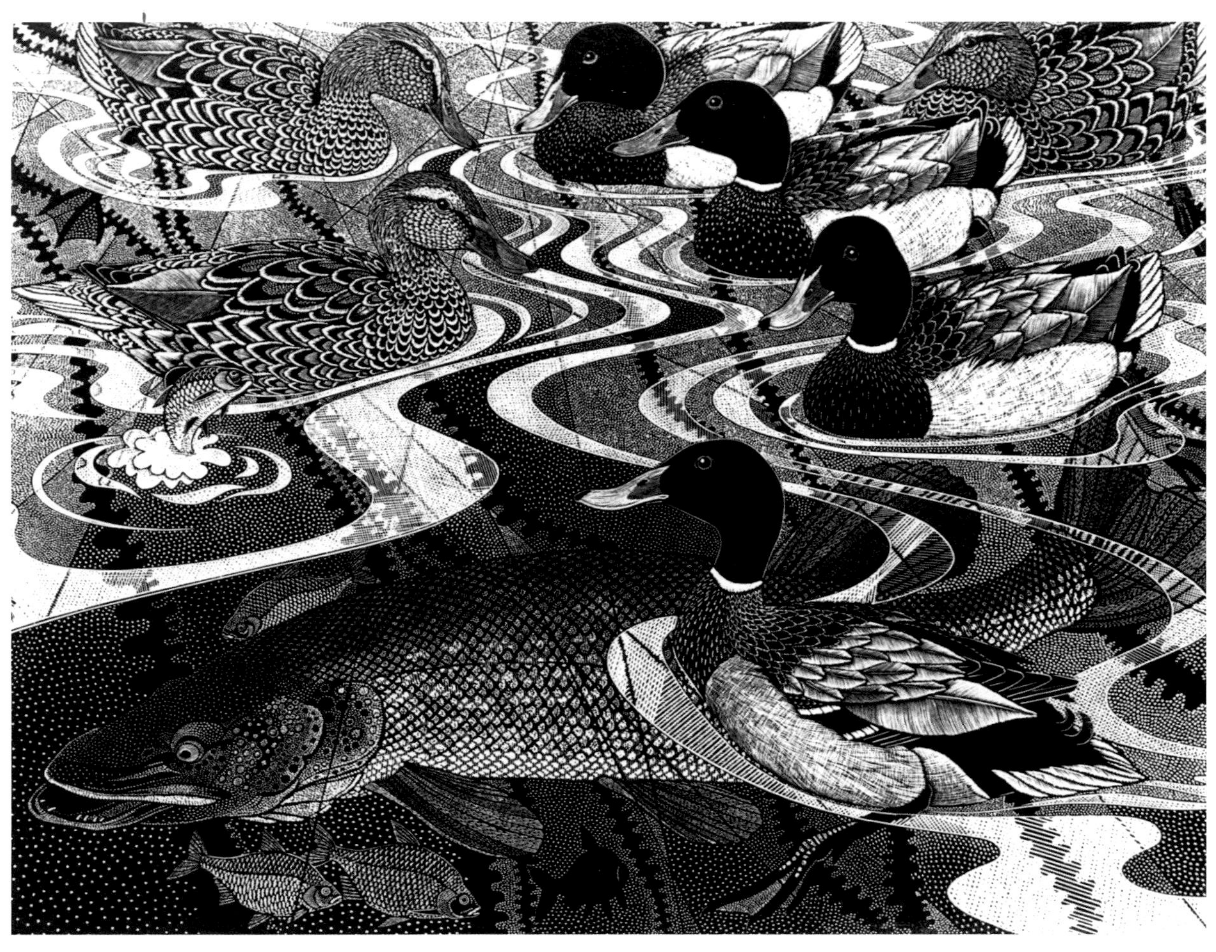

Above: Colin See-Paynton (1946 –), UK.
Mallard and Pike. *Wood engraving, 19cm x 25cm. Inscribed Paynton A/P 150.*
This is typical of his work, showing at once life above and below the surface of the water,
with detailed, complex patterned decoration in each.

Facing page: Keisei Kobayashi (1944 –), Japan.
Illusional Planet. *Wood engraving, 55cm x 50.5cm. Inscribed 1/1.*
It is most unusual for an artist to take all the time and trouble to make a work
such as this and make only one print from the block.

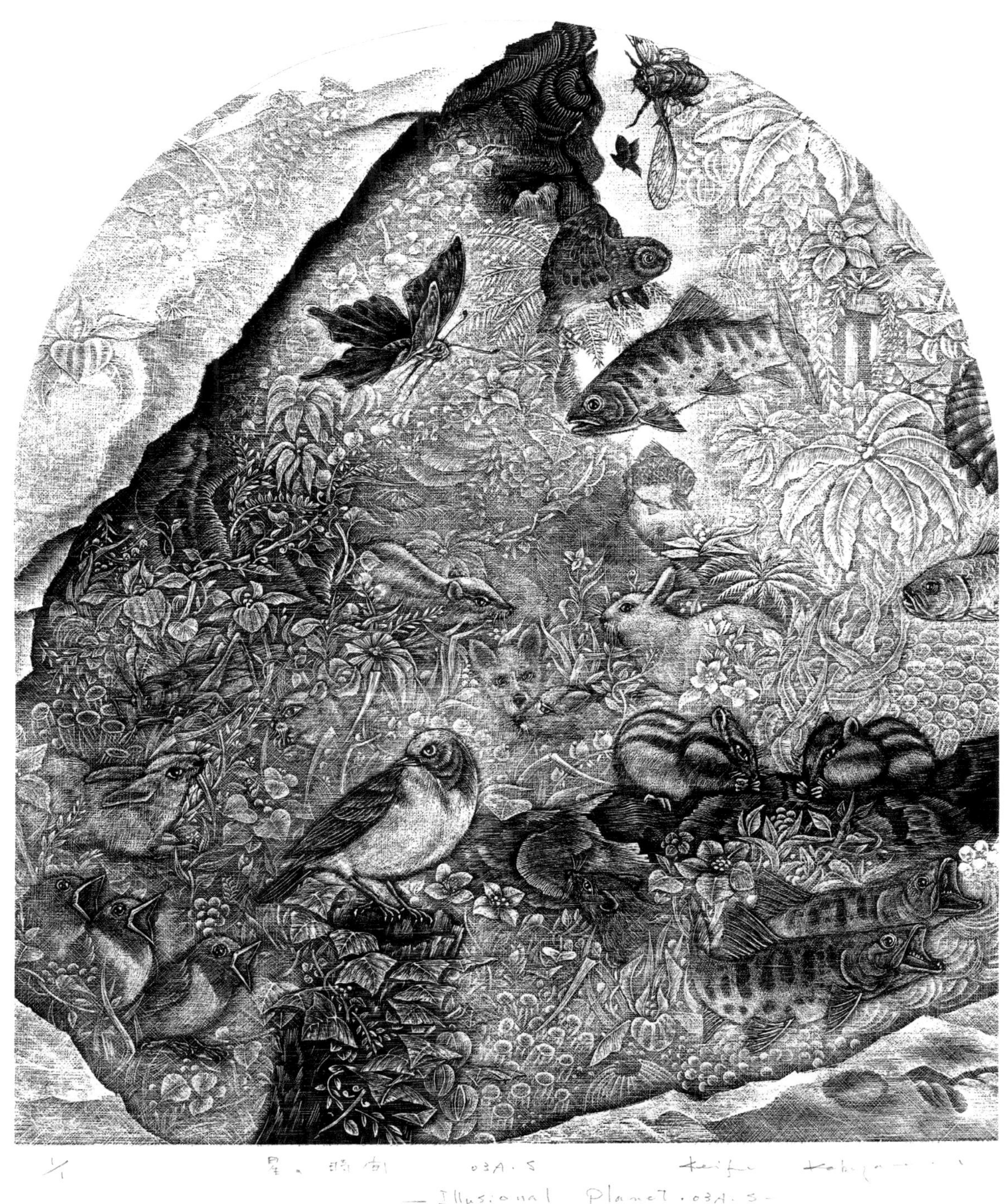

星の明向
Illusional Planet .03A.5.

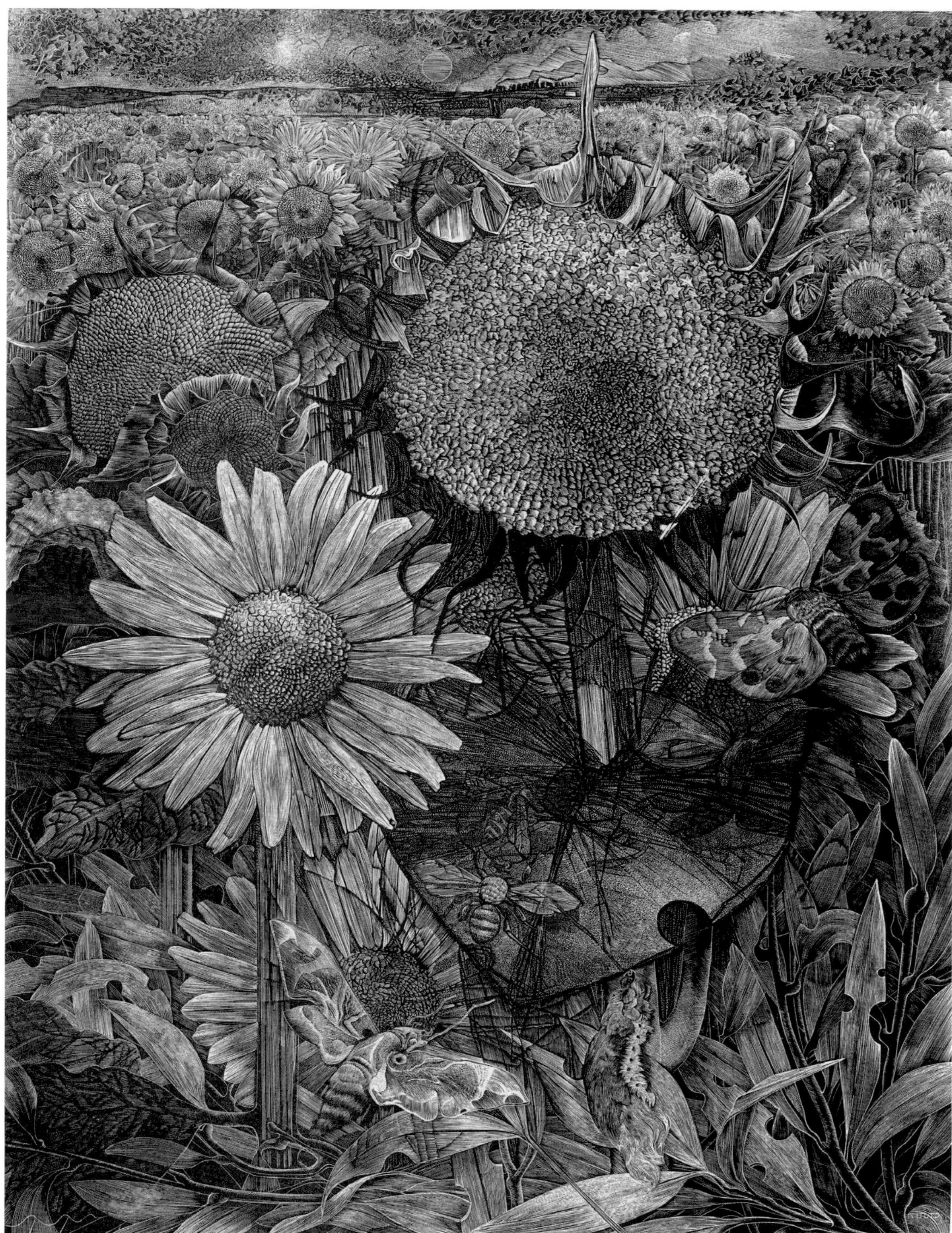

George Tute, RE, RWA
(1933 –), UK.
Sunflower Fields.
Wood engraving, 40cm x 30cm.
Inscribed and dated 1982, 35/75.

Julia Manning (contemporary), UK.
Cormorants.
Etching, 48.5cm x 32.5cm.
Inscribed: "The common cormorant or
shag lays eggs inside a paper bag
The reason you will see no doubt
It is to keep the lightning out." 7/100.
The humorous inscription is a quotation
from the nonsense poem
'The Common Cormorant' by
Christopher Isherwood (1904-1986).

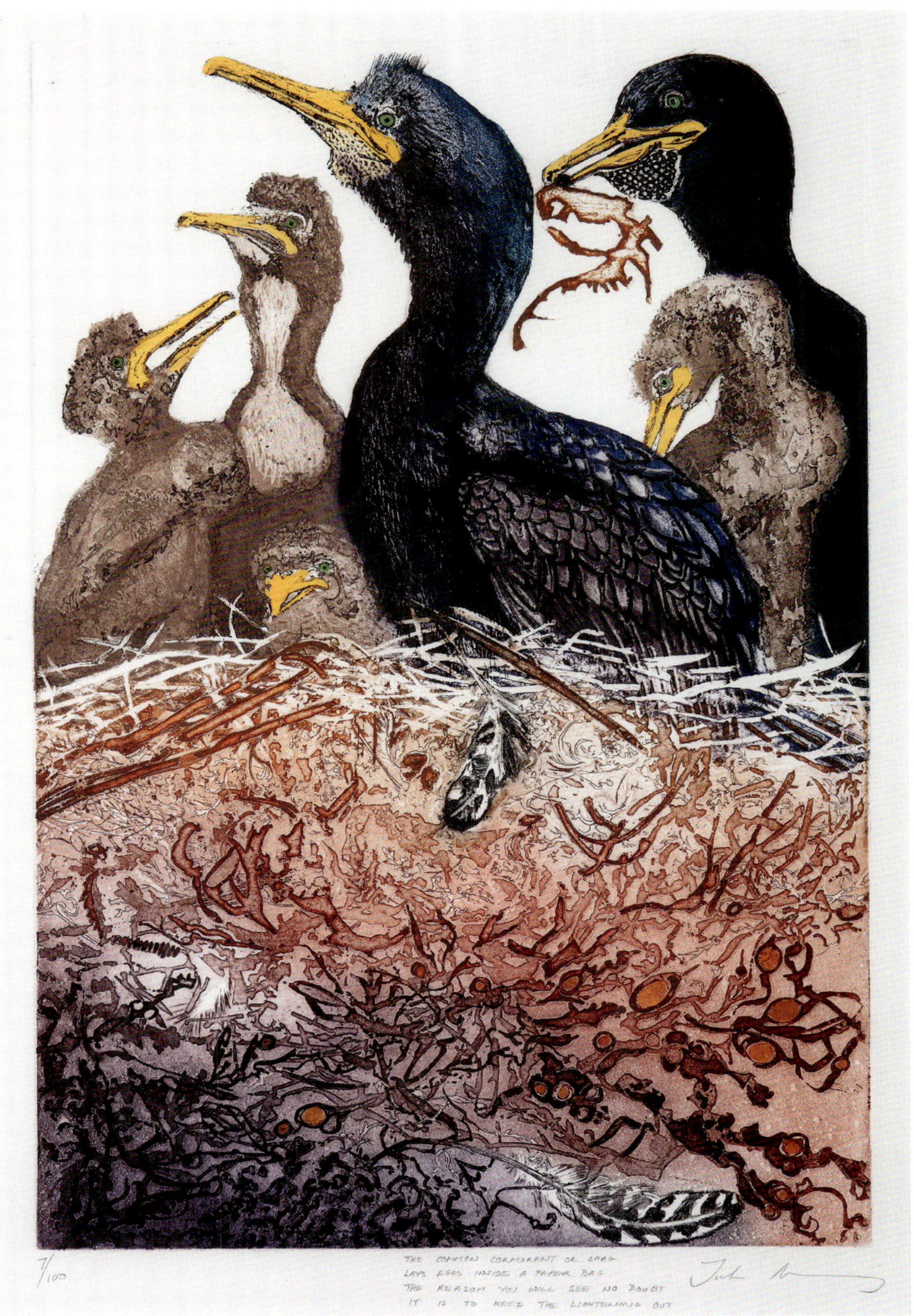

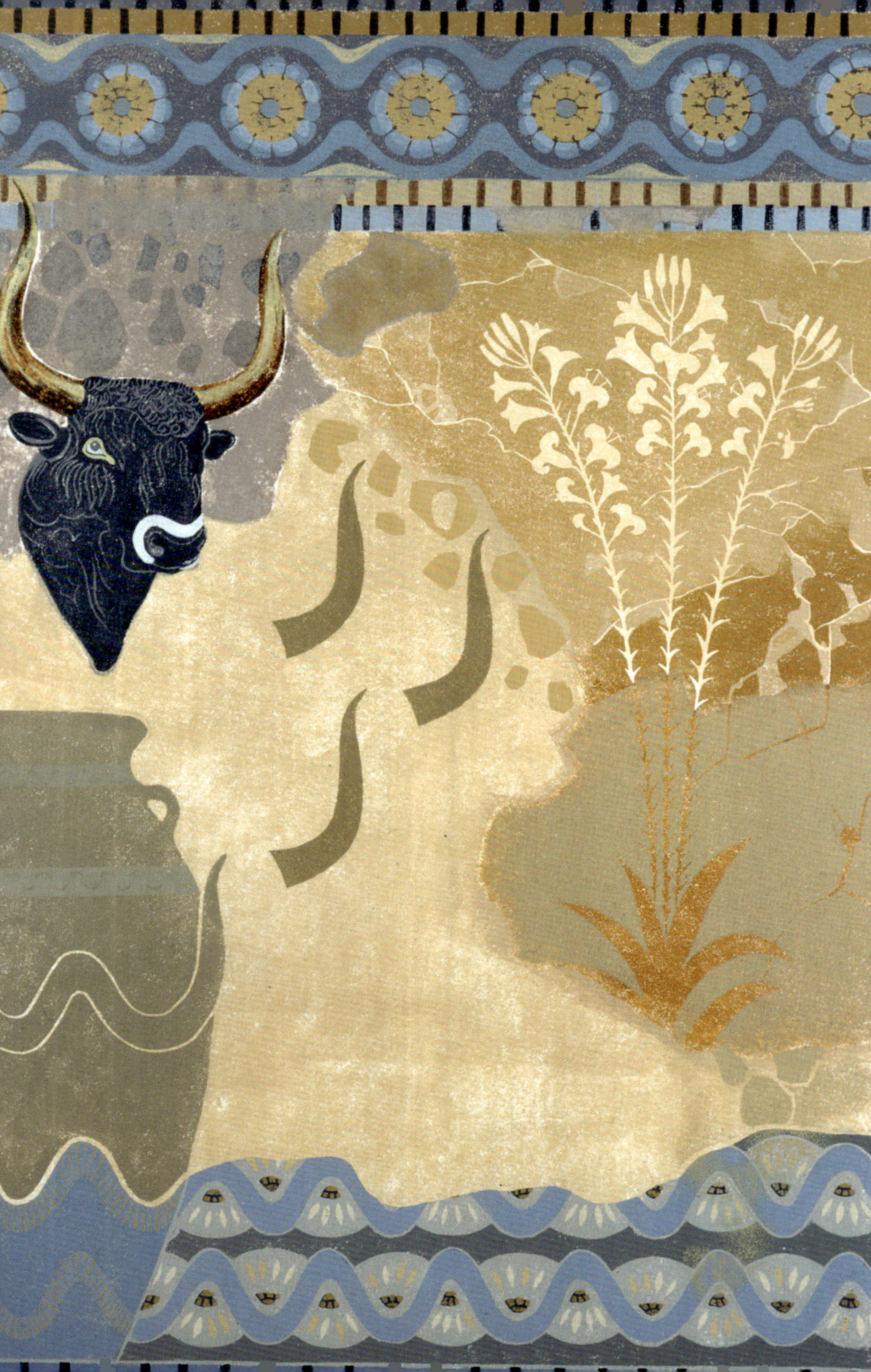

Ben Venuto (1928 –), UK.
Ode to Knossos.
Reduction linocut,
71.5cm x 45cm.
A 'reduction print' is a
technically difficult one in
which all the colours are
applied from one block.
Picasso described it as the
'suicide method' because of
its unforgiving nature.

ROOKS AND BOOKS

You may be like me when you visit a museum or art gallery. Sometimes I am looking at the pictures, the sculptures, or whatever, just to see what is in the collection. Sometimes I am looking for a specific subject in many media – that can be very interesting. So here are two examples of this approach. I am looking for rooks and books – both are uncommon subjects in most art museum collections.

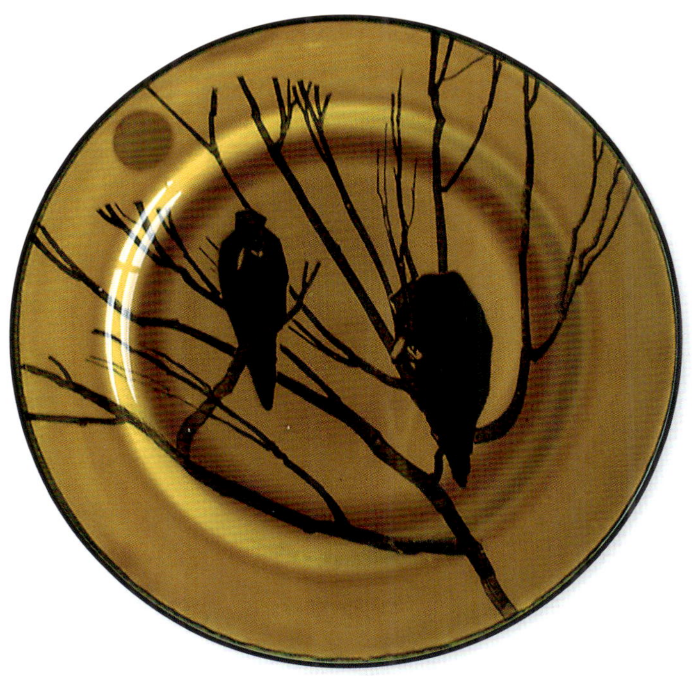

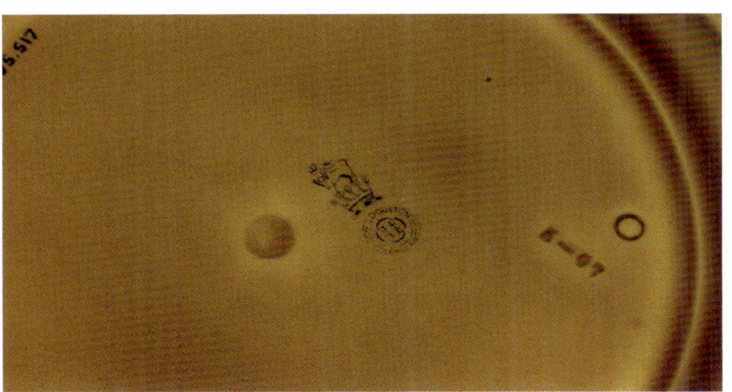

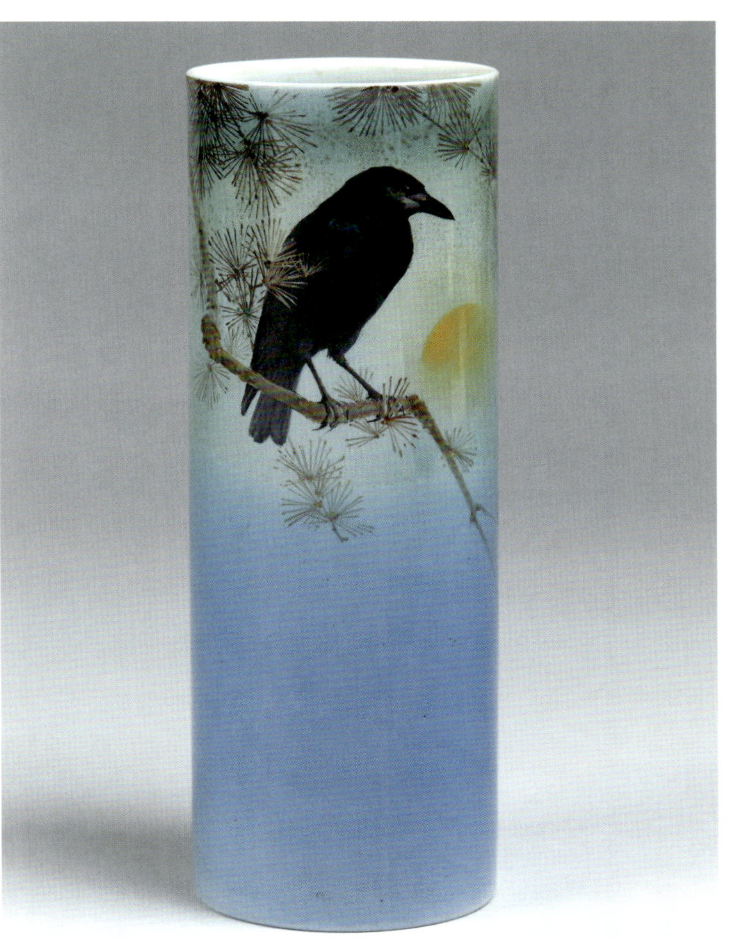

*Left: unknown artist, UK. **Two Rooks and Setting Sun**. Royal Doulton ceramic plate (1902-1922). Diameter 26.7cm. The impressed "5 - 07" on the base probably indicates manufacture of the plate in May 1907, although the artistic style suggests a later date for its decoration. The Royal Doulton mark was used from 1902-1922.*

*Above: Harry Allen (1899-1950), UK. **Rook and Setting Sun**. Royal Doulton Titanian ware cylindrical vase (21.2cm x 7.4cm). Titanian ware used titanium oxide in the glaze. This produced a wide range of blues, from dark to almost white. The 1920s were a time of much experimentation at the Doulton factory at Burslem, Stoke-on-Trent, under Charles R. Noke, Senior Designer and later Art Director.*

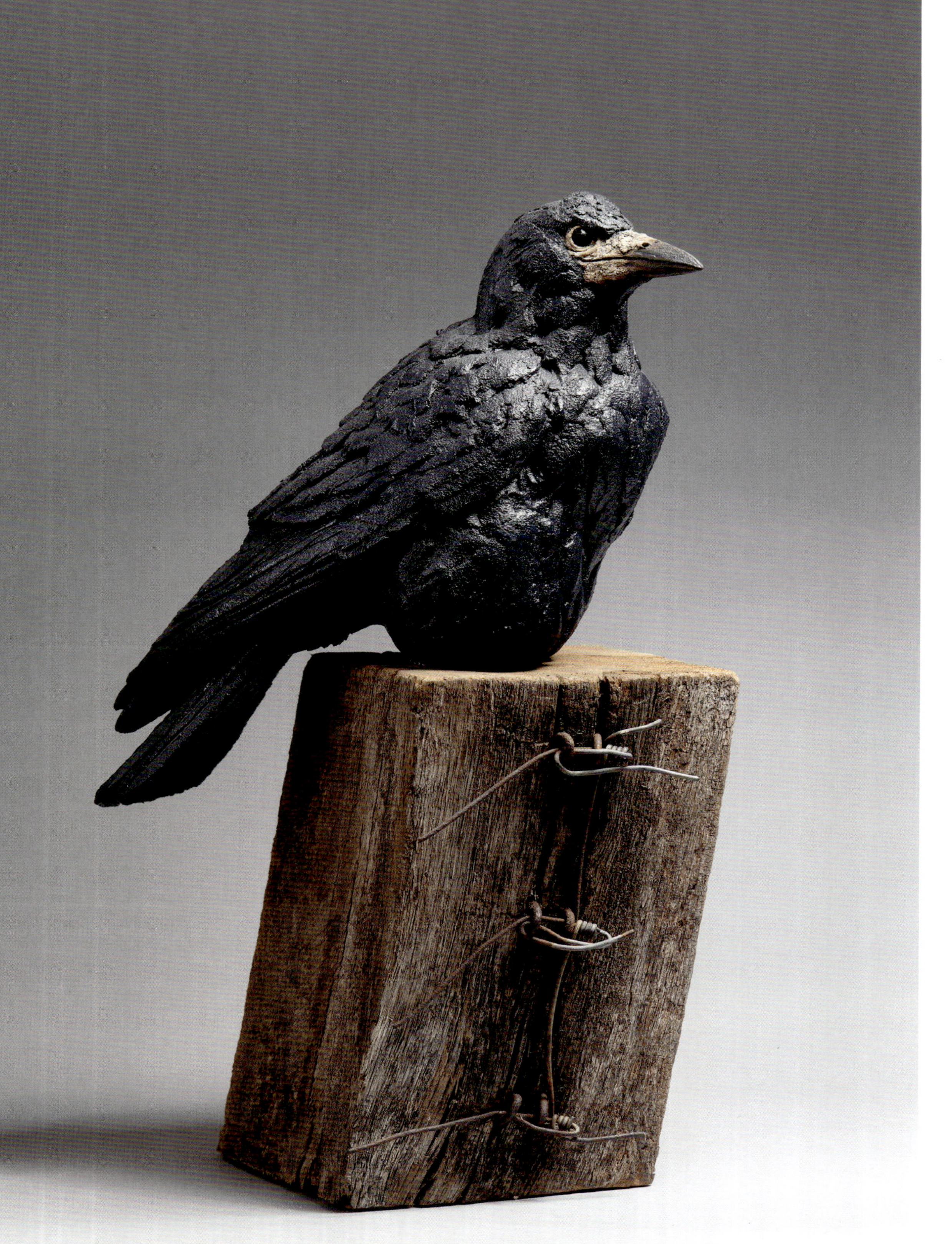

Simon Griffiths (contemporary), UK. *Rook*. Ceramic on part of an old oak fence post, 50cm x 30cm x 25cm. The decision by the artist to cut the fence post obliquely and leave the attached barbed wire was a stroke of genius!

Books are not usually regarded as works of art. Occasionally, however, artist binders or publishers consciously decide to make the cover (rather than the dust jacket) lovely to look at and to handle, as much as the contents to read.

COMMERCIAL BINDINGS CLEARLY INSPIRED BY NATURE

Both these books are examples of mid-nineteenth-century book publishers using expensive and technically difficult bindings on the outside of their best-quality colour-printed pages inside.

Below left: pressed black papier-mâché with red cloth backing on 'Coinage of the British Empire' by Henry Noel Humphreys, published by Jackson & Sons, 1855.

Below right: pressed leather binding (patented by Frederick Leake) of 'Gray's Elegy', published by Longman & Co, London, 1846.

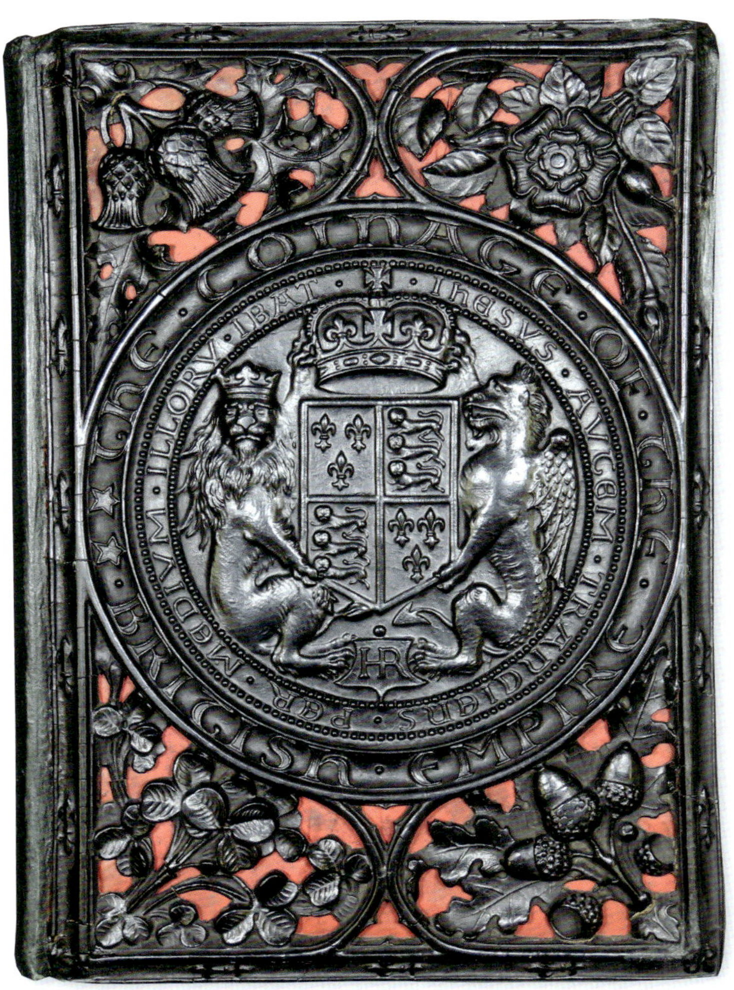

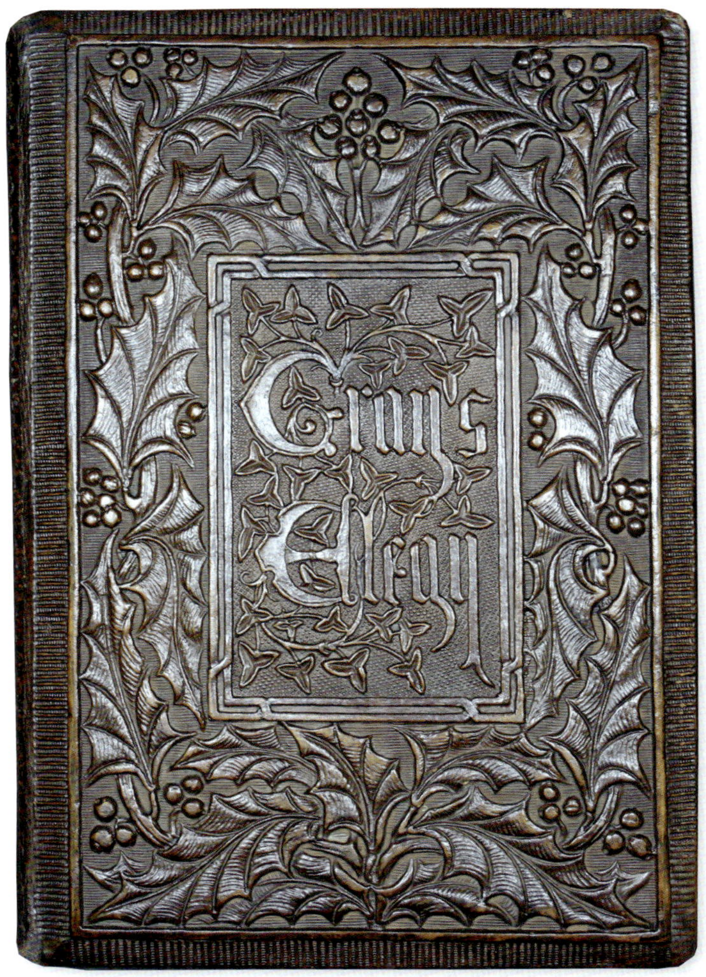

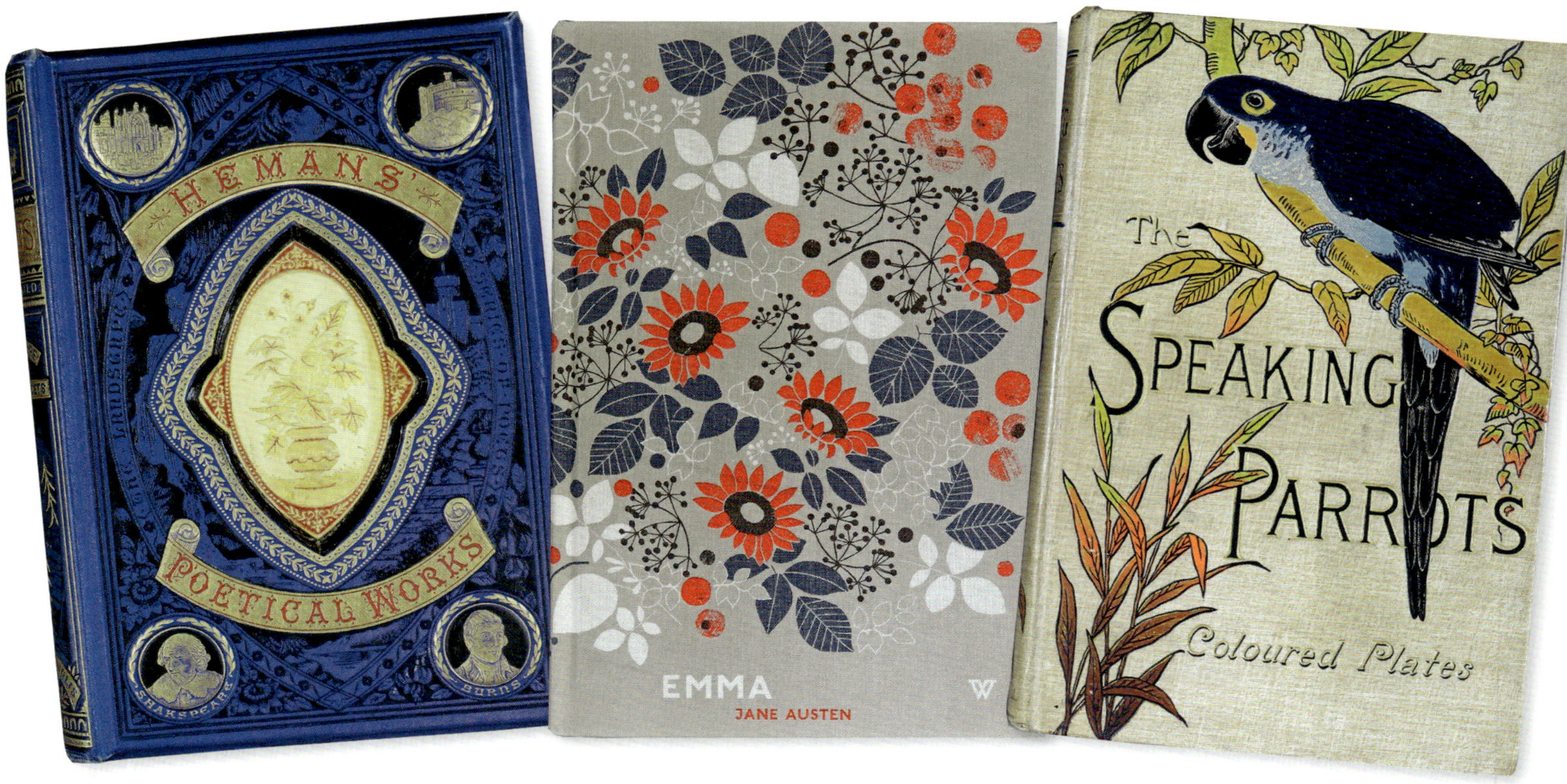

*Above left: ornate, embossed and recessed gilt floral panel on a commercial binding for 'Hemans' Poetical Works',
19.5cm x 14cm x 3.5cm, published by Gall & Inglis, Edinburgh, 1882.*

*Above centre: Amy Gibson (contemporary), UK. Floral design on cloth-covered hard binding on 'Emma' by Jane Austen,
24cm x 13.5cm x 3cm, published (and donated) by White's Books, London, 2009.*

*Above right: design artist unknown. 'The Speaking Parrots' (1912) by Dr Karl Russ,
published by Upcott Gill, London. 20cm x 13.5cm x 3cm.*

DESIGNER BINDINGS (USUALLY 'ONE-OFF' WORKS BY BINDER-ARTISTS)

Right: William Perry, 1863. Wood carver to HM Queen Victoria.
Carver, binder, author and photographer. 19.5cm x 14.5cm.
Signed by the author/maker.
The front of a book, with solid oak covers back and front, hand-carved
with floral swags, and a central photographic print of an ancient oak
tree in Windsor Great Park. The oak for the book came from this tree
that had recently died. The photograph is protected by a thin convex
panel of glass. The carving was done and the text of the book written by
the same man for this publication, limited to six copies. One copy was
presented to HM Queen Victoria. The tree shown was thought to be the
Maiden Tree mentioned in Shakespeare's 'Merry Wives of Windsor'.

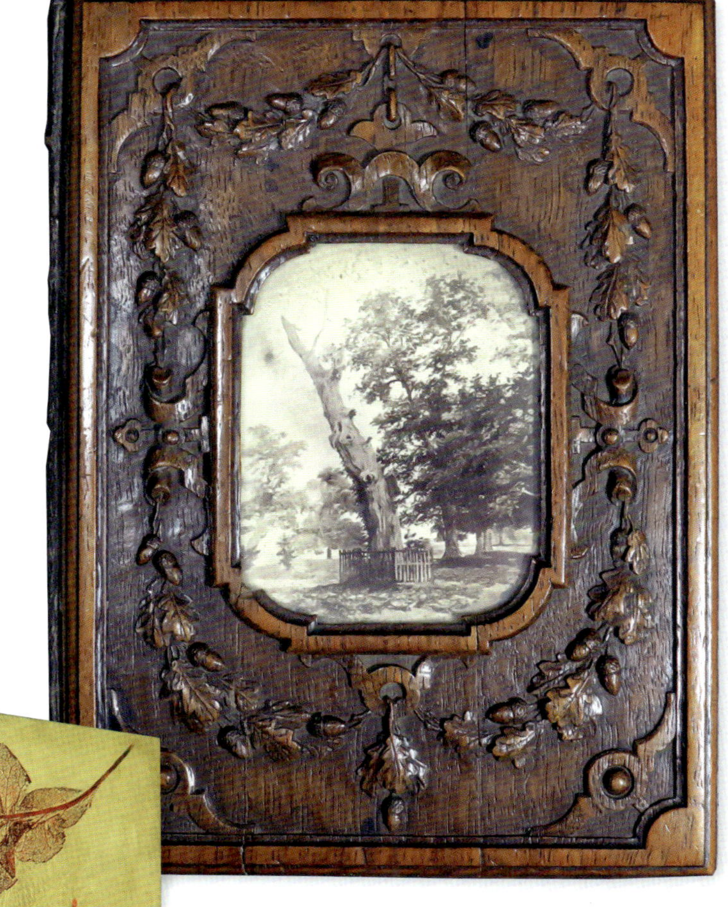

Left: unknown binder (initials "R.M.W.S."), UK.
Leaf skeletons on calf leather binding of
'Four Hedges: a Gardener's Chronicle'
by Clare Leighton, published by Victor
Gollancz, 1935. 26cm x 20cm x 3cm.

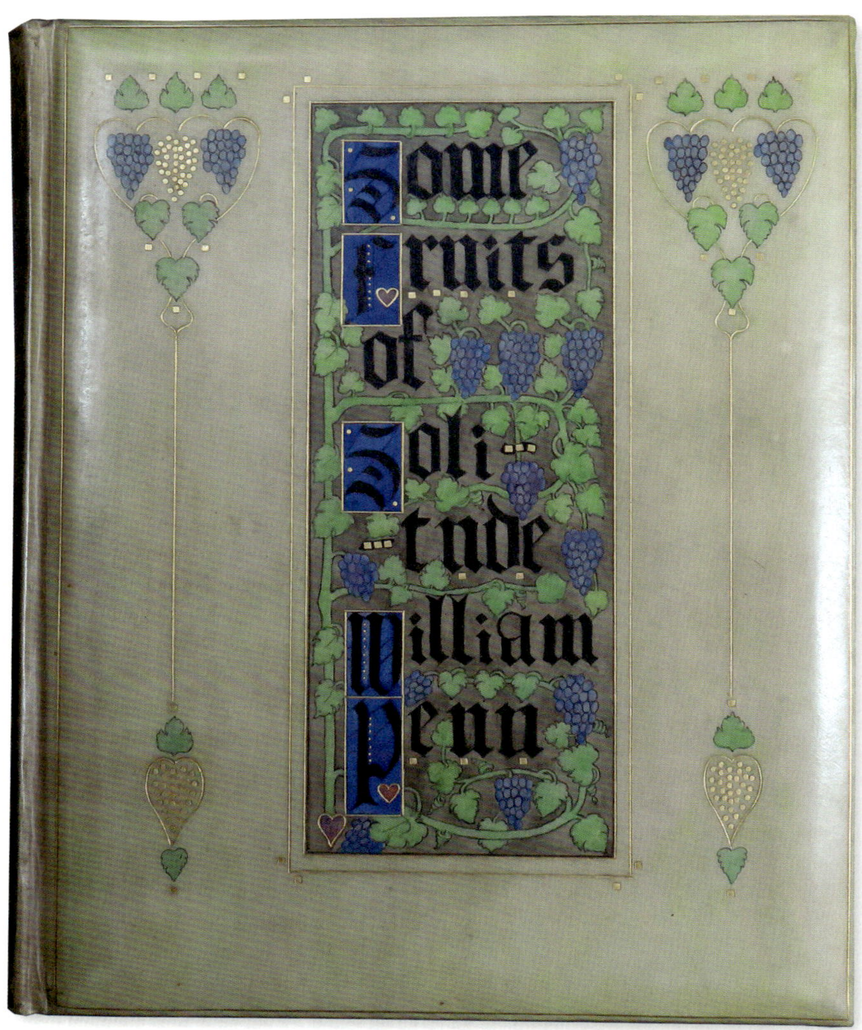

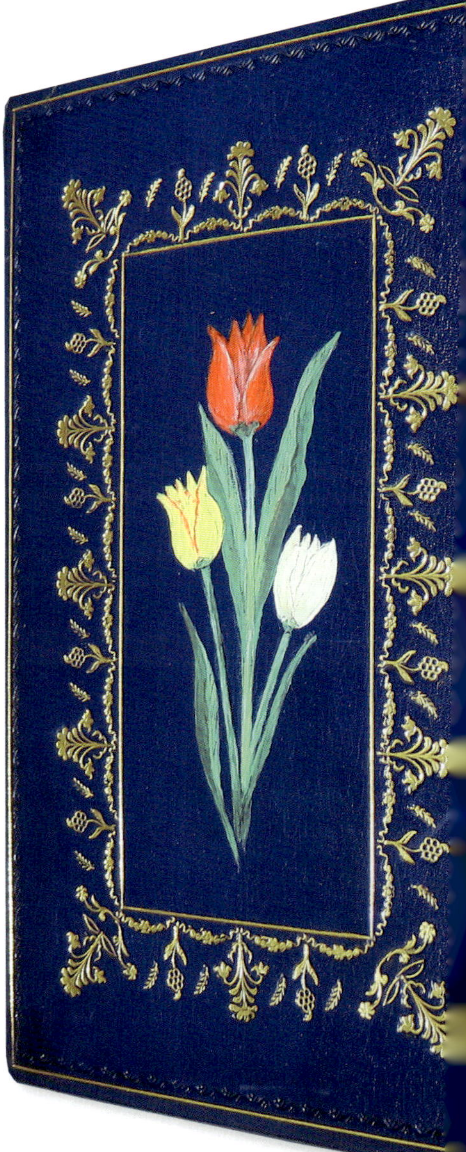

Left: Cedric Chivers, artist /binder of Bath, Somerset, UK. 'Vellucent' binding (semi-transparent vellum) in typical Art Nouveau style on 'Some Fruits of Solitude' by William Penn, with a foreword by Edmund Gosse. 1901. 19.5cm x 13cm x 3.5cm.

Right: Mary Martin (died 2000), UK. One-off 'designer' leather book binding of 'The Art of Botanical Illustration' by Wilfrid Blunt. 22cm x 15cm x 3.5cm.

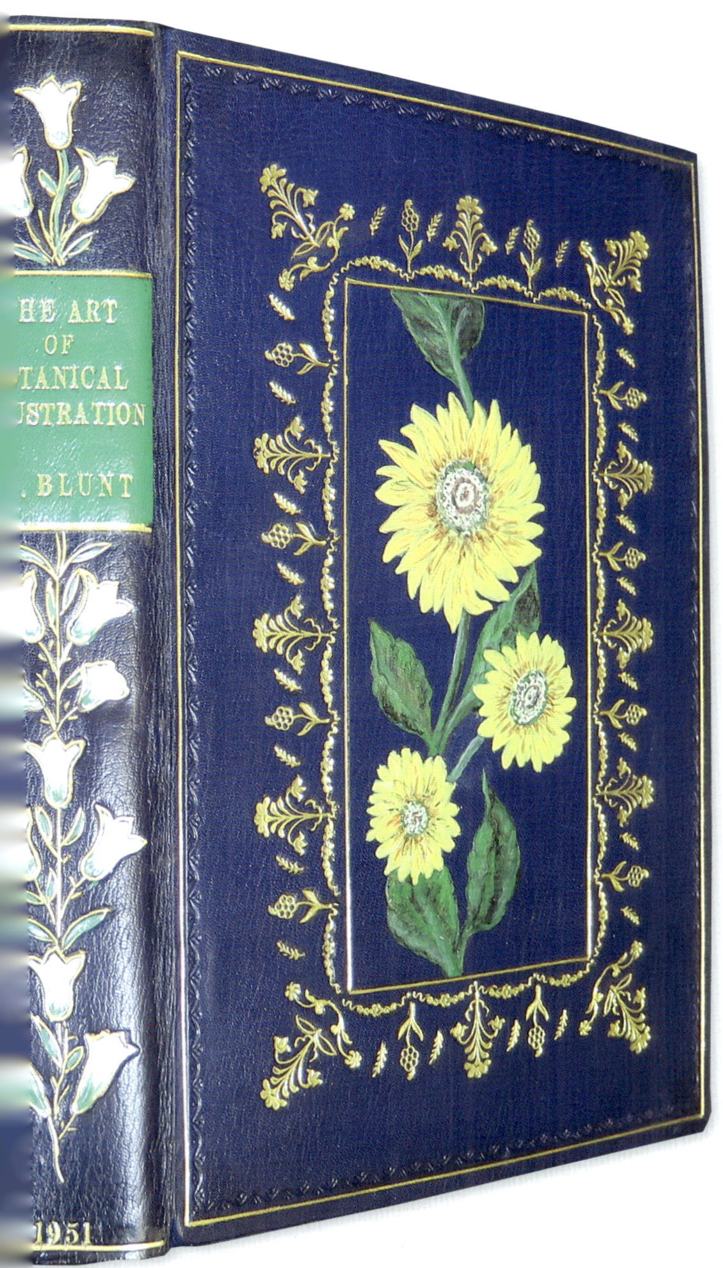

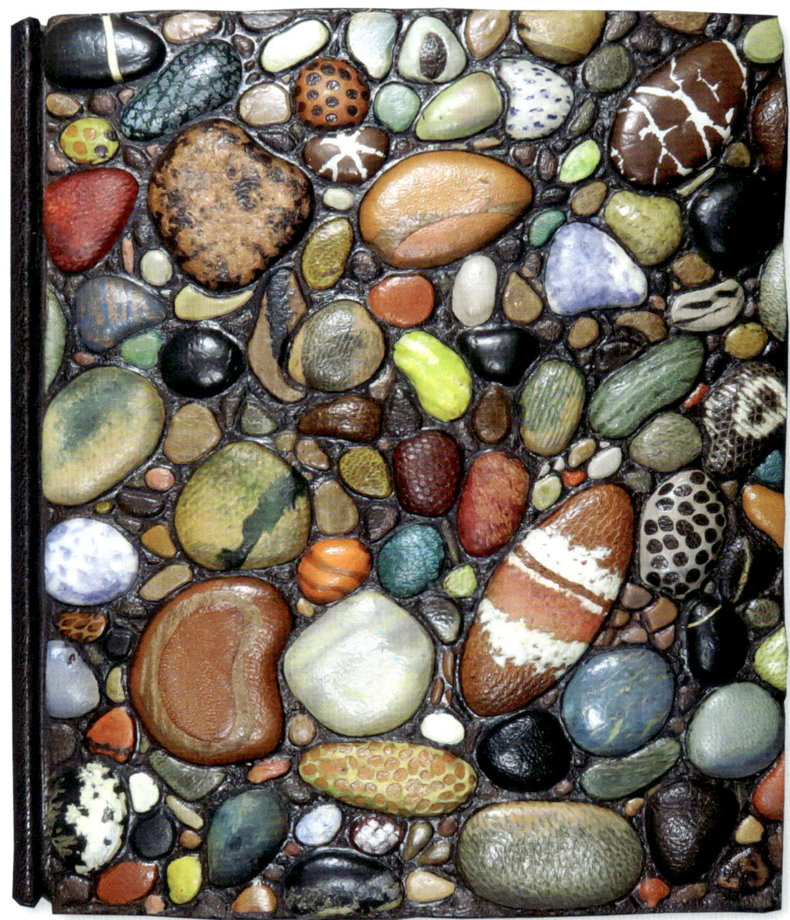

Above: George Kirkpatrick, UK. 2009.
Multi-leather binding and contents, 'Alphabets of Stone collected from
British beaches' – a series of photographs of sea-shore pebbles with
apparent alphabet-like letters on them. 17.5cm x 15cm x 2.5cm.
A wide range of very carefully chosen leathers (padded) have been used on
the back and front to create the impression of a beach of pebbles.

SCULPTURE

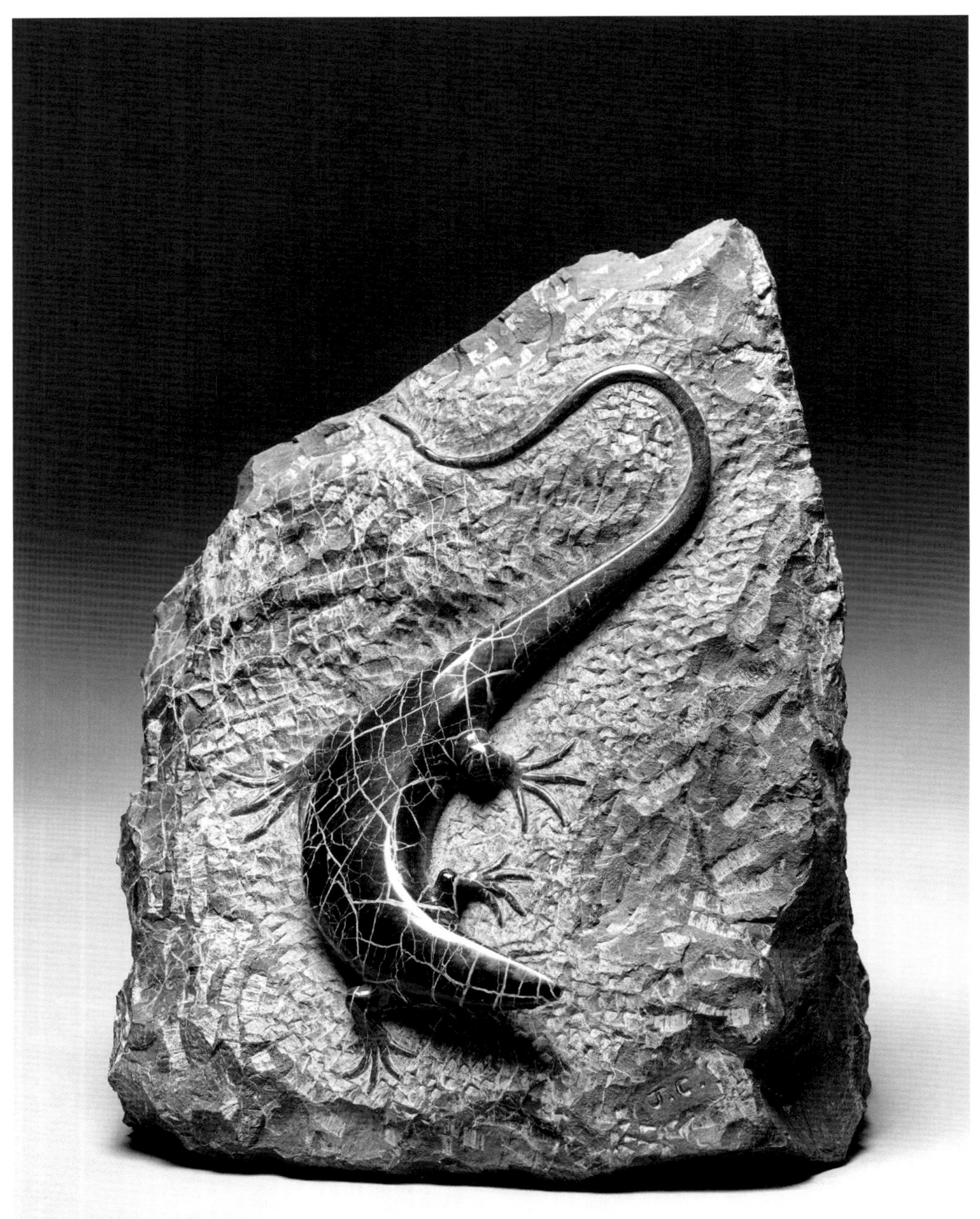

*John Carlyon (1917–1982), UK. **Lizard**.*
Signed "J.C" (lower right).
Carved from serpentine stone from
The Lizard peninsula, Cornwall, one
of the few places this stone is found.
29cm x 20cm x 13cm. This softer-than-
most stone can be polished to reveal
the natural colours within it – as here.
Nothing has been added.

Facing page: Erik and Martin Demaine (contemporary), USA.
Natural Habitat.
Origami, watercolour on folded paper. 33cm x 28cm x 33cm.
This piece was designed to include small vinyl frogs which, the artists said, could be omitted or included. They are not shown here. The sculpture was made by glueing together two sheets of art paper of different colours with an archival PVA glue before folding.

Right: Geoffrey Dashwood (1947 –), UK. **Cormorant**. *Bronze, 69cm x 50cm x 72cm.*
Signed "Dashwood A/C".

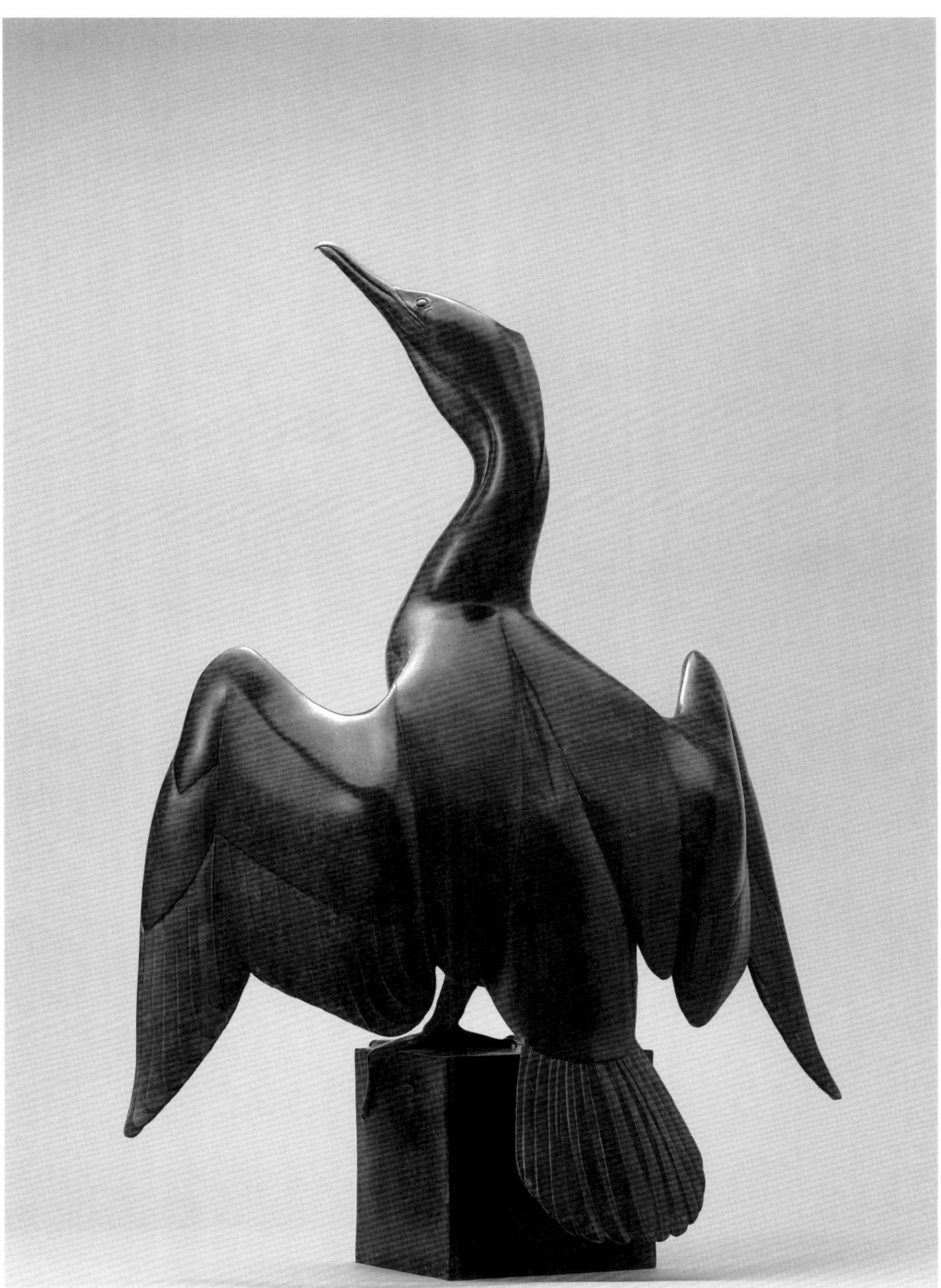

INLAID STONE

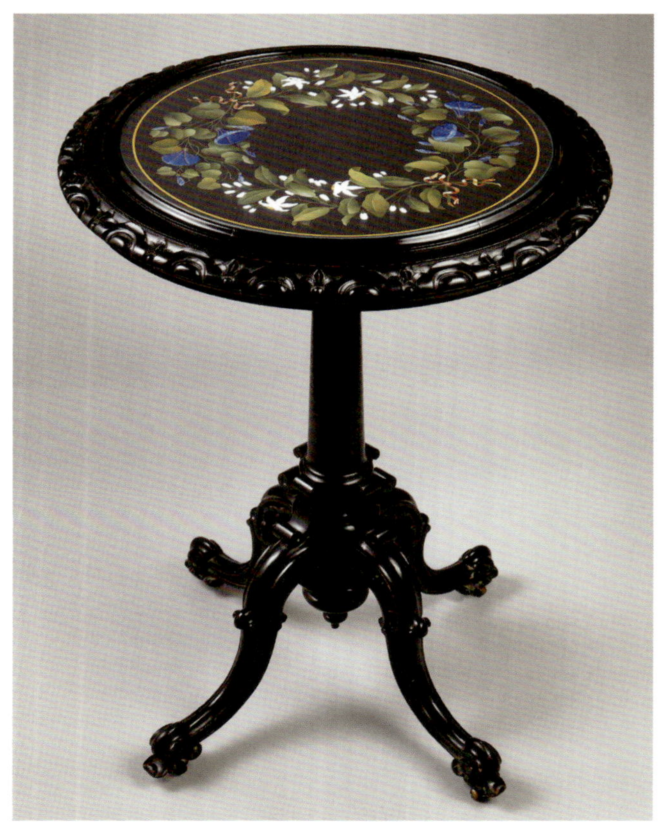

Below (detail) and left: Italian inlaid stone table top, diameter 53.5cm, in an English 'ebonised' mahogany table. Table height 73.5cm. The black so-called 'marble' is actually polished limestone in these and in the following pieces.

Bottom: a further detail showing blue morning glory flowers made of lapis lazuli.

Table bought with the aid of a grant from the MGC V&A Purchase Grant Fund.

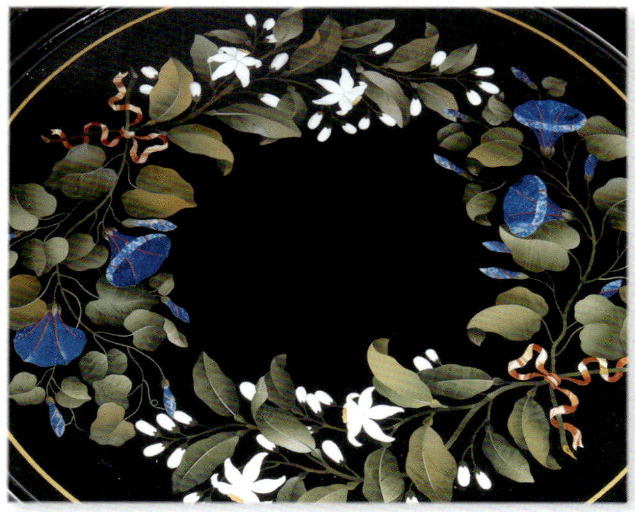

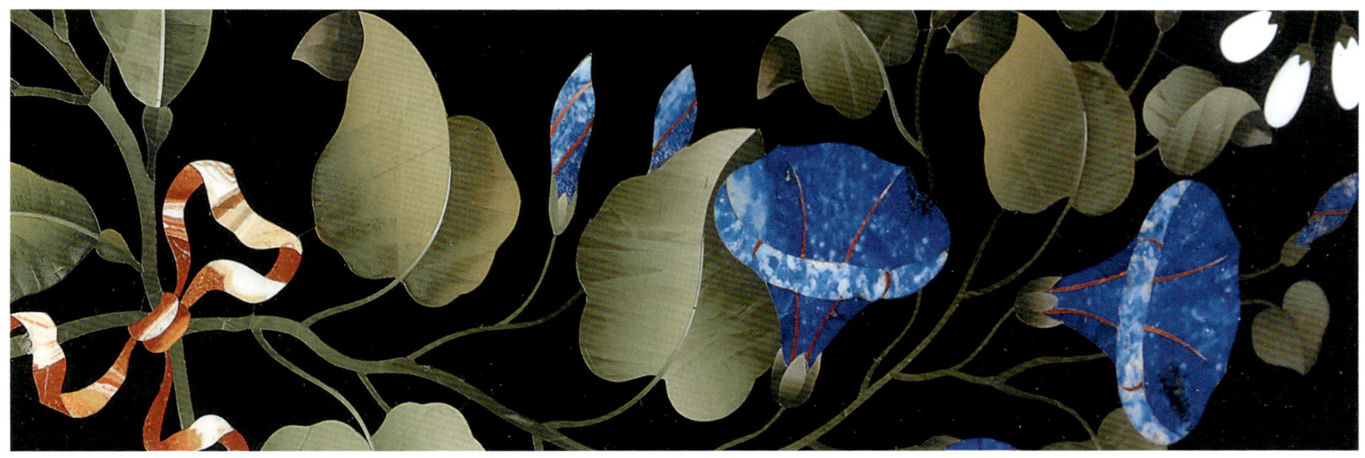

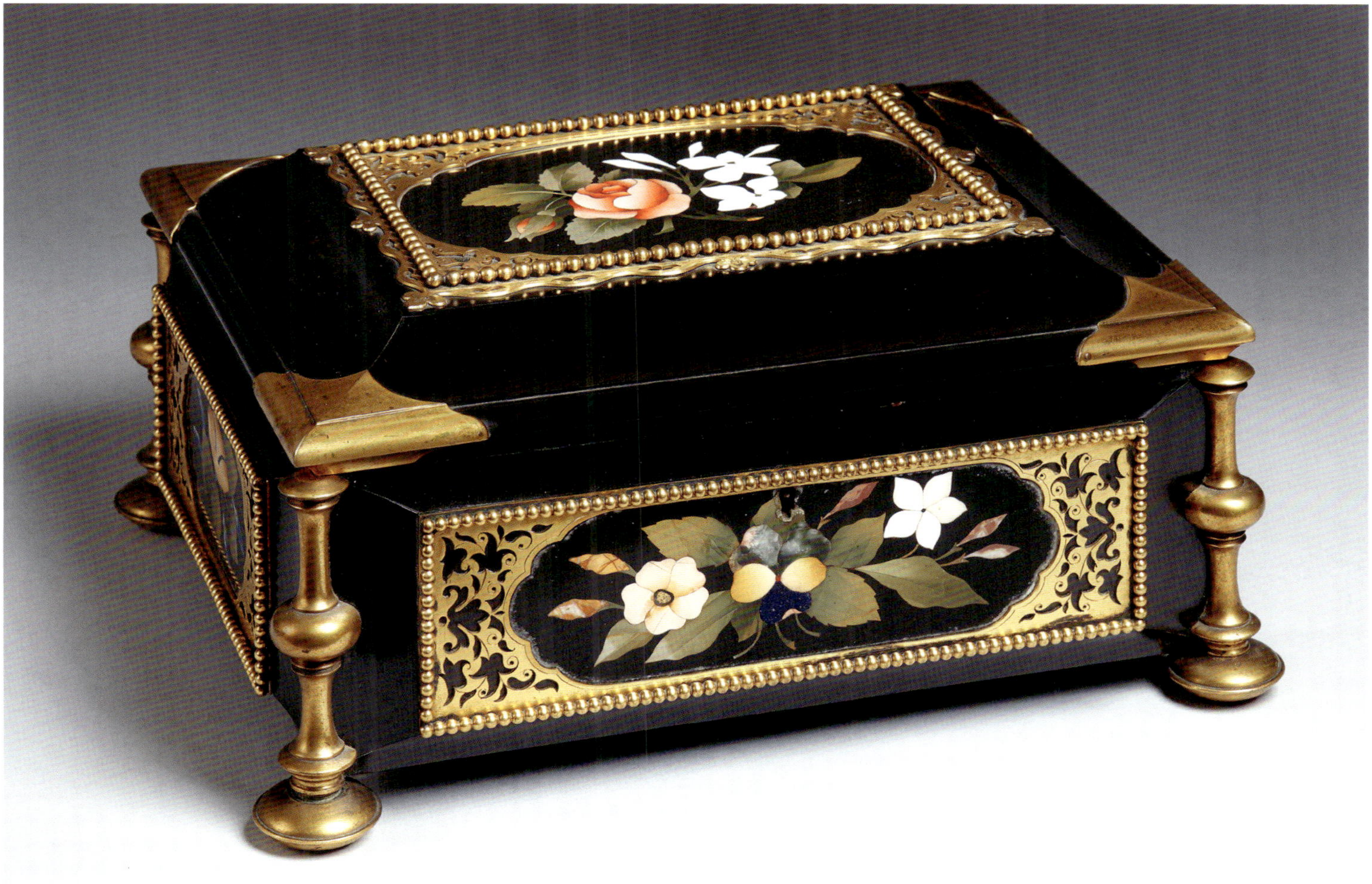

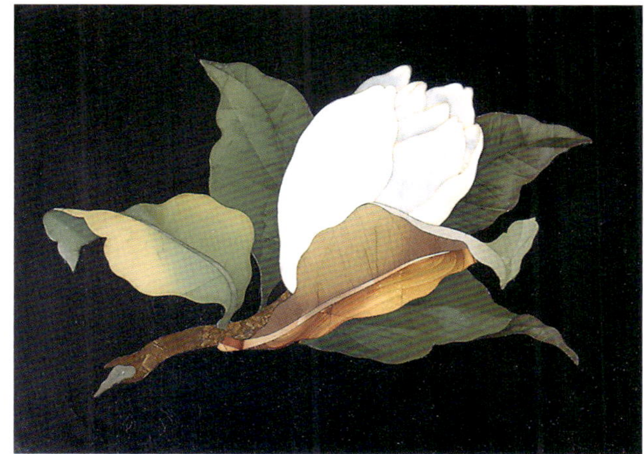

Above: no maker's name or date, late 19th century. Scarce Italian ebonised wood casket with decorative brass fittings and inlaid stone panels. 15.7cm x 33cm x 26.5cm. A similar casket is in the Los Angeles County Museum, California, USA.

Right: unknown maker, Florence, Italy, c.1870. **Magnolia**. *Inlaid stone panel. 12.9cm x 17.4cm. Typical of the Florence style.*

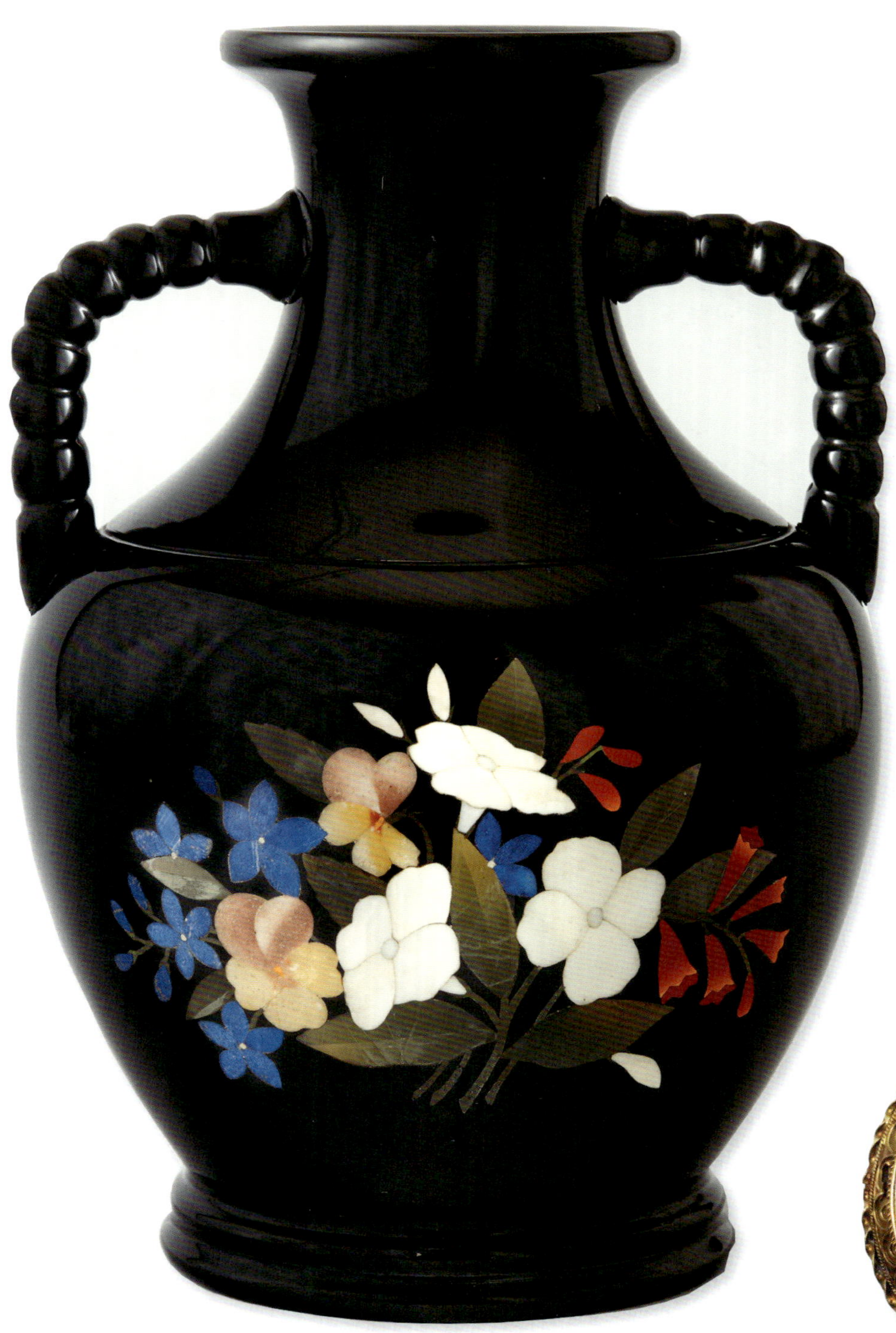

Left: unsigned, Derbyshire inlaid limestone vase (one of a pair). 26cm x 17cm diameter. Because Florentine pietre dure craftsmen made their work from thin, flat sheets, any piece such as this, with the inlaid stone on a curved surface, must be English. However, although the body is typically English, the handles were almost certainly imported from Italy!

Below: signed "Montelatici Frères Lungarno Nuovo 12, Florence". Gold-framed brooch, made c.1870, Montelatici, Florence, Italy. 4.9cm x 4cm x 5cm. A typical Italian floral brooch in gold mount.

Kent Ullberg (1945 –), born
Sweden, works Texas, USA.
Ring of Bright Water.
Impressed "Ullberg A/P".
Stainless steel.
65.5cm x 29cm x 29cm.
The sculptor has become
famous for his monumental
works in stainless steel.

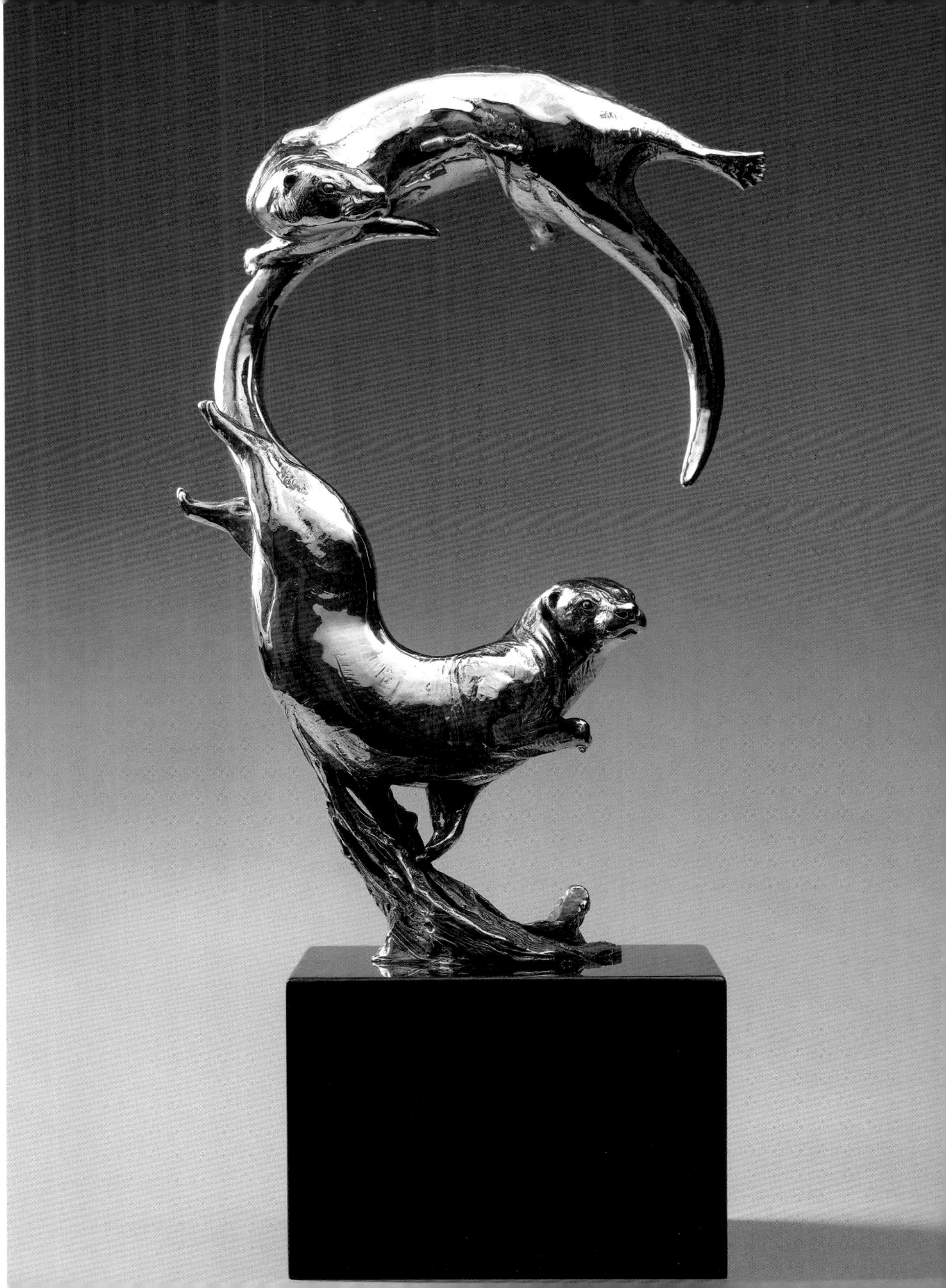

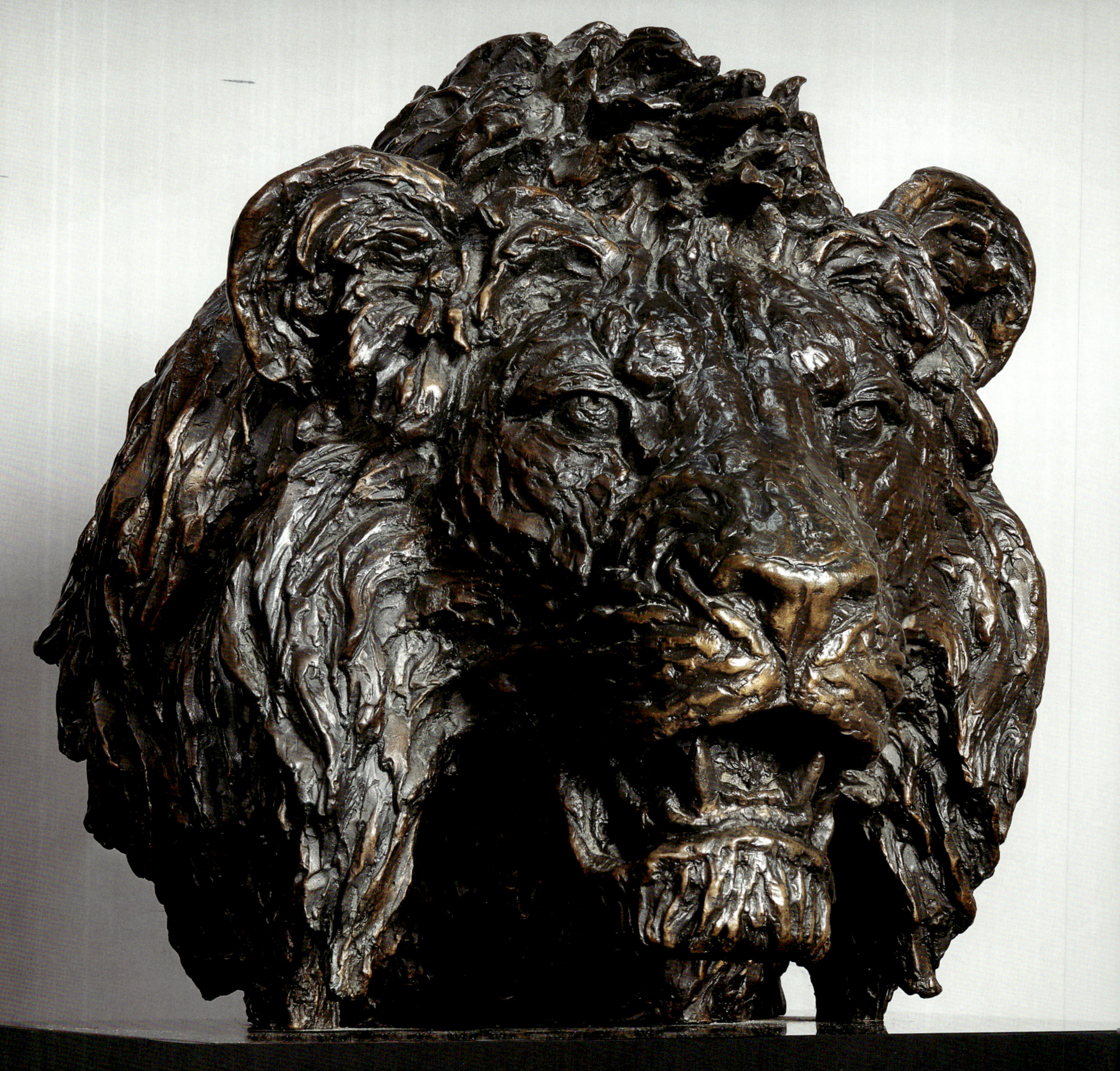

Left: William Timym (1901/2–1990),
Austria; and, from 1938, UK.
Lion's Head.
Life-size, bronze.
53cm x 42cm x 65cm.
Signed and dated W. Timym 5/10, 1974.

Right and below: William Timym, UK.
Preparatory pencil sketches
for the bronze, which was modelled
first in plasticine.

Many sculptors are skilful with pencil,
pen, ink and charcoal. Timym was
particularly gifted in this way. He
made some notable portrait paintings
during the Second World War.

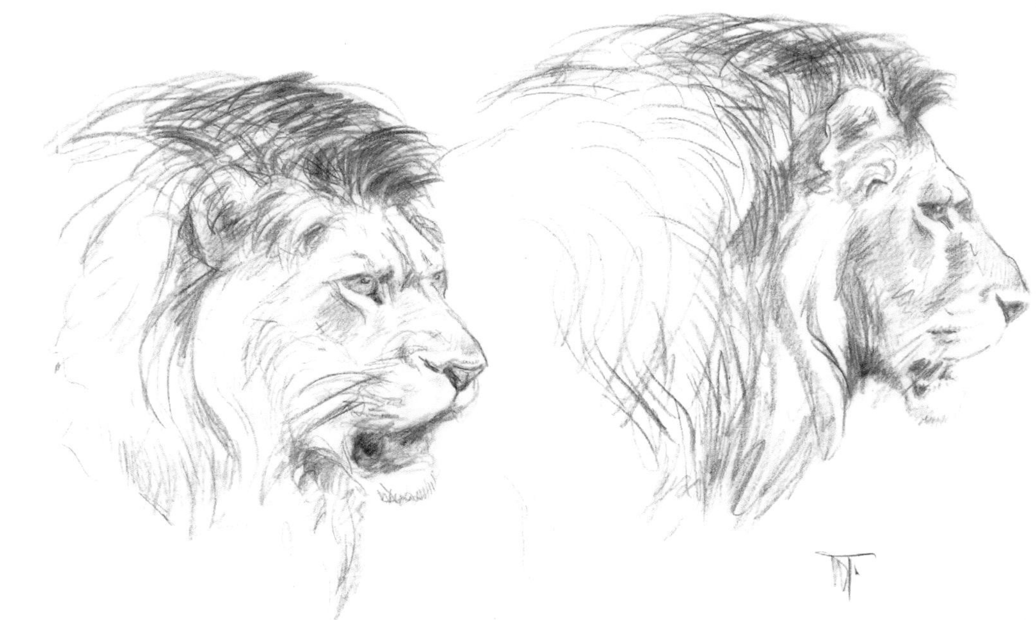

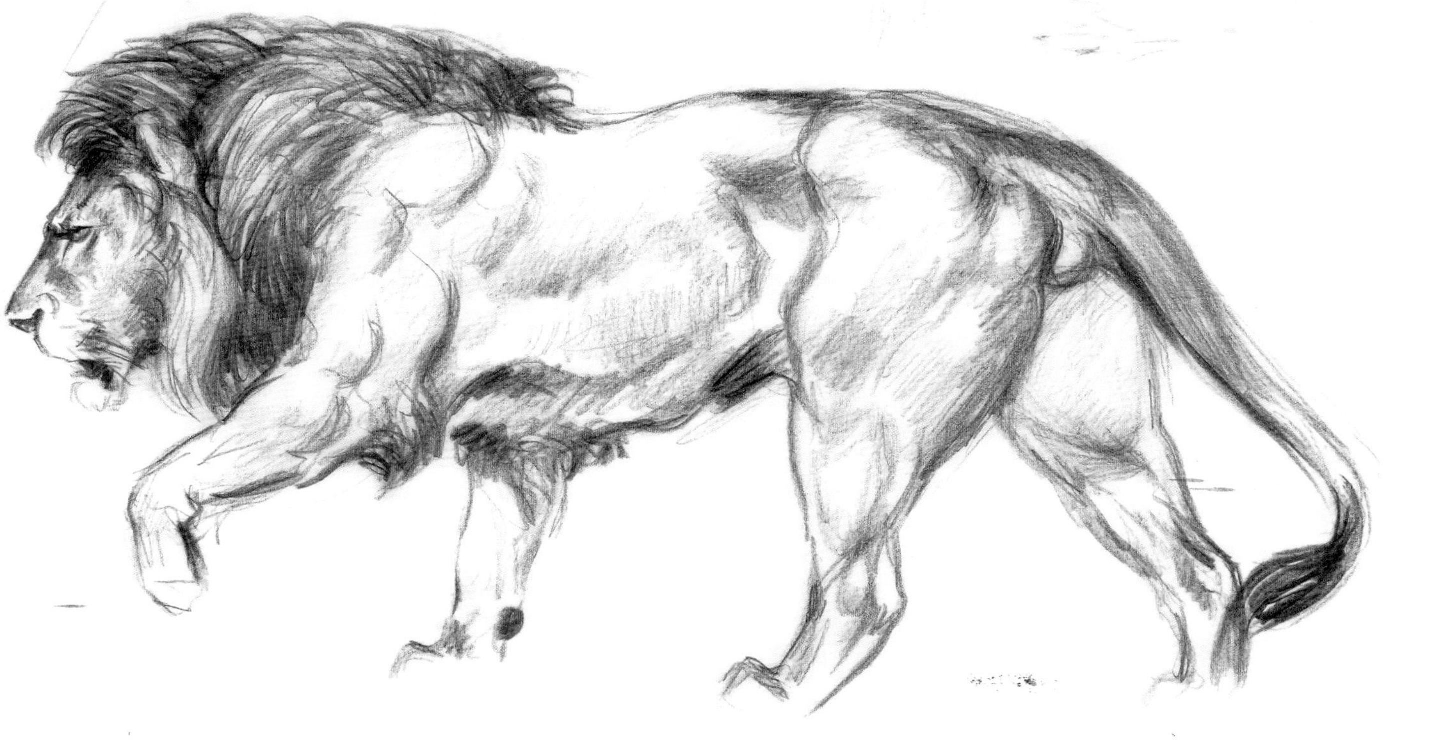

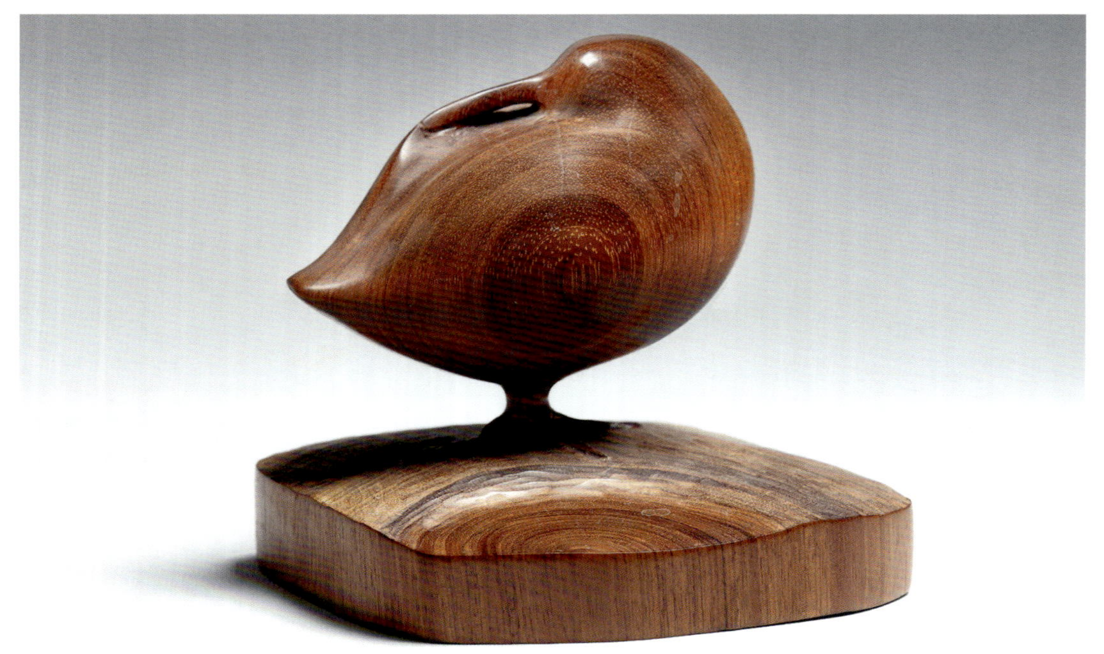

Harry R. (Hank) Tyler Jr.
(1944 –), USA.
Dunlin Sandpiper.
Bubinga wood.
16.5cm x 20cm x 15cm.
Signed and dated 1983.

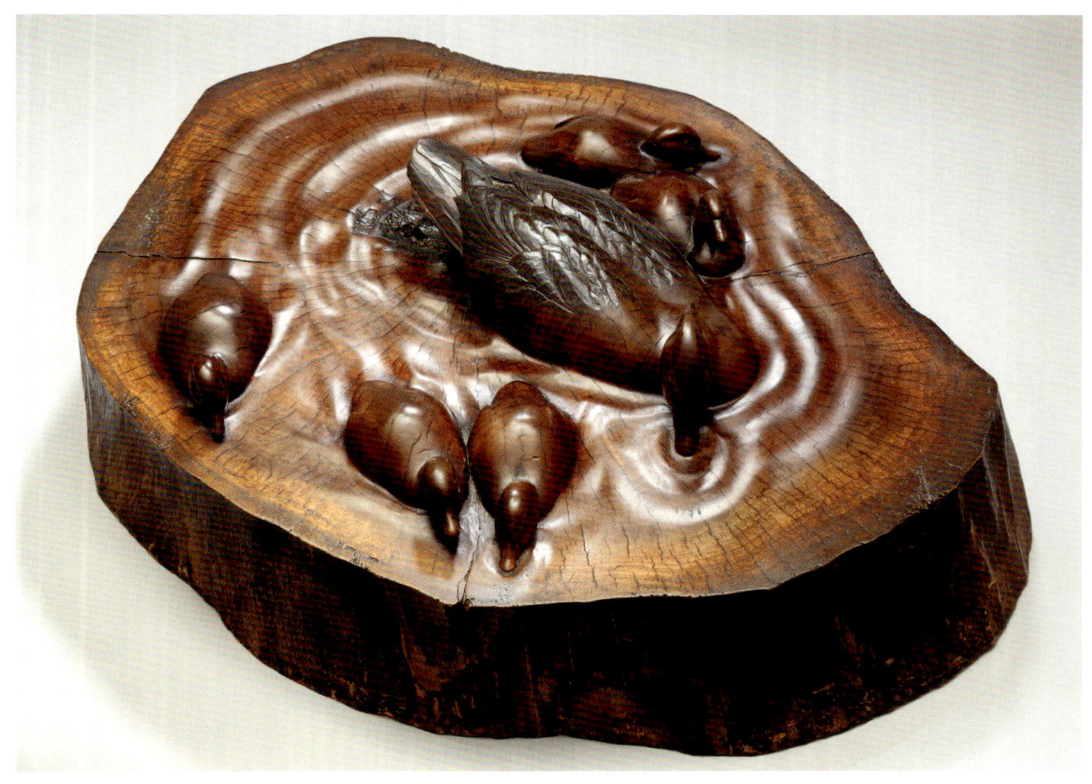

John Sharp (1943 –), USA.
Wood Duck.
Black walnut tree section.
19cm x 71cm x 50cm.
Signed "J. Sharp '78".

Harry Pootoogook
(1935-2010), Inuit,
Baffin Island, Canada.
Musk Ox.
Soapstone, with inlaid bone horns.
38cm x 14cm x 57cm.
Not signed.

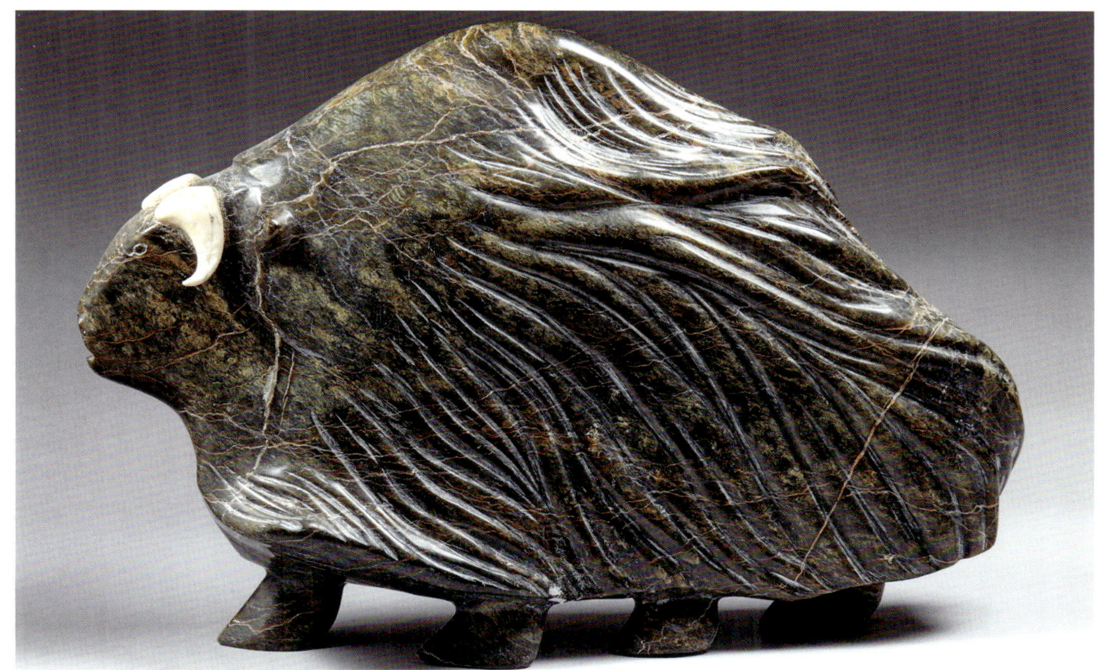

Korean sculptor unknown,
20th century.
Carp.
Bronze casting.
19cm x 8.5cm x 43cm.
A contemporary copy of a popular
17th-century Korean design.

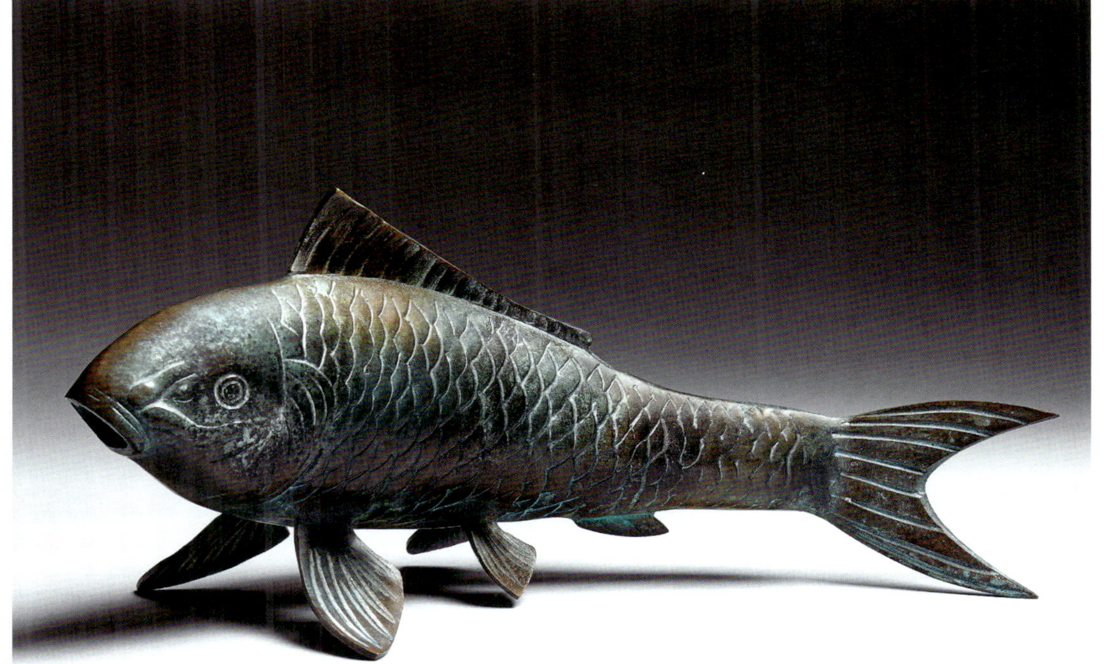

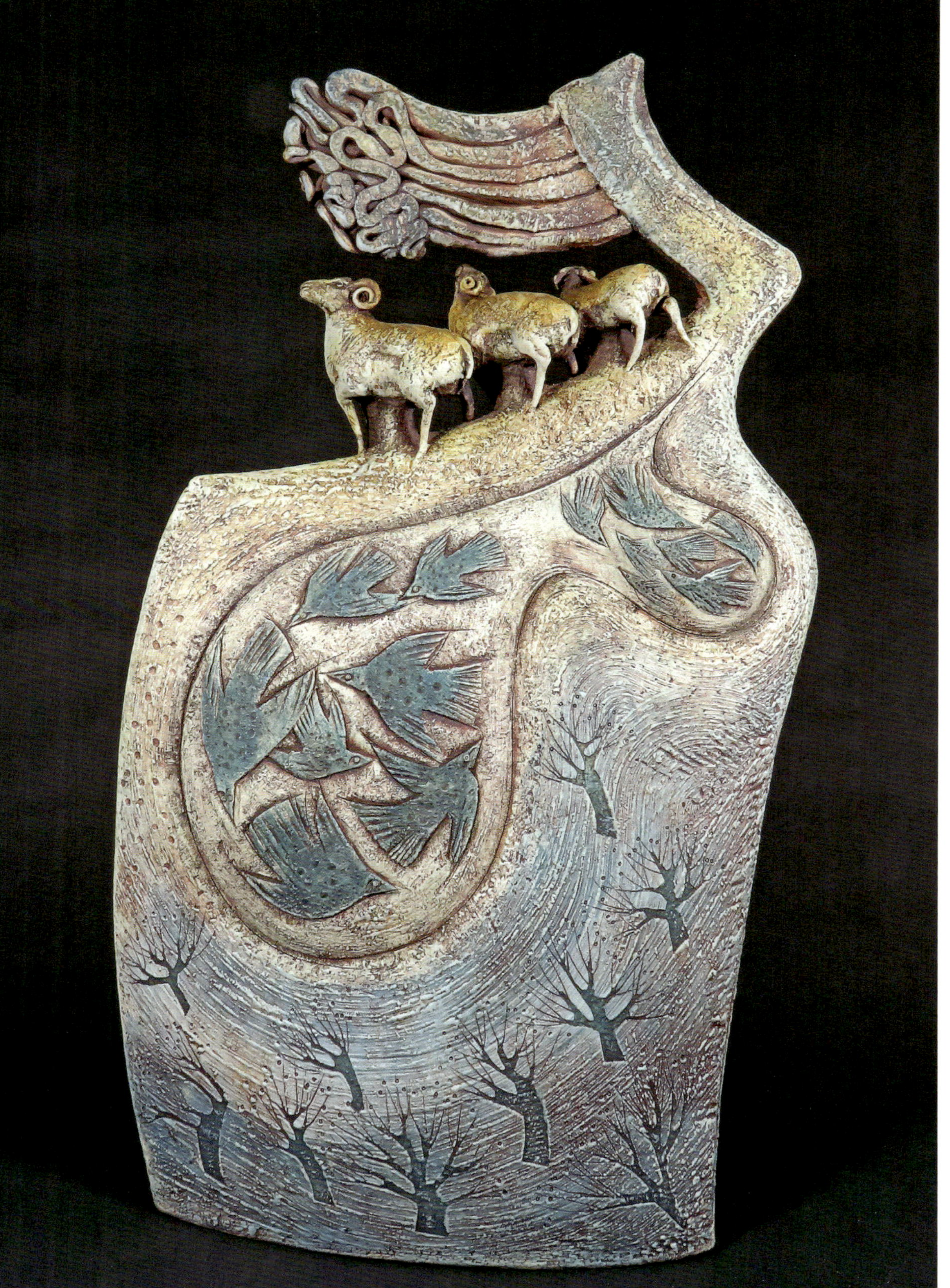

*Blandine Anderson
(contemporary), UK.
Sevens. Stoneware.
46cm x 26cm x 12cm.*

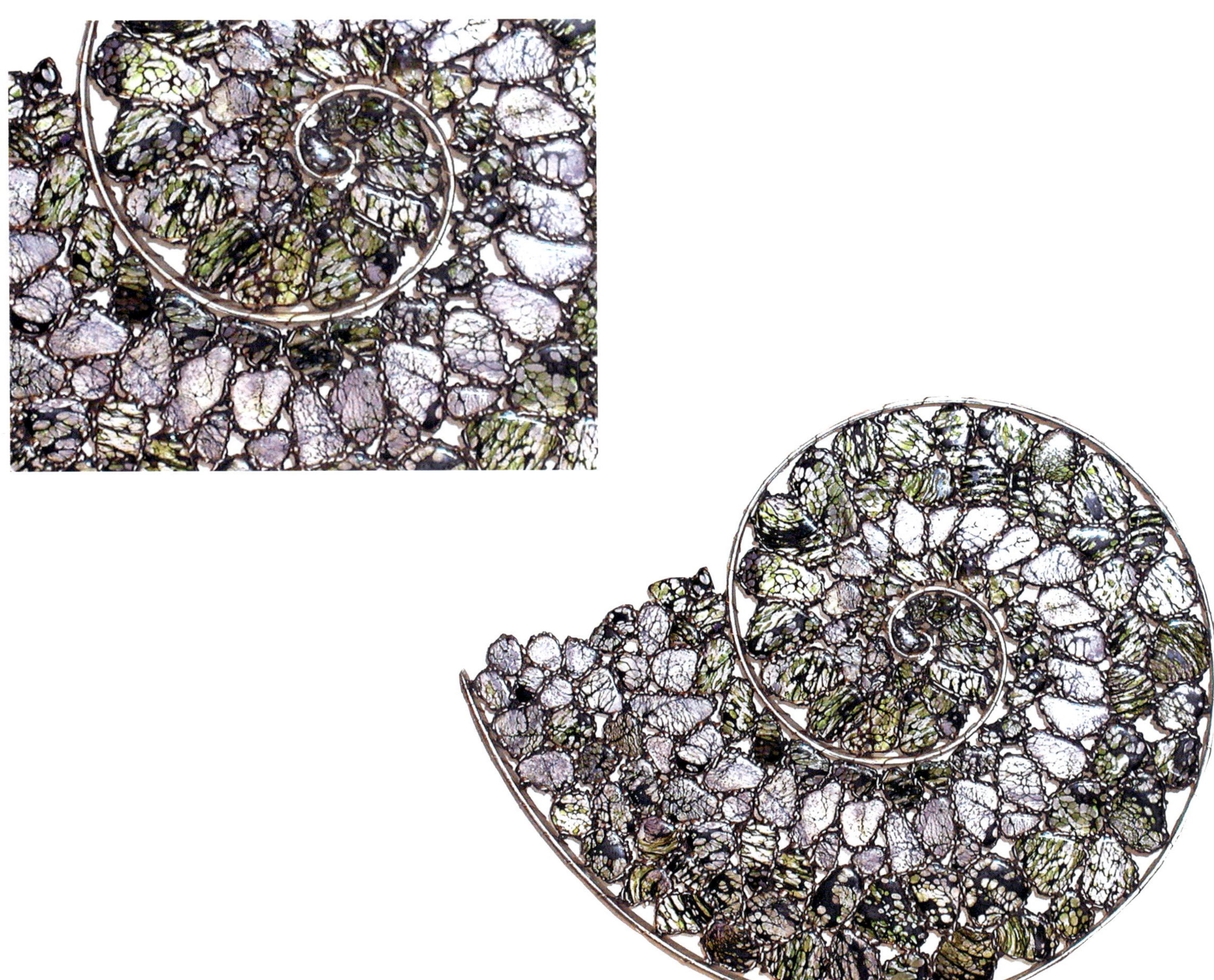

Above (detail) and right: Gill Hobson (contemporary), UK.
Spiral. *Hand-made cabochons of lead crystal glass, held in copper collars, soldered to others and copper wire to fix to the steel spiral support, standing on a natural stone. 64cm x 69cm x 27cm (inc base).*

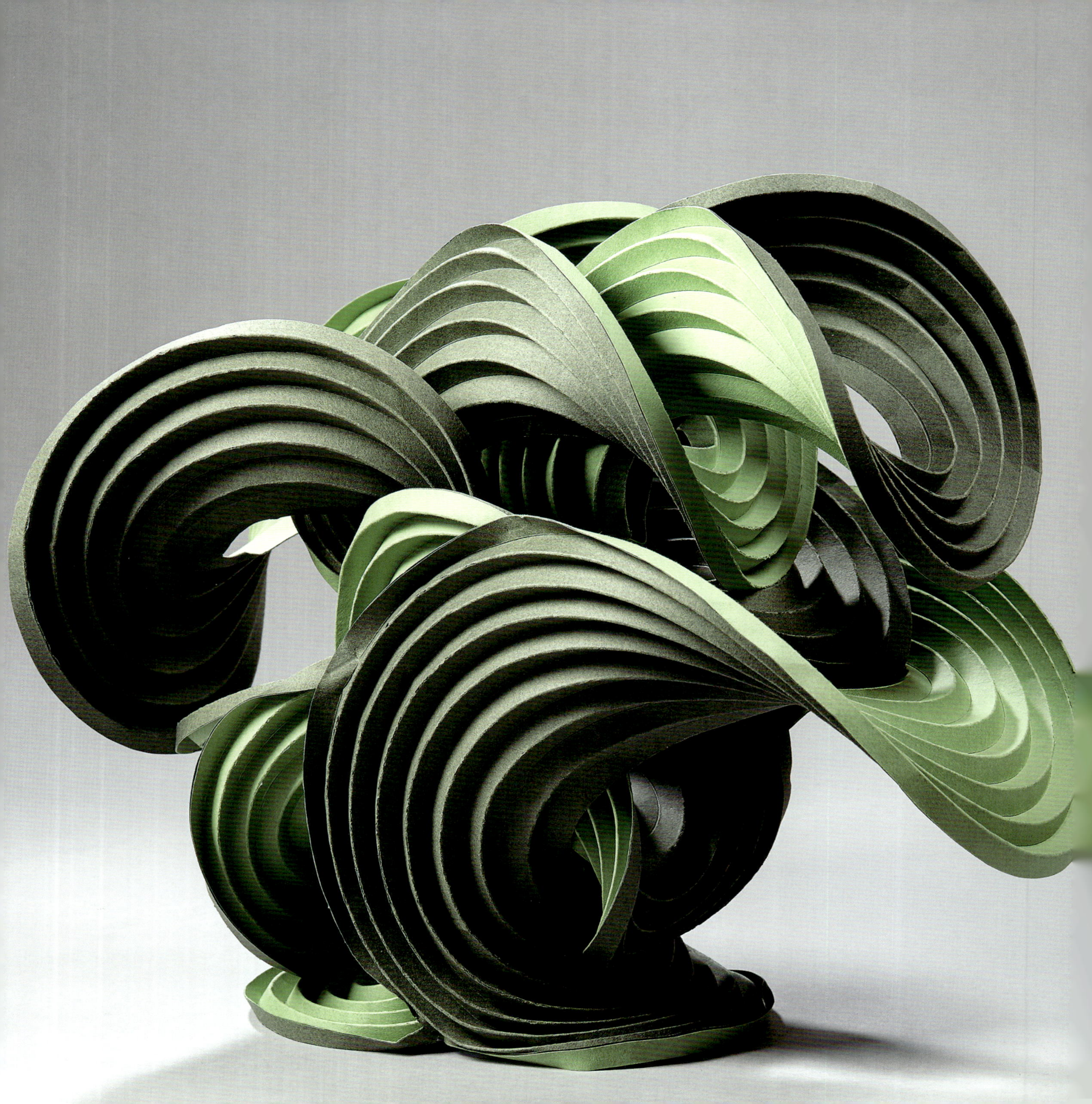

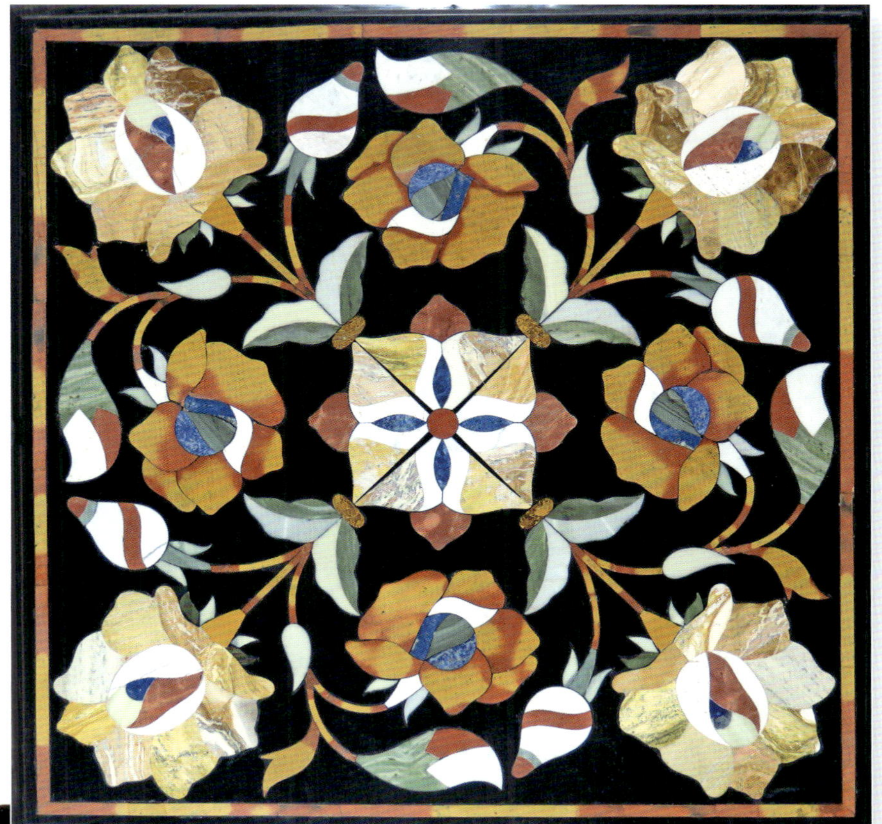

*Right: unidentified Afghan family working
in Kashmir, India, 20th century.
Decorative stone panel incorporating
pieces of blueish
(poor-quality) lapis lazuli.
56.2cm x 56.2cm x 2.8cm.*

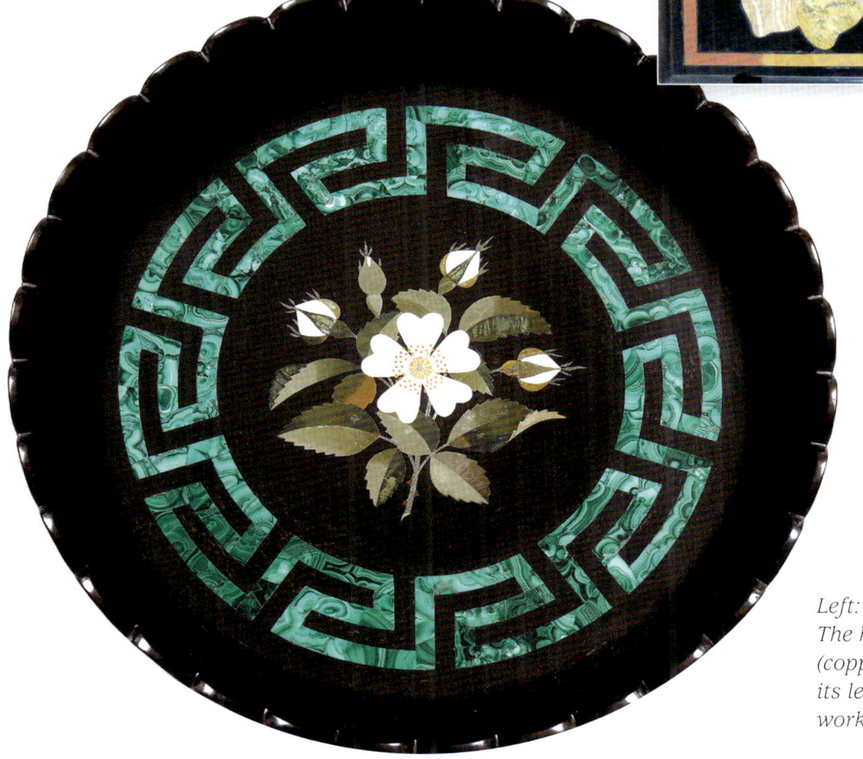

*Left: unsigned, typically Derbyshire, dish, made c.1870.
The key pattern ring in the decoration is made of malachite
(copper carbonate). The design and detail of the central rose,
its leaves and their stems is all typically English
workmanship. 4.8cm x 30cm diameter.*

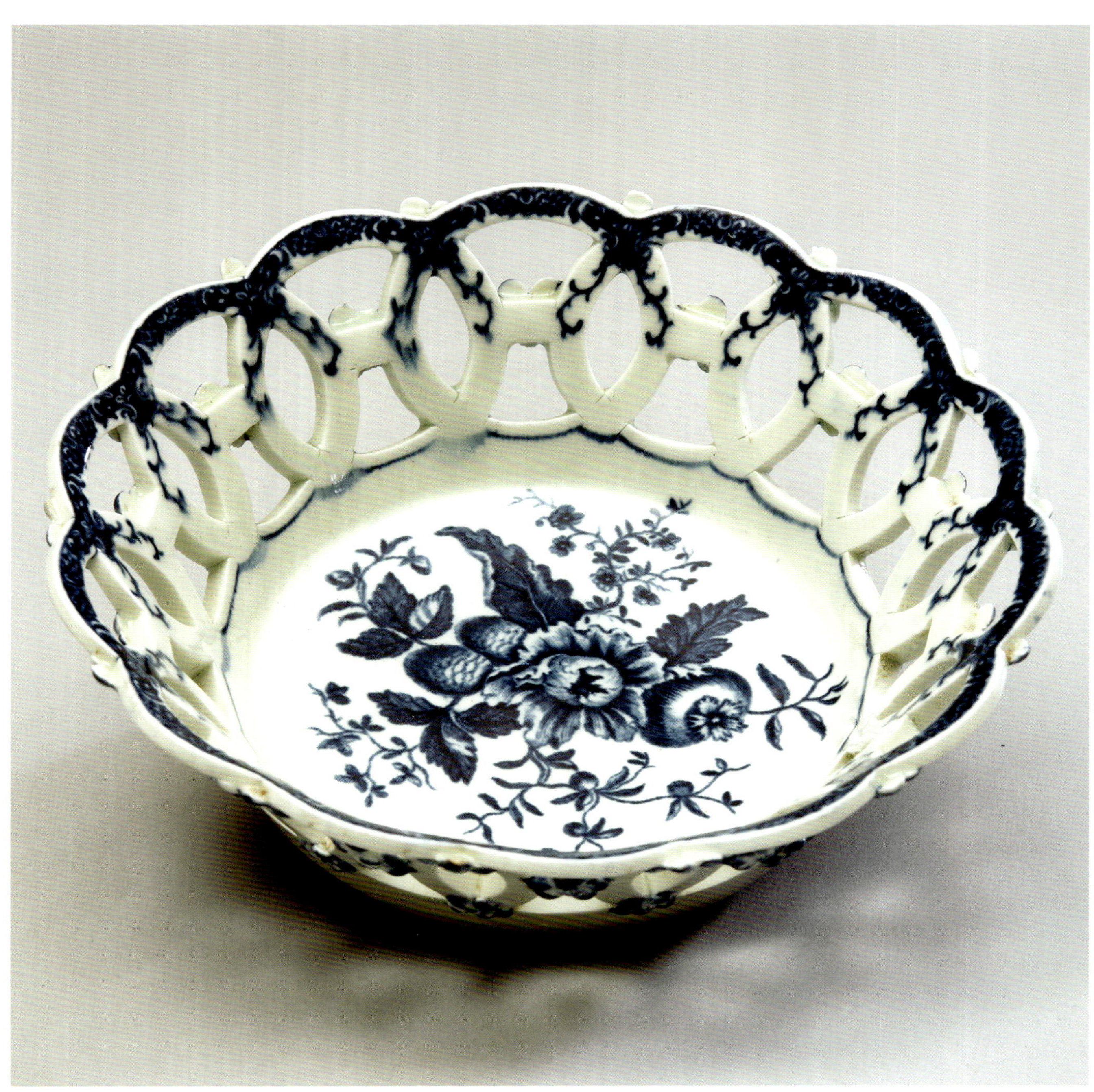

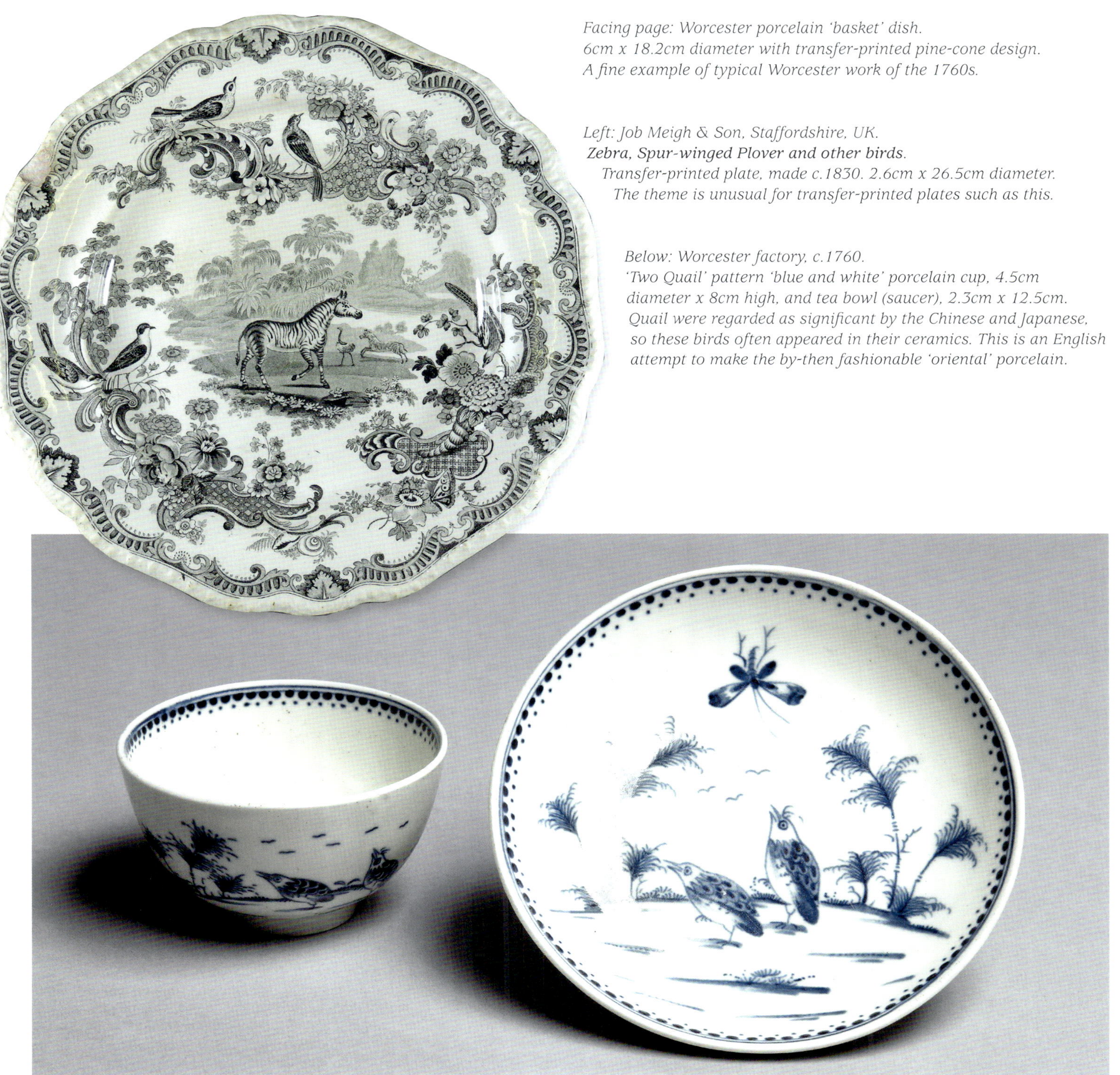

Facing page: Worcester porcelain 'basket' dish.
6cm x 18.2cm diameter with transfer-printed pine-cone design.
A fine example of typical Worcester work of the 1760s.

Left: Job Meigh & Son, Staffordshire, UK.
Zebra, Spur-winged Plover and other birds.
Transfer-printed plate, made c.1830. 2.6cm x 26.5cm diameter.
The theme is unusual for transfer-printed plates such as this.

Below: Worcester factory, c.1760.
'Two Quail' pattern 'blue and white' porcelain cup, 4.5cm
diameter x 8cm high, and tea bowl (saucer), 2.3cm x 12.5cm.
Quail were regarded as significant by the Chinese and Japanese,
so these birds often appeared in their ceramics. This is an English
attempt to make the by-then fashionable 'oriental' porcelain.

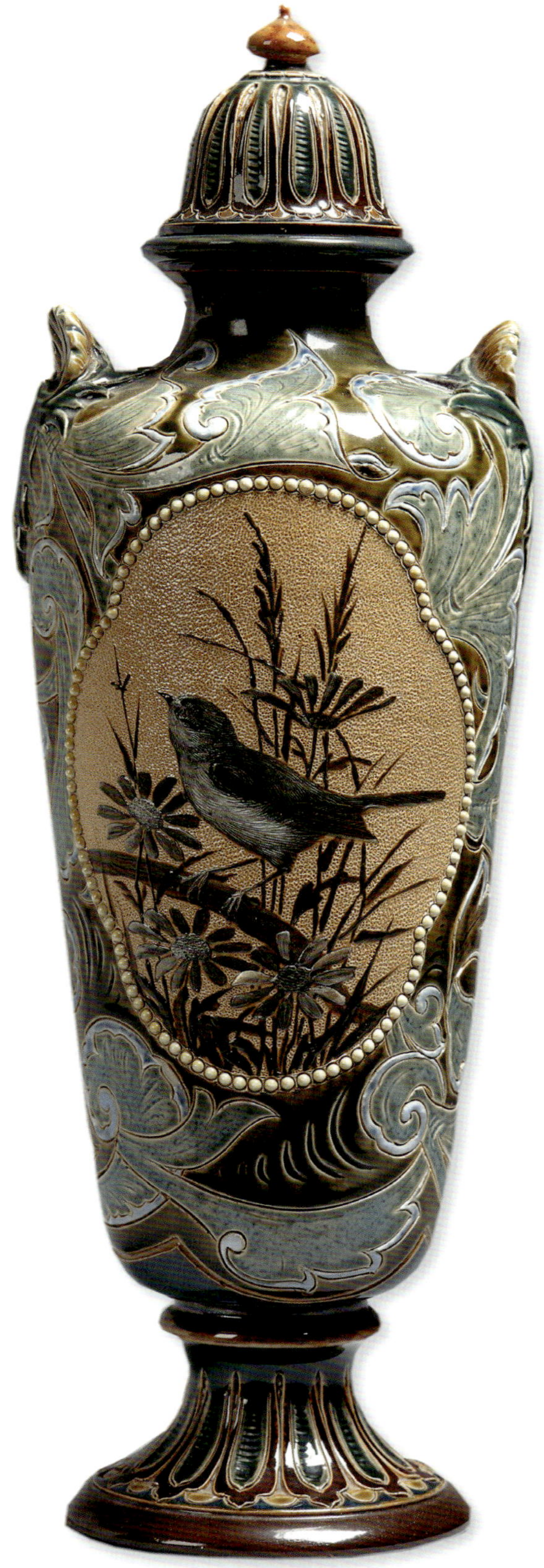

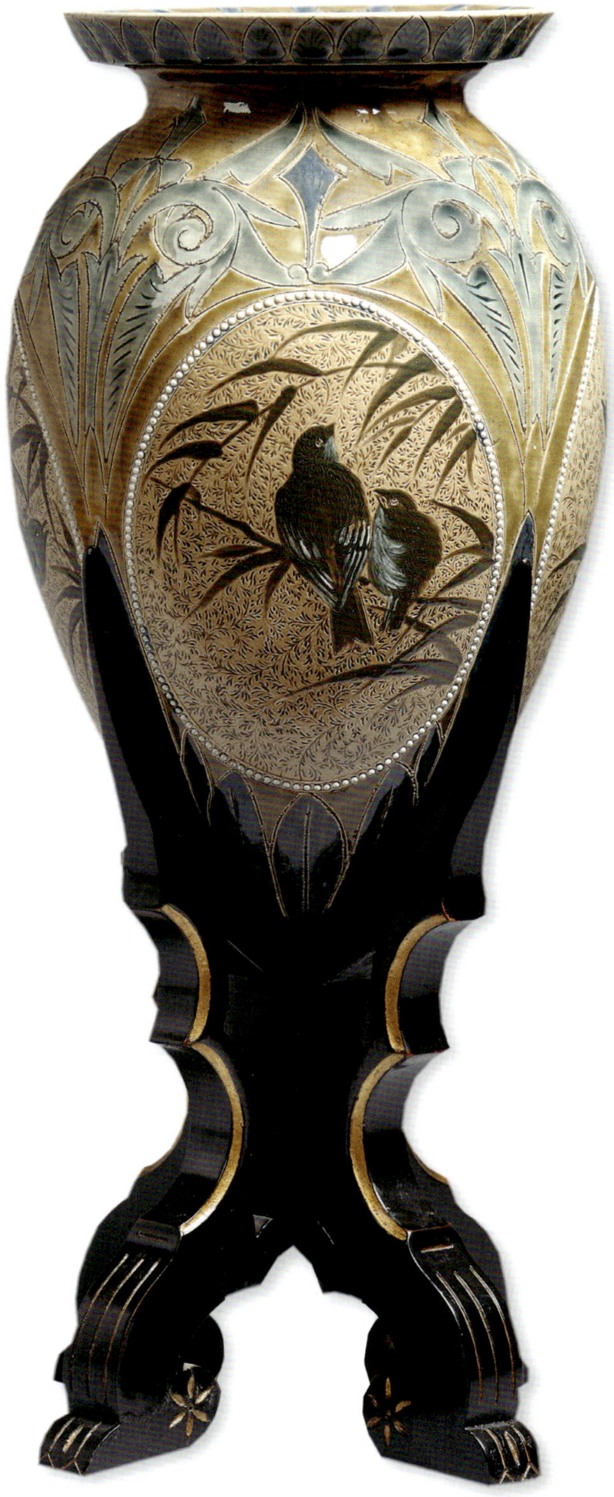

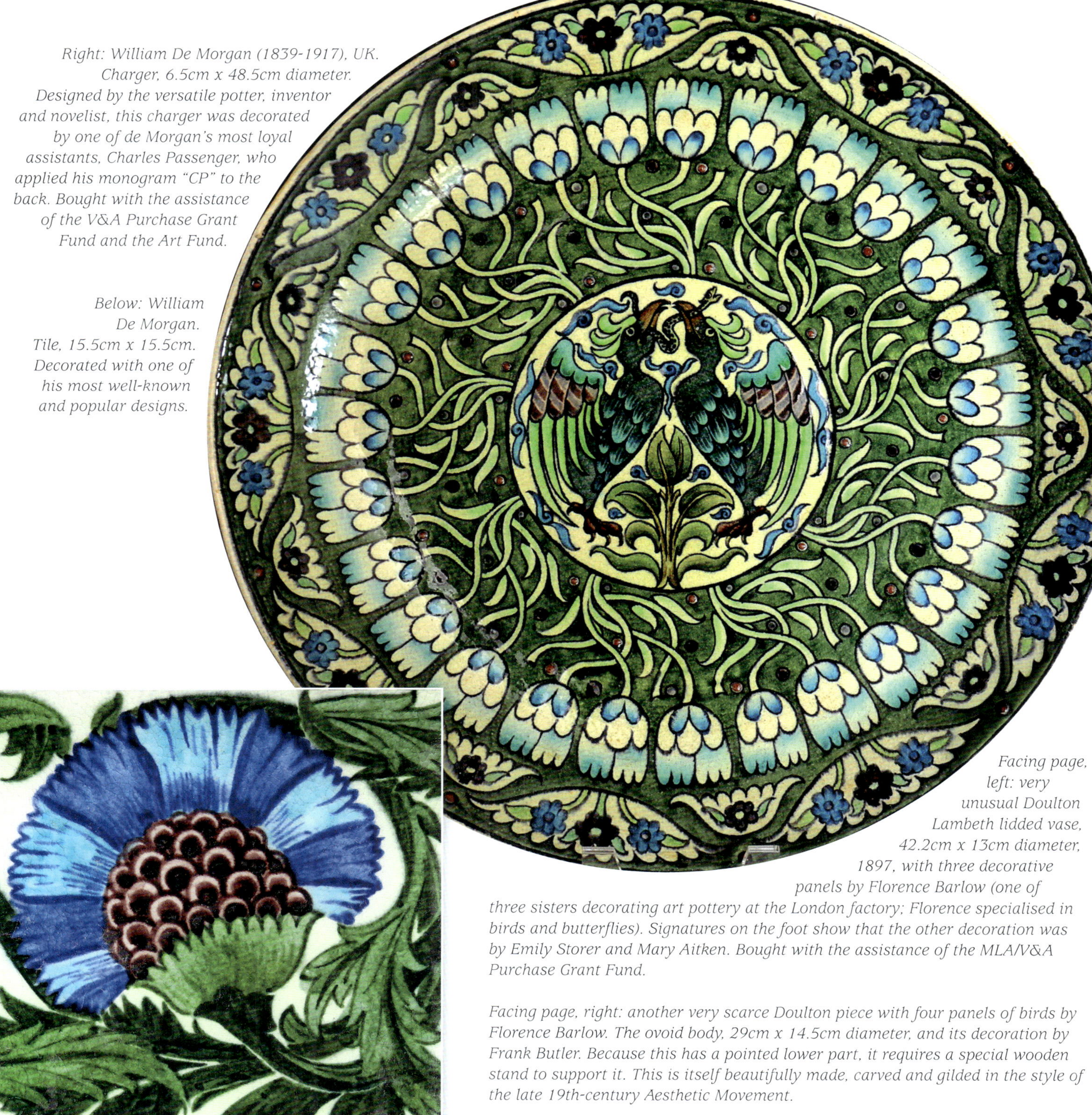

Right: William De Morgan (1839-1917), UK. Charger, 6.5cm x 48.5cm diameter. Designed by the versatile potter, inventor and novelist, this charger was decorated by one of de Morgan's most loyal assistants, Charles Passenger, who applied his monogram "CP" to the back. Bought with the assistance of the V&A Purchase Grant Fund and the Art Fund.

Below: William De Morgan. Tile, 15.5cm x 15.5cm. Decorated with one of his most well-known and popular designs.

Facing page, left: very unusual Doulton Lambeth lidded vase, 42.2cm x 13cm diameter, 1897, with three decorative panels by Florence Barlow (one of three sisters decorating art pottery at the London factory; Florence specialised in birds and butterflies). Signatures on the foot show that the other decoration was by Emily Storer and Mary Aitken. Bought with the assistance of the MLA/V&A Purchase Grant Fund.

Facing page, right: another very scarce Doulton piece with four panels of birds by Florence Barlow. The ovoid body, 29cm x 14.5cm diameter, and its decoration by Frank Butler. Because this has a pointed lower part, it requires a special wooden stand to support it. This is itself beautifully made, carved and gilded in the style of the late 19th-century Aesthetic Movement.

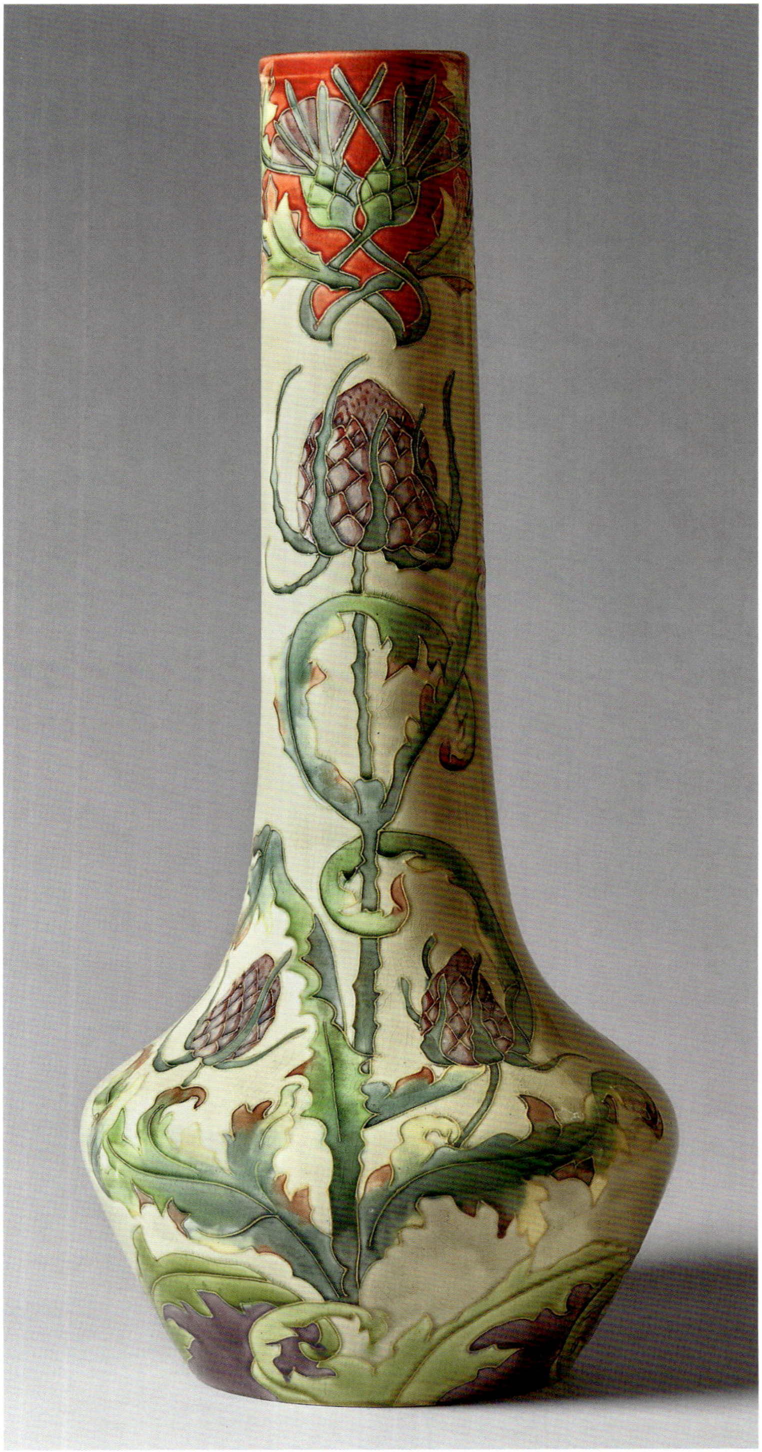

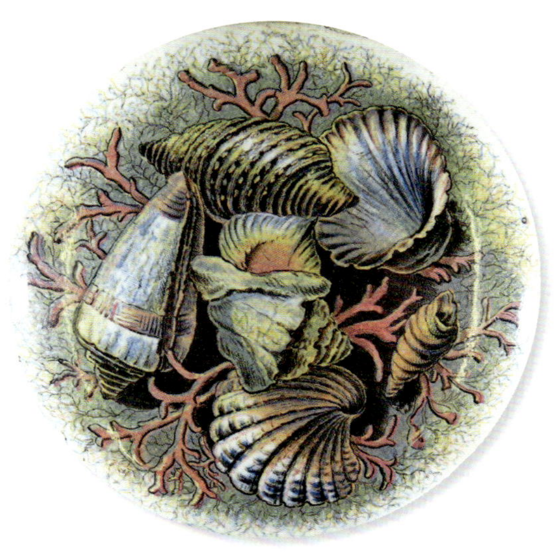

Above: F. & R. Pratt factory, Staffordshire, late 19th/early 20th century. Pot lid 'Pegwell Bay' – sea shells, 1.7cm x 10.2cm diameter. Designed to hold such foods as fish paste. A wide variety of designs were produced in a deliberate (and successful) attempt to promote the purchase and collecting of these. Designs based only on nature are scarce.

Left: Longchamps factory, Paris, France, c.1900. Long-necked vase with stylised artichoke design in the Art Nouveau style. 59cm x 25cm max diameter.

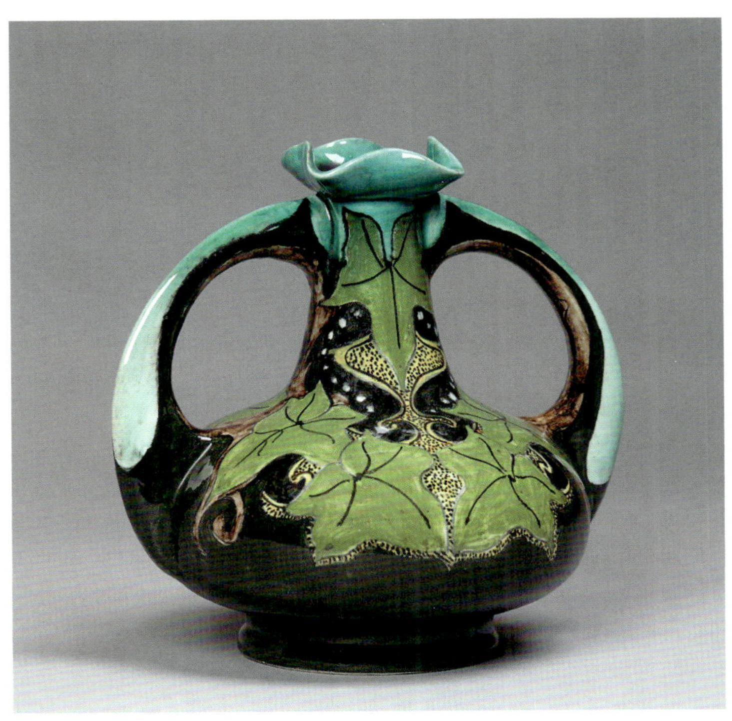

Above: artist unknown, Brantjes & Co, made in Purmerend, north of Amsterdam, The Netherlands, c.1910. Handled vase, 18cm x 17cm.

Right: Burmantofts Art Pottery, Leeds, UK, c.1900. Handled vase, 31.5cm x 17cm. Not signed or dated.

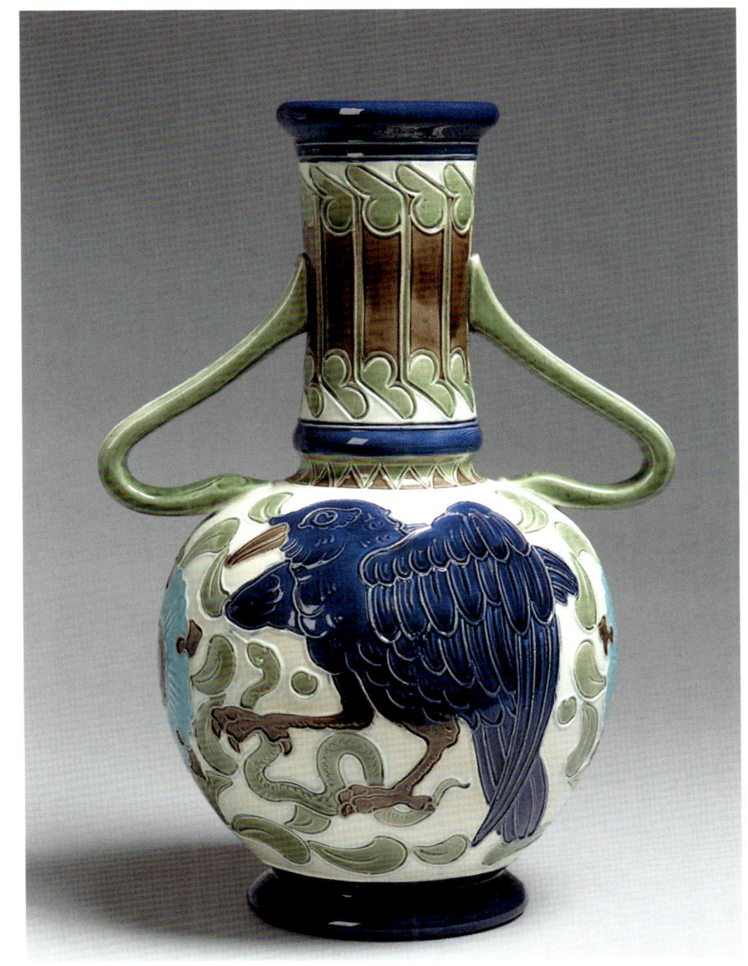

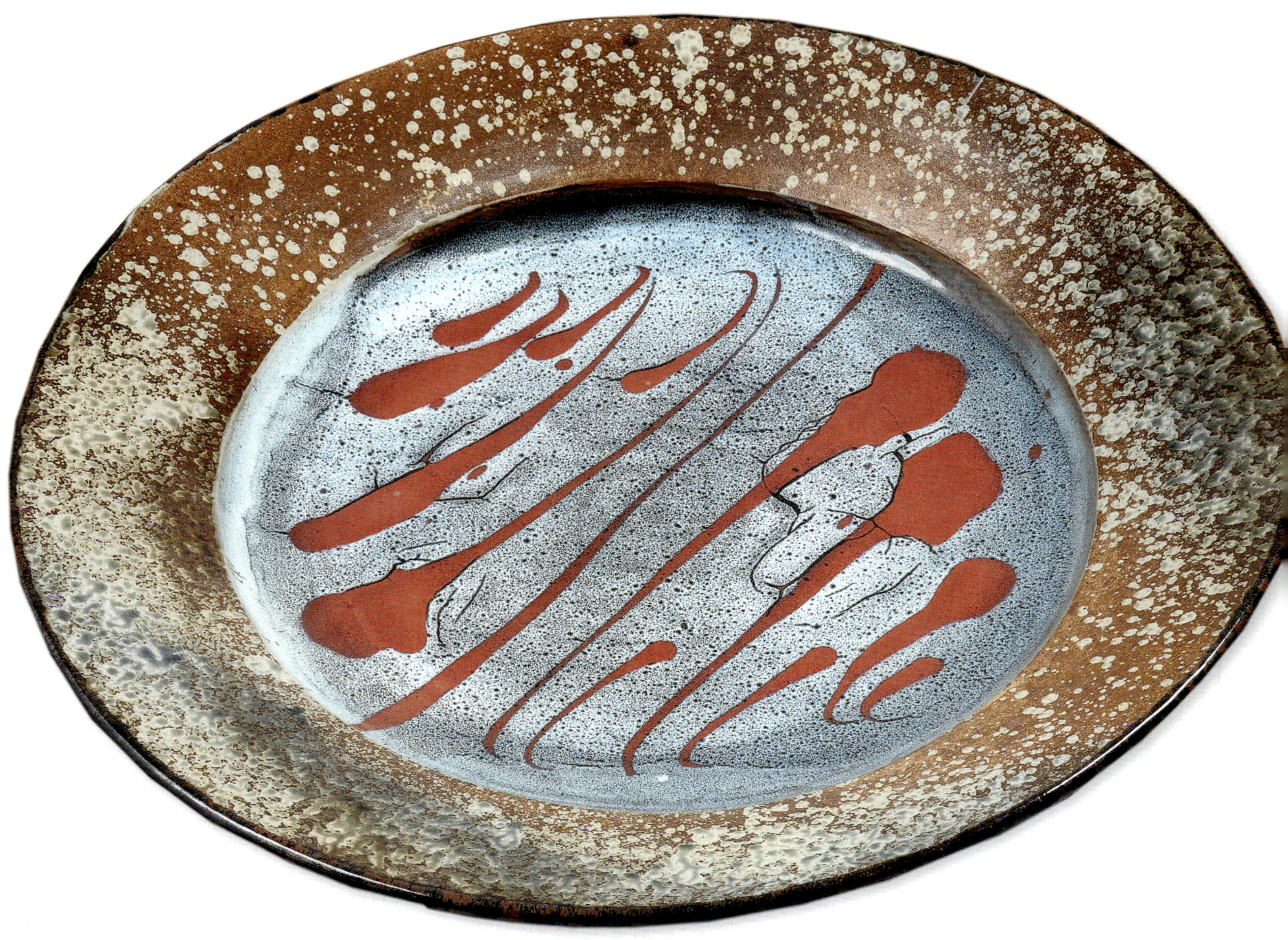

Above: David Frith (1937 –), UK, 2015.
Unusually large stoneware charger – bigger than many private kilns
are able to accommodate – 73cm diameter x 11.2cm deep.
Before firing this must have been some 80cm wide and larger still when
newly thrown, requiring great technical skill.

Facing page: Elizabeth Gray (1928 –), UK, 2012.
Handmade 'Hare' earthenware pot, 30cm x 30cm.
Inscribed on base, "I made this pot in 1997 for the garden. After 15
years I brought it in, cleaned, dried and painted it before decorating it
with monoprinted tissue-paper and gold leaf. Elizabeth Gray."

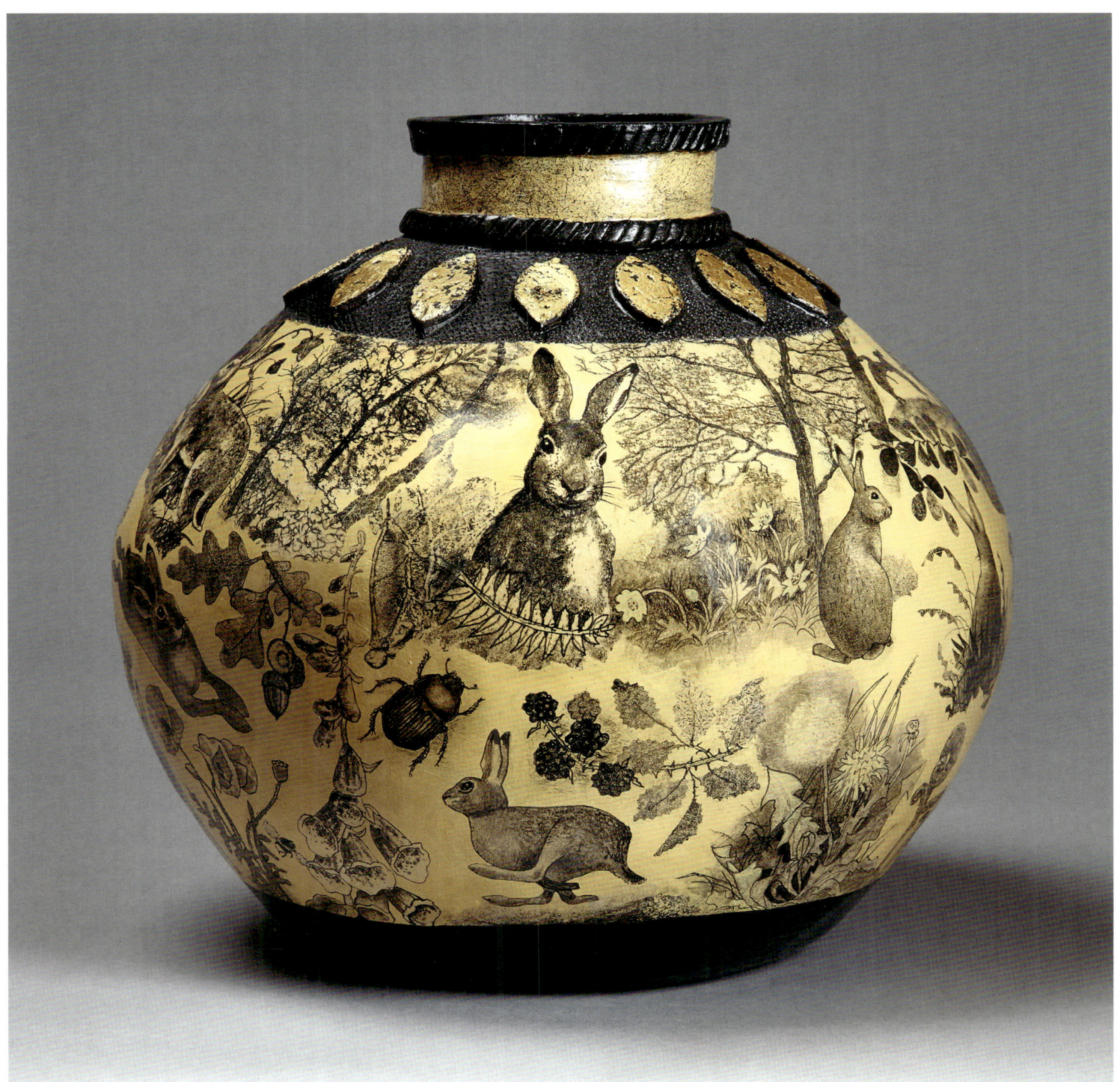

GLASS

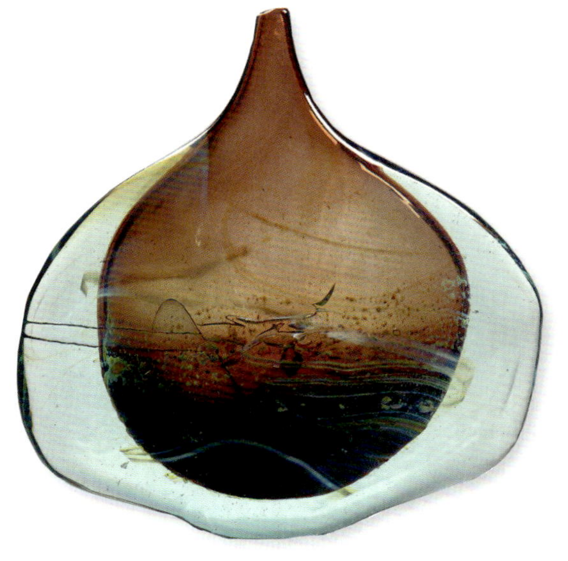

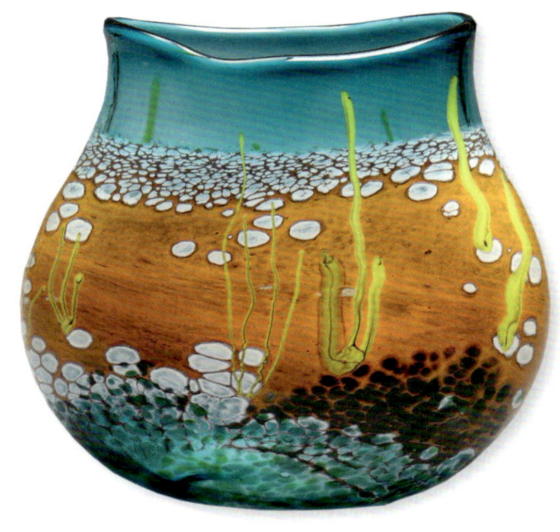

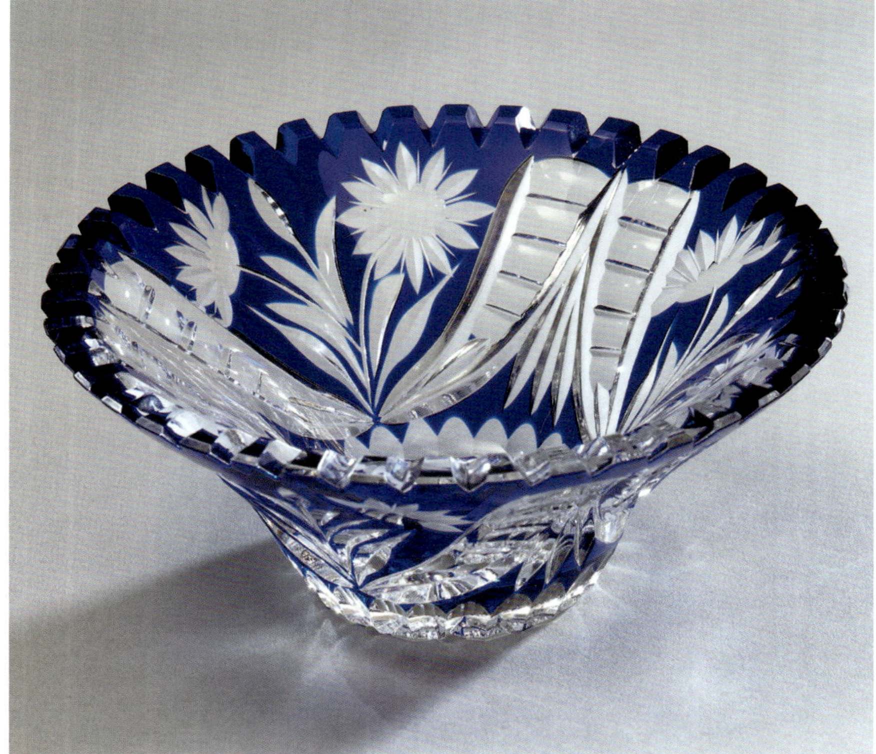

Above left: Michael Harris (1933-1994), UK, worked in Malta 1968-1972.
Blown flat glass bottle, 27cm x 27cm x 7cm. Inscribed on base "Michael Harris, Mdina Glass, Malta".

Above right: Siddy Langley (contemporary), UK.
Seabed*, glass vase, 21cm x 21.5cm x 11.2cm.*
Engraved on base "Siddy Langley, 2003".
Sidi's hobby is scuba diving so she has often seen the scenes below the surface of the sea.

Left: unknown artist, probably made at Stourbridge (48 miles north of Nature in Art), c.1860/70.
Cut, cased (layered) glass, 7cm x 17.5cm diameter.

Facing page, top left: James Powell & Sons, London, UK, c.1900. Whitefriars glass bowl, 9.5cm x 25.5cm.

Facing page, bottom left: unknown artist and maker, Bohemia, c.1890. Gold on glass vase, 26.8cm x 6.2cm. Typical Art Nouveau, from the region in which the style started.

Facing page, right: Bob Crooks (1965 –), UK.
Contours and Reflections*, blown glass, 51cm x 31cm x 12cm.*

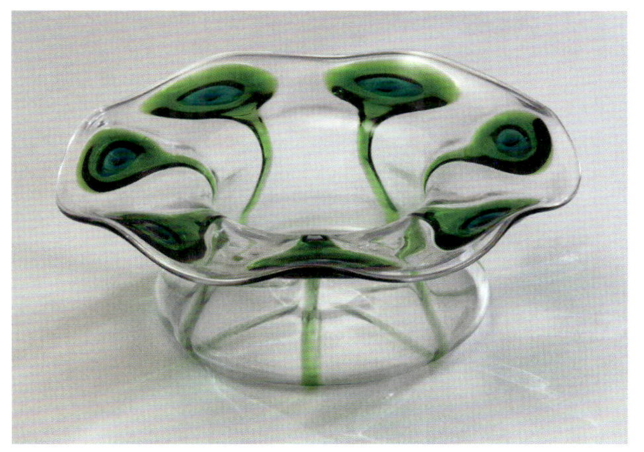

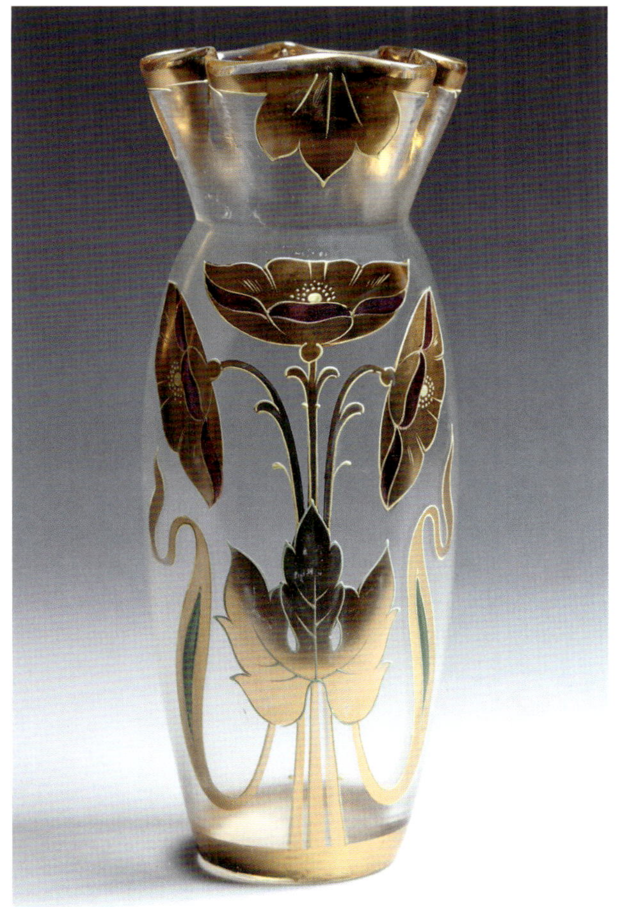

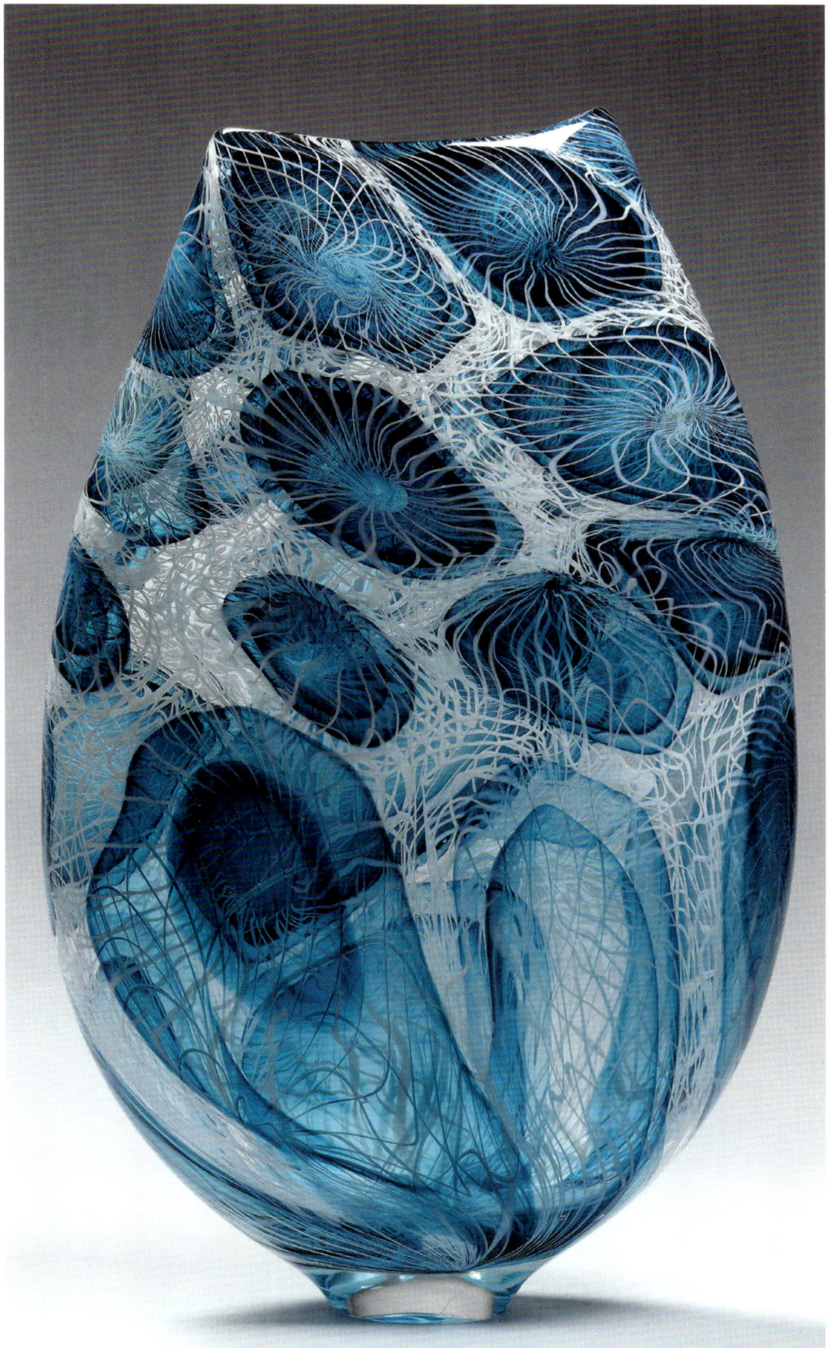

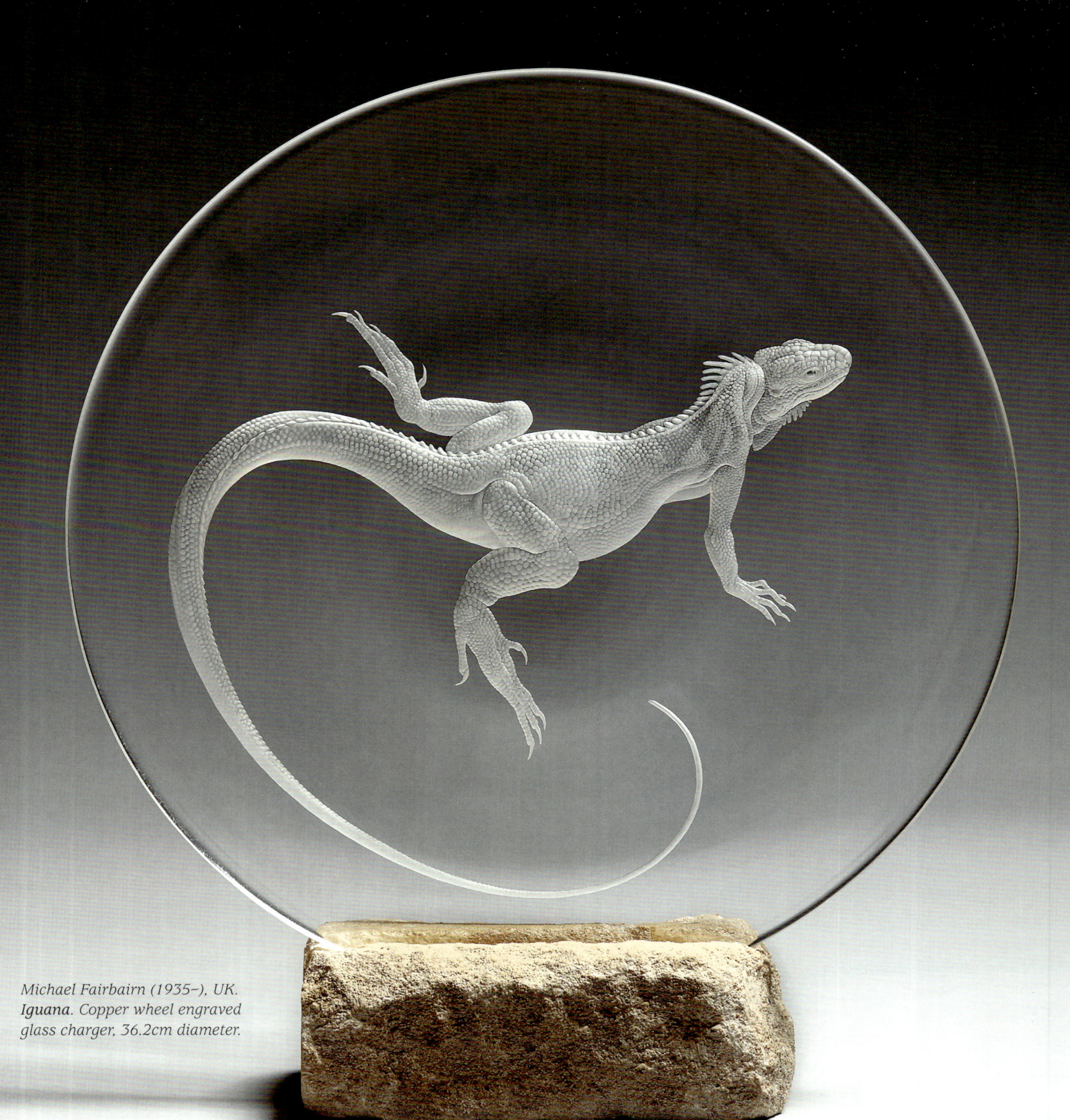

Michael Fairbairn (1935–), UK.
Iguana. *Copper wheel engraved*
glass charger, 36.2cm diameter.

Right: Elizabeth Gray (1928 –), UK. *Sea Shells*.
Découpage of images of real shells painted
in watercolour on paper, cut out and stuck to
the inside of a commercially made glass vase.
36cm x 20cm. Signed and dated 2012.

Below: Jonathan Harris (1965 –), UK
(son of Michael Harris, page 76). *Treescape*.
Internally carved, cased glass,
51cm x 31cm x 12cm, 2017.

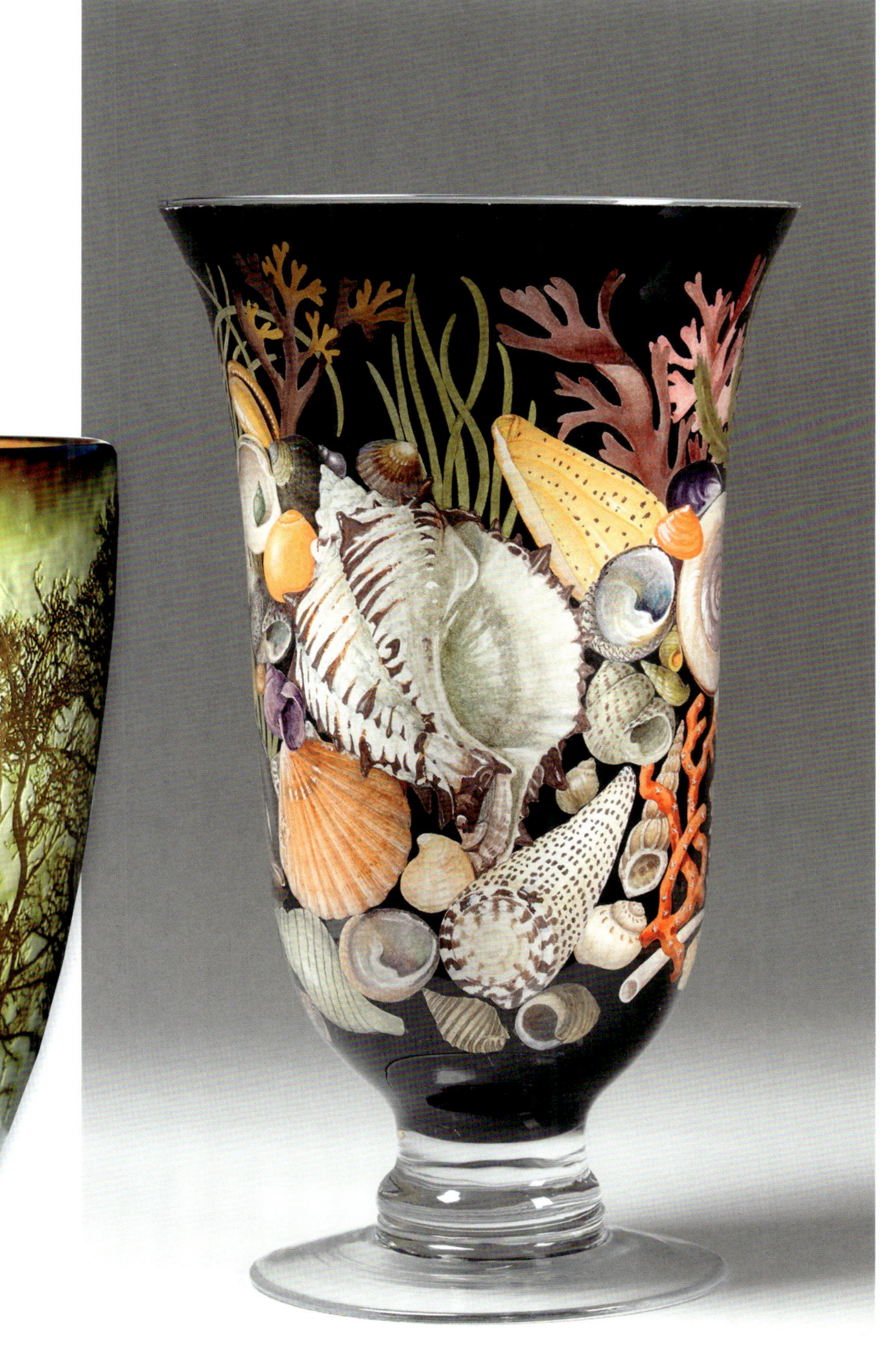

NATURAL ART

Brian Dickie (contemporary), Scotland, UK.
Ancient Strength.
Two Juniper tree stumps from peat bogs in Glencoe, Scotland, said to date from c.3000 BC.
130cm x 63cm x 55cm.
Like many sculptures, a two-dimensional image does not convey the power of this piece.

Water-worn wood found in a river bed in Korea by the unknown artist who had it mounted thus.
114cm x 23cm x 23cm.
Japan, 20th century.

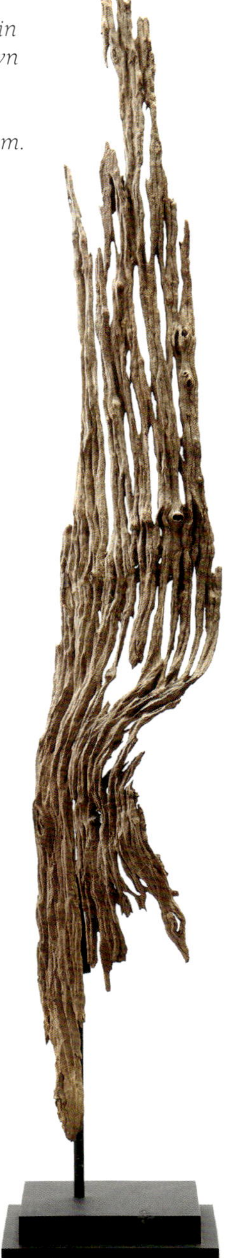

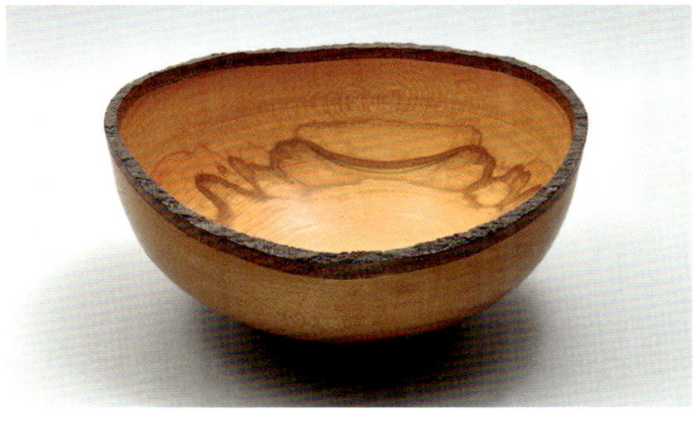

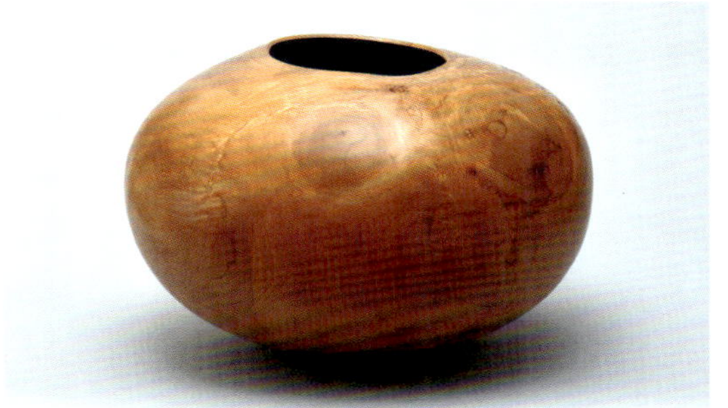

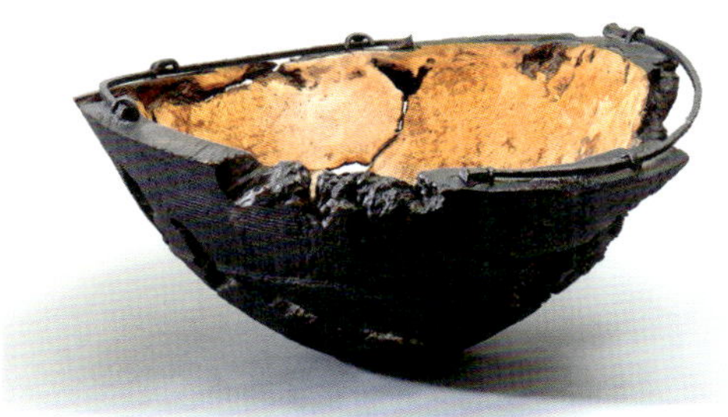

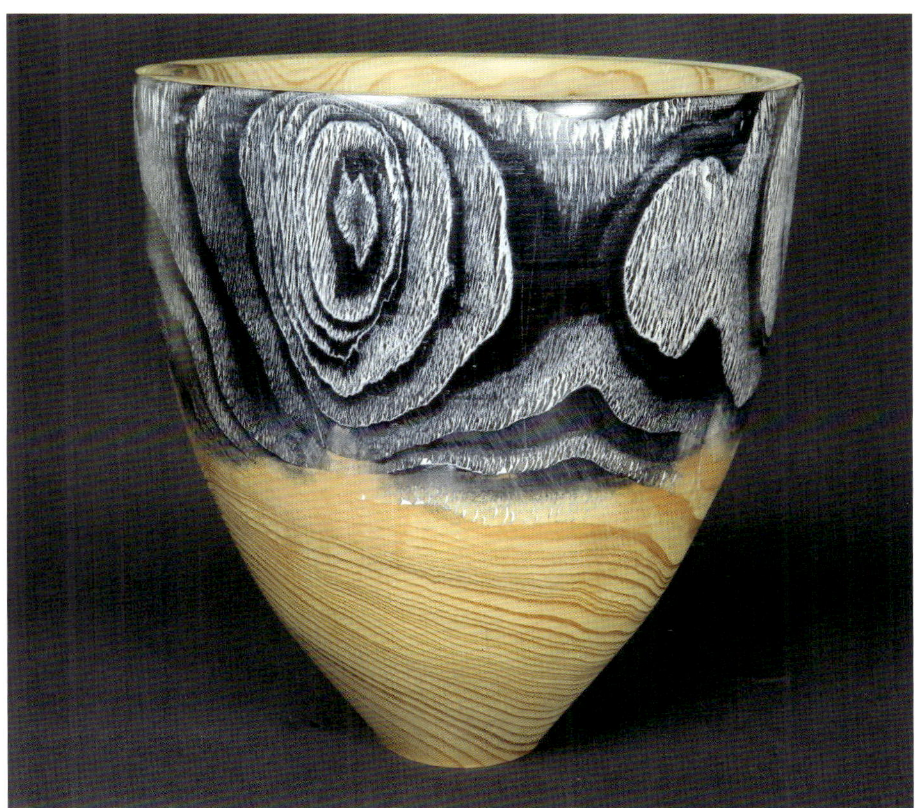

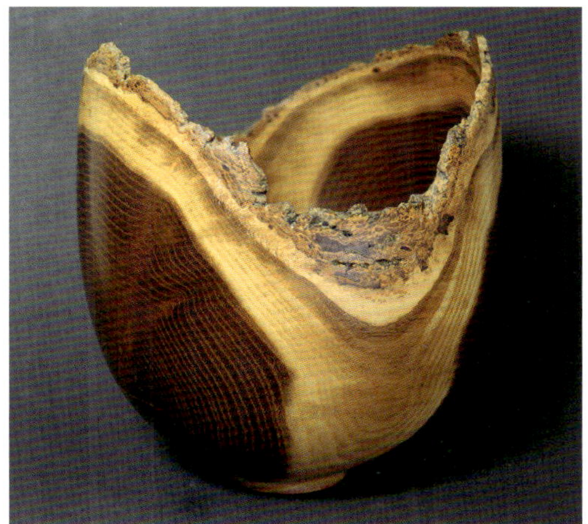

Top: Bert Marsh (1932 – 2011), UK.
Bowl made in 1990 from spalted chestnut wood, retaining its bark. 7.2cm x 19.3cm. Spalting is the name given to discolouration of wood by a fungus.

Middle: Phil Irons (contemporary), UK.
Sycamore wood bowl, 35cm x 54cm, turned while the wood was green (unseasoned). It is very difficult to turn green wood so thin without it splitting.

Bottom: Mike Scott (contemporary), UK.
Lime burr elm bowl, 32cm x 66cm. After turning on a lathe, the outside was burned to blacken it and then polished. The rim was completed and strengthened with wrought iron. Purchased with the assistance of the V&A Purchase Grant Fund.

Above: Maurice Mullins (contemporary), UK.
Cedar wood bowl turned and partly stained black, and then white rubbed into it to reveal the natural grain of the wood. 1990. 15cm x 14cm.

Left: Bert Marsh, UK.
Mulberry wood bowl, 135 x 112mm, retaining its natural bark. 1991. To achieve this, Marsh has turned the wood along the grain of the tree, rather than the more usual across the grain. The pale wood beneath the bark is the sap (recently grown) wood.

Below: a thin, translucent slice of 'Landscape agate' in a silver mount, from Russia. 6.5cm x 7.5cm x 5mm. This is simply a thin, polished slice of agate, lit partly by the white behind it.

Bottom left: Opalescence in Labradorite (a scarce, natural mineral), polished, 17.8cm x 24cm x 7cm. Light rays reflected from the mineral are slightly distorted, creating the impression of many different colours. This effect is critically altered by the direction of the incident light and the position of the viewer's eyes.

*Bottom right: Brian and Jenny Blanthorn (contemporary), UK. **Double pebble**. Laminated, ground and polished colourless sheet glass, 18.5cm x 45.5cm x 8cm. Signed and dated on base "B.C & J.S. Blanthorn. 17.11. 02". Purchased with the assistance of the V&A Purchase Grant Fund and the Art Fund. Distortion of the light reflected from within the 'pebble' causes opalescence.*

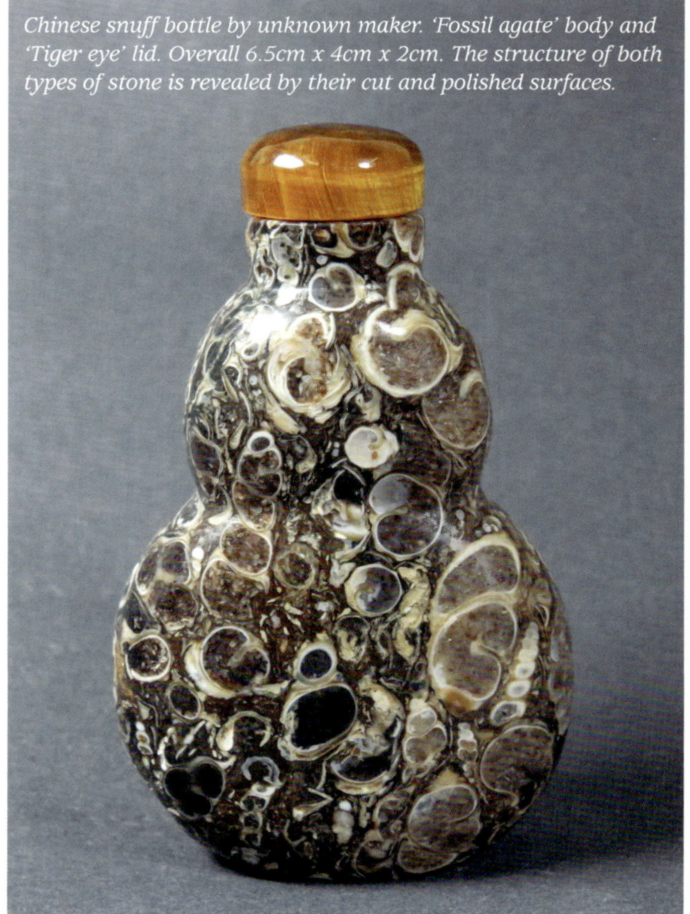

Chinese snuff bottle by unknown maker. 'Fossil agate' body and 'Tiger eye' lid. Overall 6.5cm x 4cm x 2cm. The structure of both types of stone is revealed by their cut and polished surfaces.

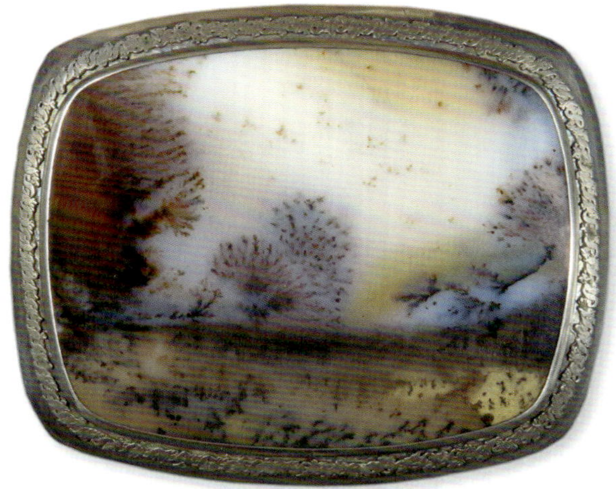

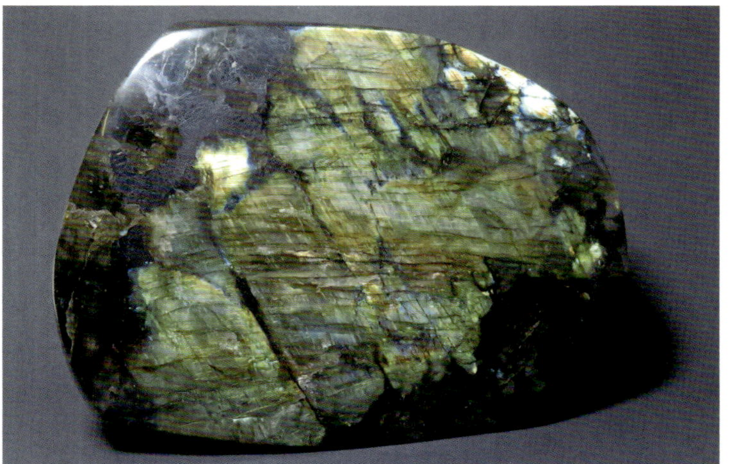

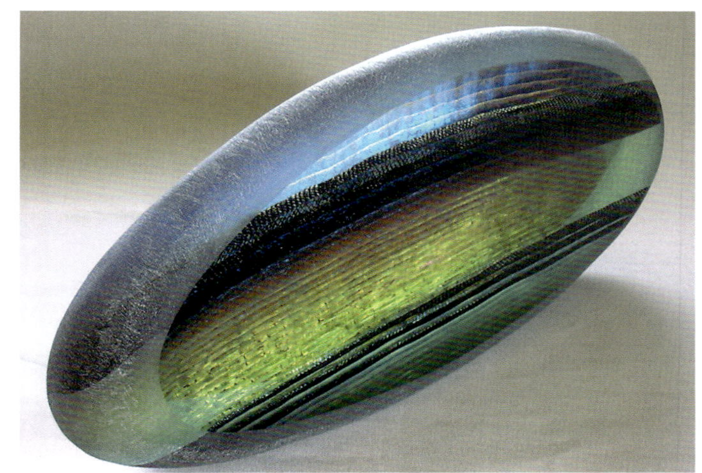

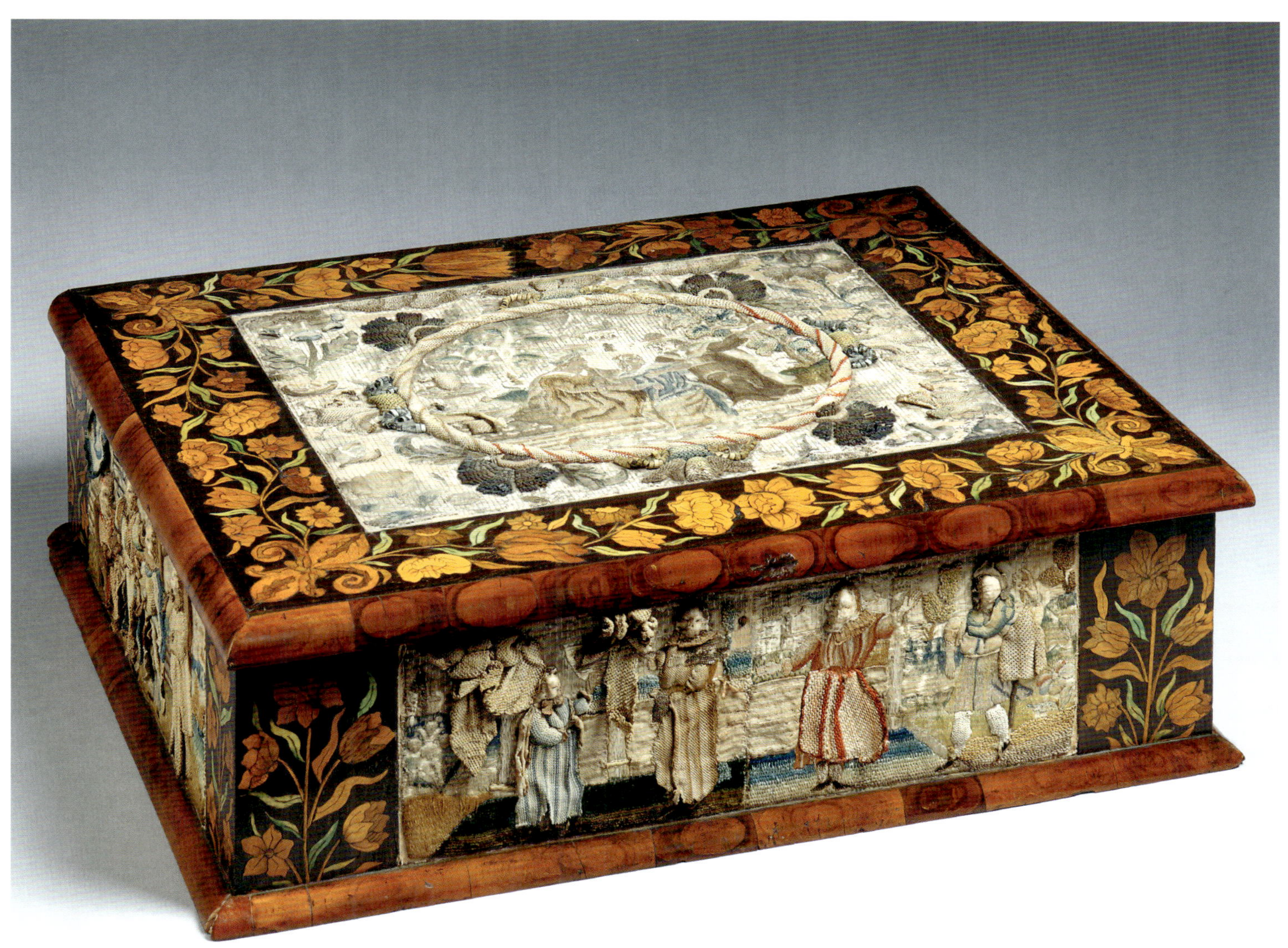

English lady's vanity cabinet, c.1660, decorated with marquetry margins and stump-work (padded and embossed) embroidery panels on the top and sides, outside and inside. 14.8cm x 53.8cm x 40.6cm. The embroideries on the outside of the box have faded but inside they are bright and clean.

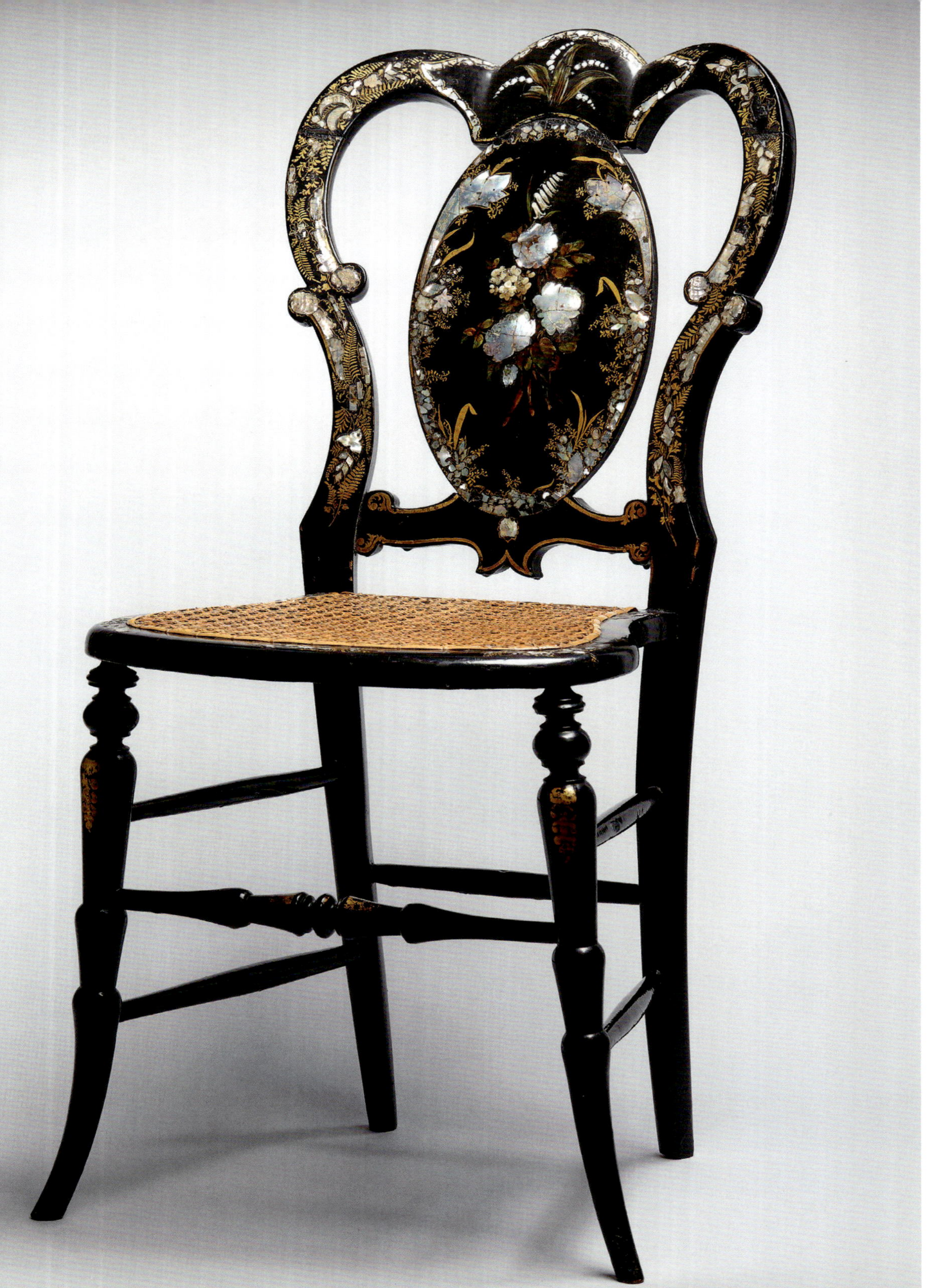

English 'Lady's chair'
made of papier-mâché
with inlaid pearl and painted
decoration, c.1870,
83cm x 38cm x 45cm.

Probably made in Wolverhampton, c.1810.
Domestic tray with raised sides, lacquered with
pseudo-oriental design of tigers, leopards and
flowers in three colours, 11cm x 61cm x 44cm.

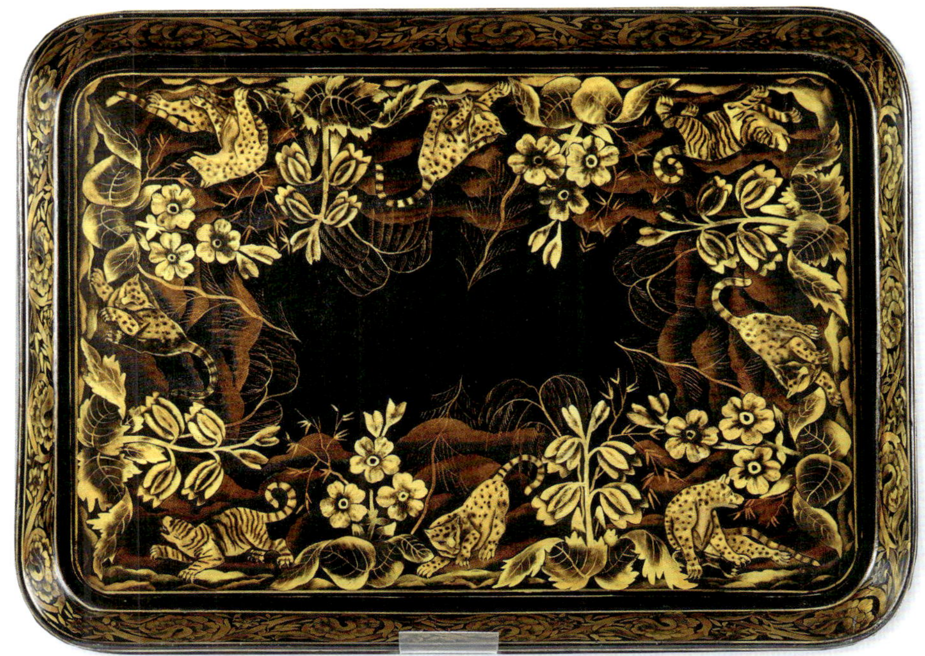

Tea caddy. Papier-mâché. English, late 19th
century. Like the chair opposite, pearl
has been inlaid in the black lacquer
and the whole highly polished, and painted
decoration applied. Such ware was
fashionable while Queen Victoria was in
mourning after the death of Prince Albert.
15cm x 21cm x 14cm.

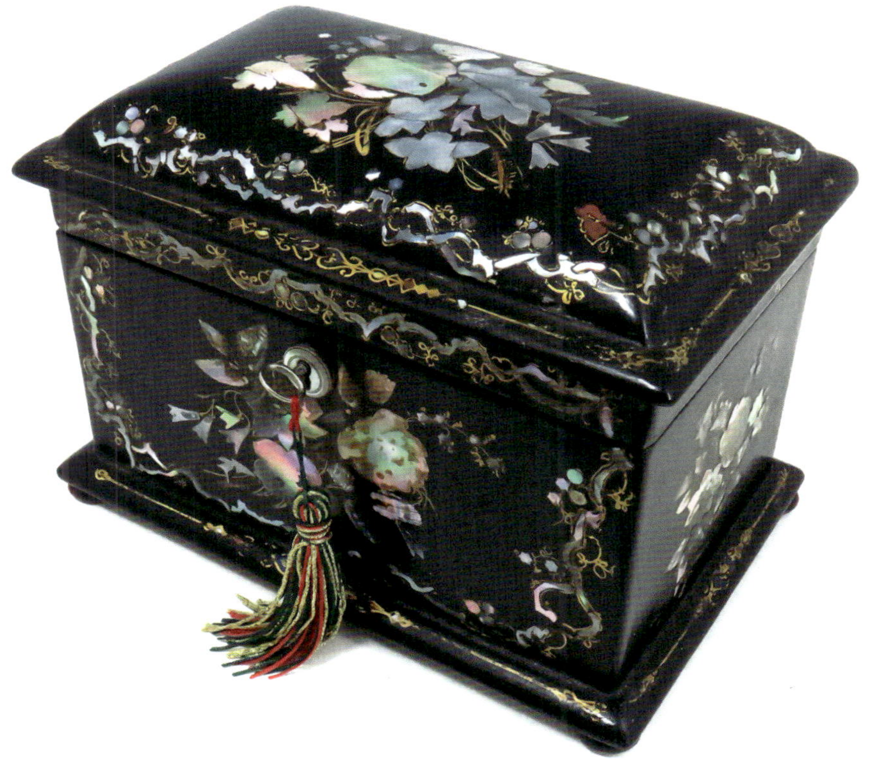

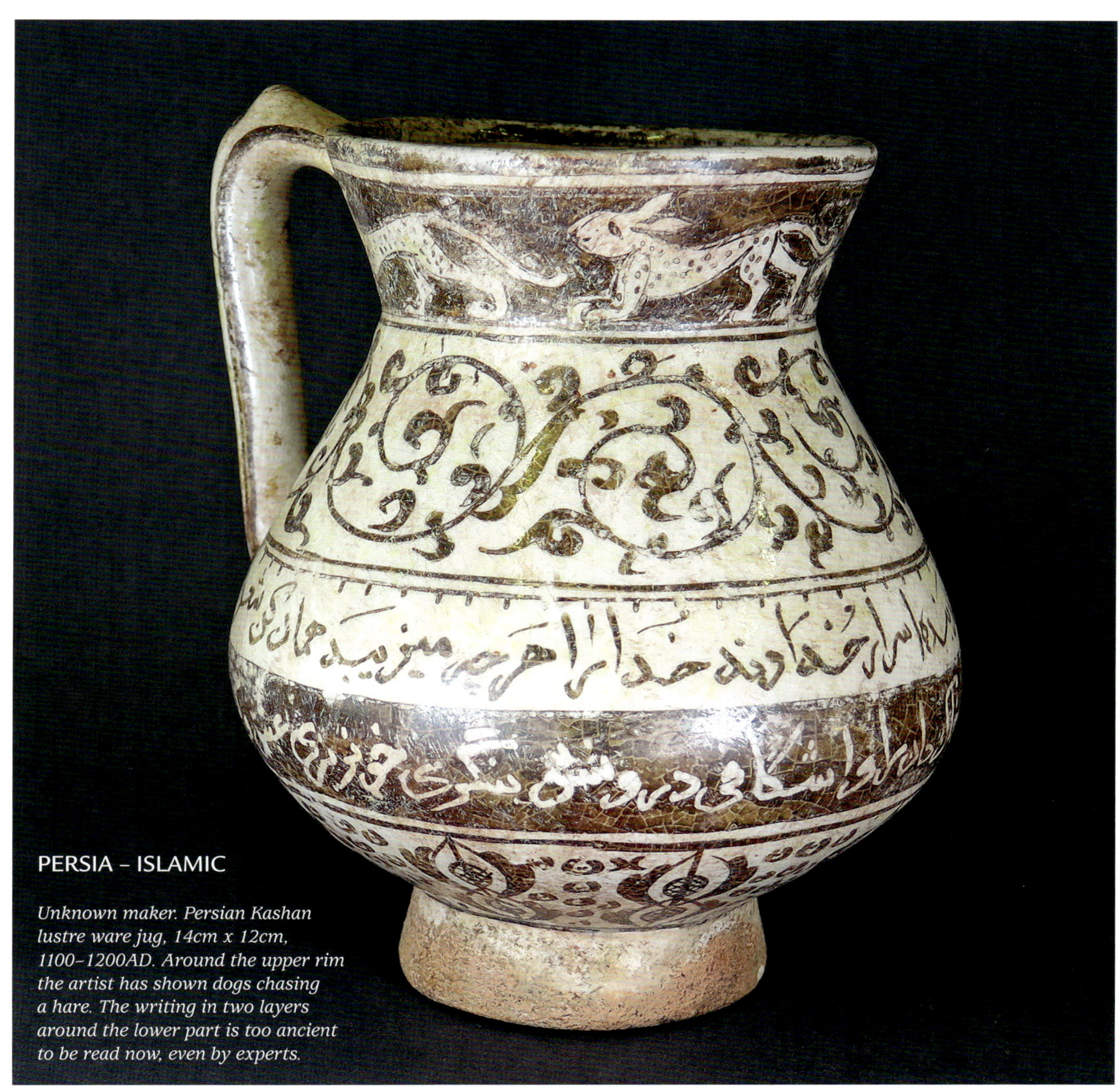

PERSIA – ISLAMIC

Unknown maker. Persian Kashan lustre ware jug, 14cm x 12cm, 1100–1200AD. Around the upper rim the artist has shown dogs chasing a hare. The writing in two layers around the lower part is too ancient to be read now, even by experts.

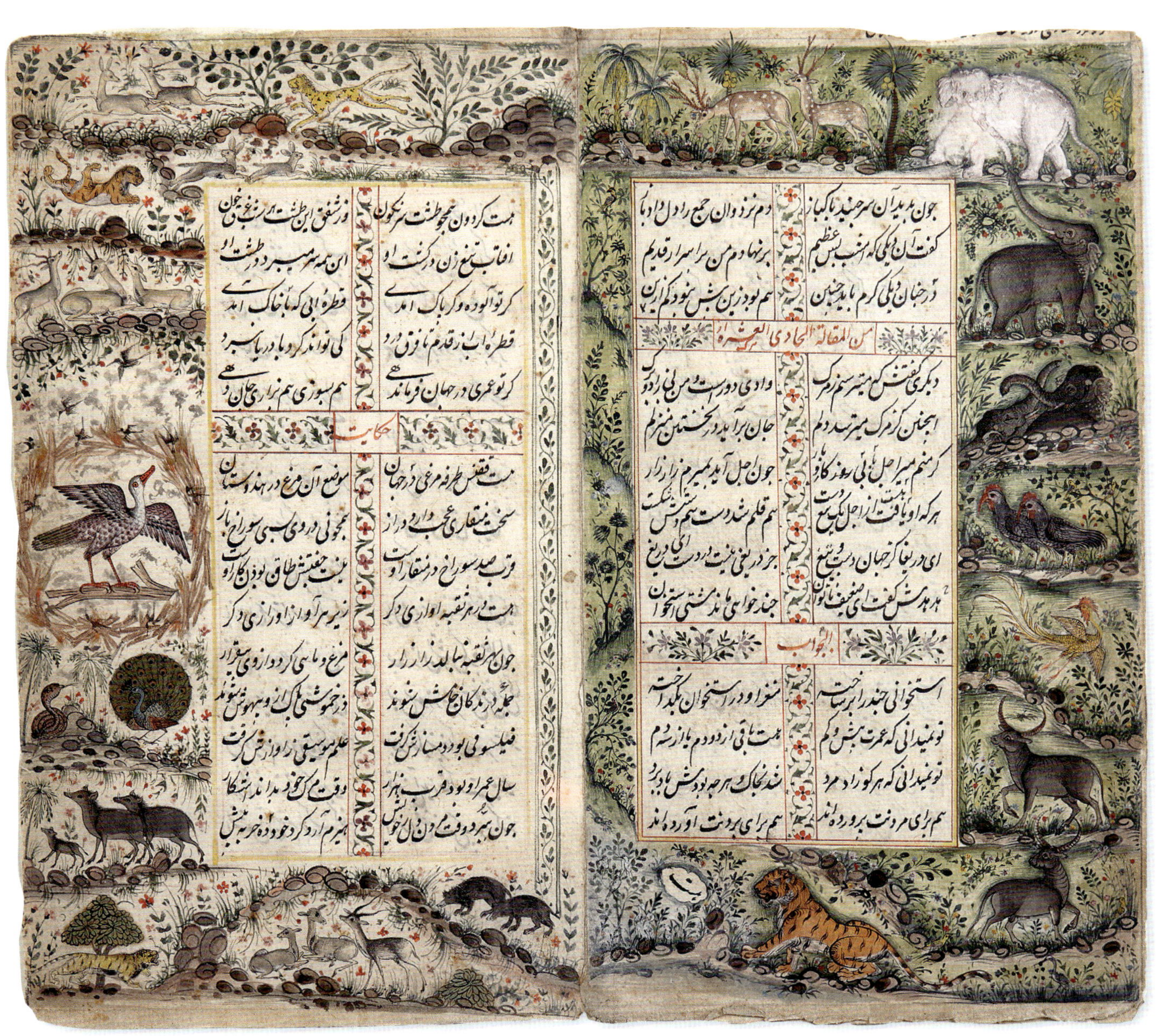

Above: unknown artist, c.1700AD. A Persian poem illustrated by an Indian artist.
Two pages from a book showing a variety of wild animals and birds, 24cm x 26cm. Such pages illustrating nature are scarce.

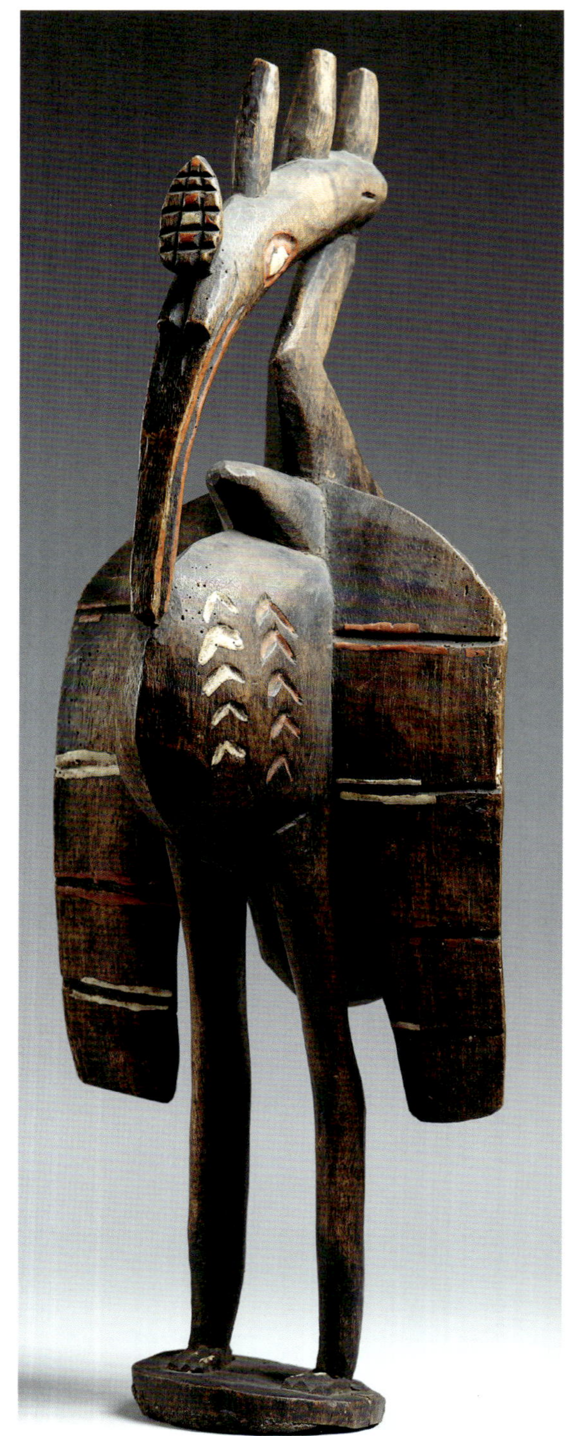

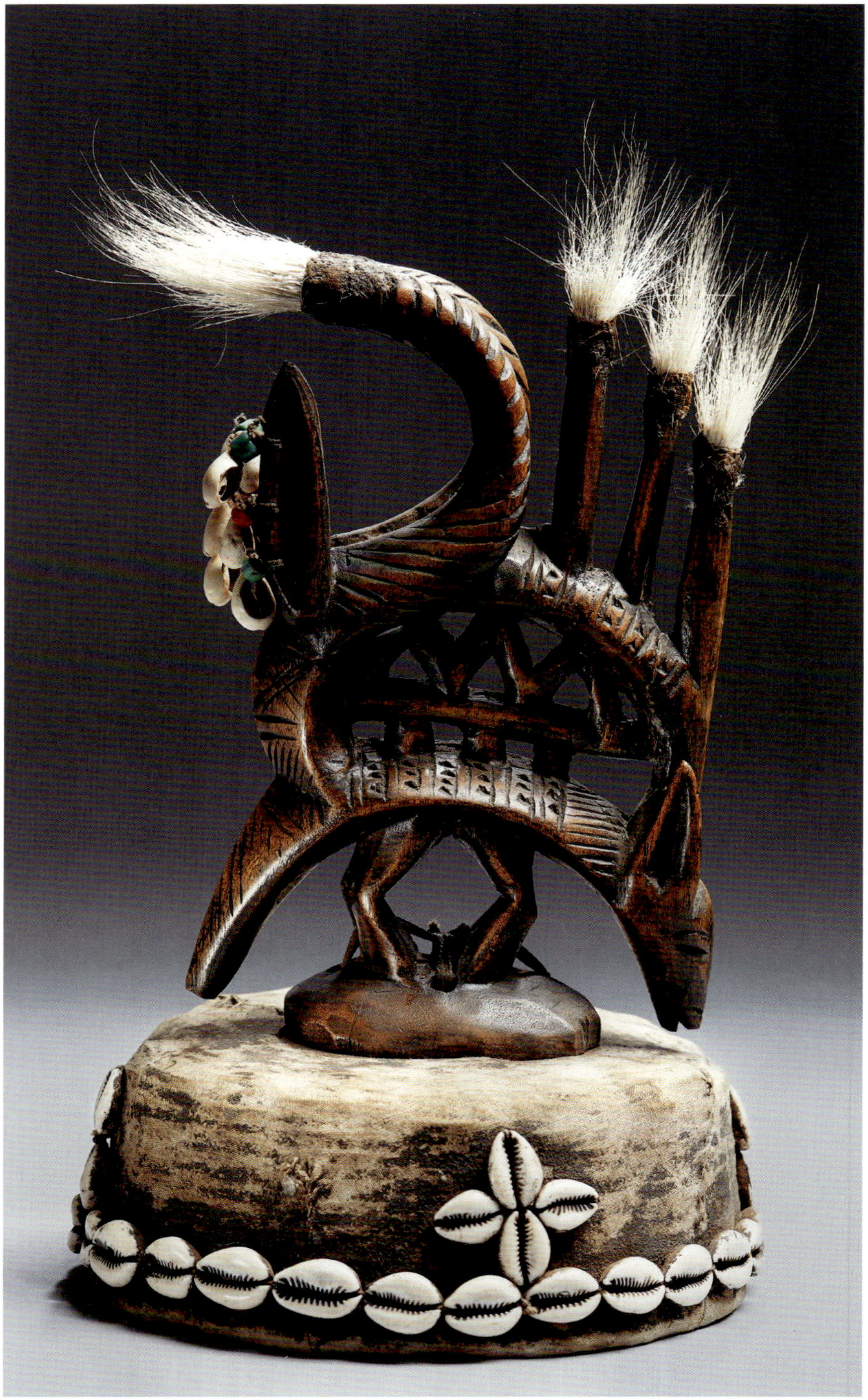

WEST AFRICAN

*Far left: unknown artist, Senufo tribe,
Ivory Coast, Africa, early 20th century.
A pregnant-looking hornbill (bird)
suggests fertility. In spite of its small
base, this was designed to be worn
on the head (as with the object to the
left) in processions around the fields.
56cm x 20cm x 250cm.*

*Left: unknown artist, Chi Wara tribe,
Mali, Africa, early 20th century.
Carved softwood decorated with beads and
feathers, on a canvas hat over a basket
frame, decorated with cowrie shells.
39.5cm x 17cm x 6.5cm.*

AUSTRALIAN ABORIGINAL

*Right: 'Man 2' of the Yulengo
Aboriginals of Arnhem Land,
North Australia, late 20th century.*
Crayfish and 2 Barracuda Fish. *Painted
on the inner side of a sheet of eucalyptus
tree bark. This has been prevented from
curling up by the stick tied tightly to each
end. The pigments used are natural earths.
78.5cm x 31cm x 3cm.*

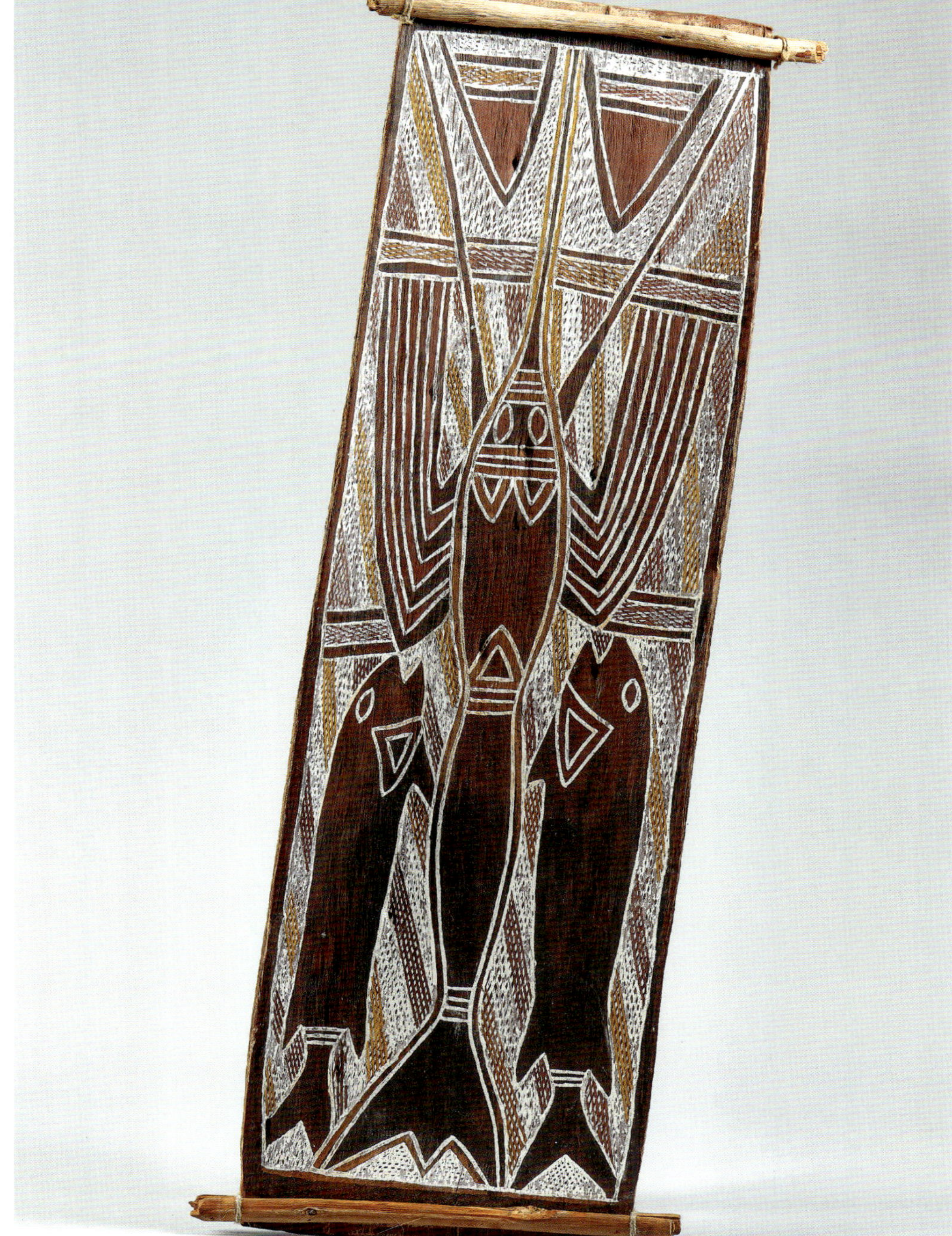

MIDDLE EAST AND ORIENTAL

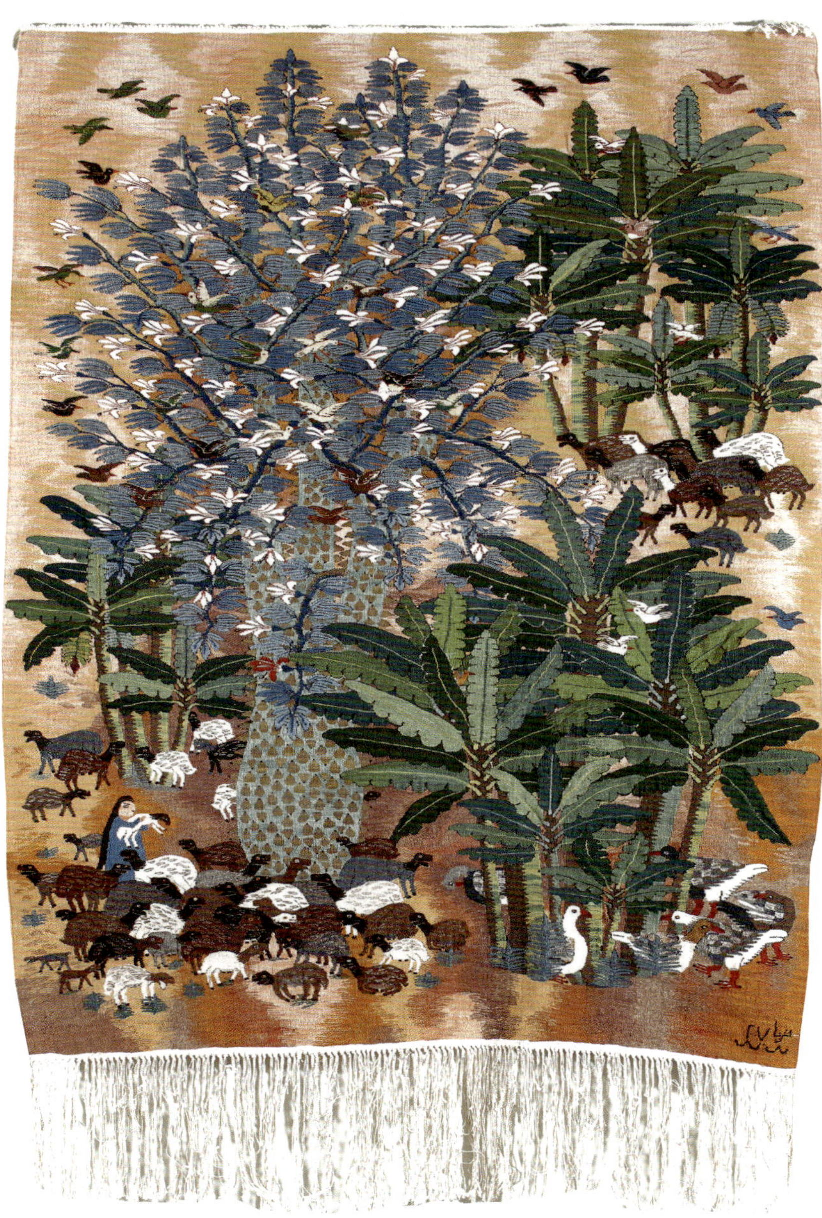

EGYPTIAN TAPESTRY

Soraia Hassan (2009), Egypt. Tapestry, 186cm x 140cm, woven in wool illustrating banana and kapok trees, birds and sheep. Made at the Wissa Wassef Art Centre, Cairo. Signed lower right.

JAPANESE WOODBLOCK PRINTS

The artist for both these prints was the same person (1877-1945), although he changed his name in 1912, as many Japanese artists did in the 19th and early 20th century.

Right: 'Ohara Koson'. **Waxwings.** *Woodblock print, 33.5cm x 18.5cm.*

Far right: 'Shoson' (the artist changed his name in 1912). Carp. Woodblock print, 36.5cm x 23.5cm. The name change is indicated by the different two-character signatures above his red seal (also changed). Carp were thought to symbolise faithfulness and longevity.

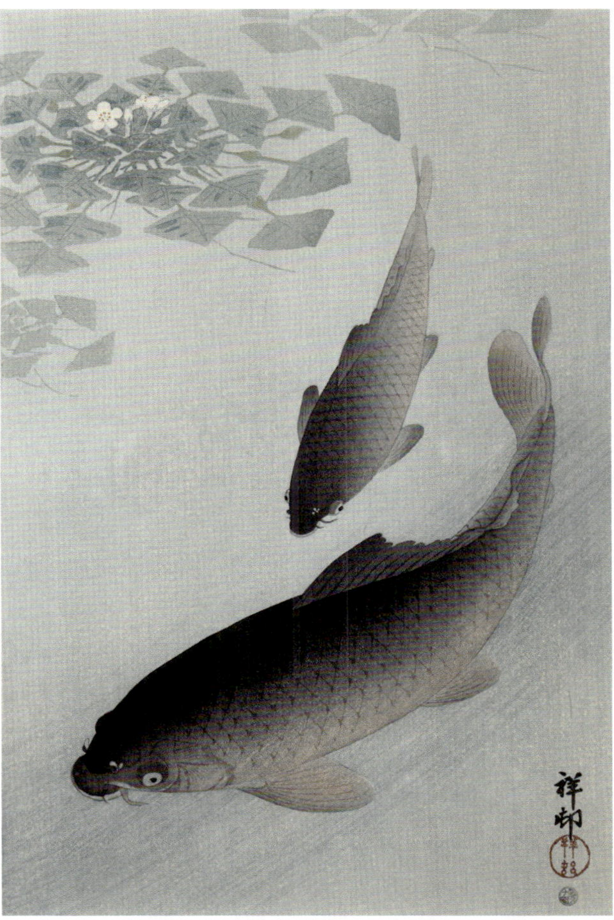

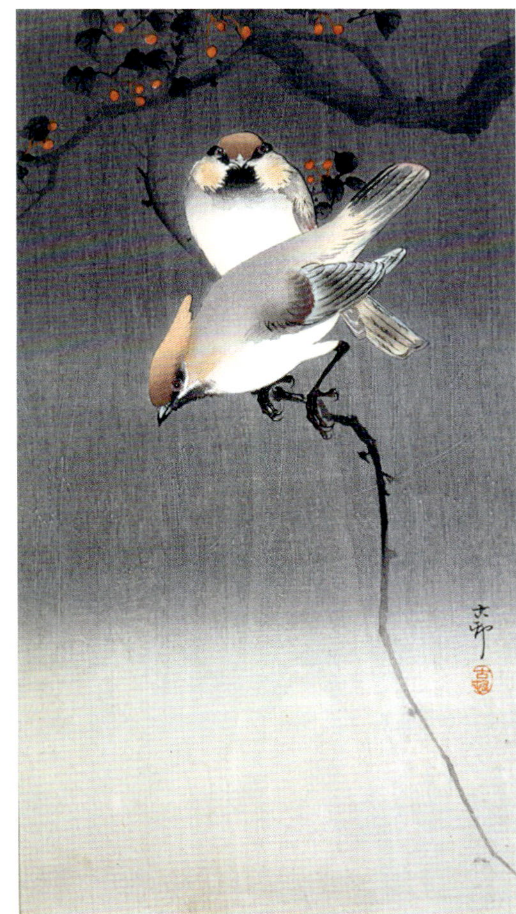

CHINESE SNUFF BOTTLES

Below: Chinese glass snuff bottle painted on the inside showing male and female mandarin ducks. The narrowness of the neck is shown in the left image by the stopper, with its snuff spoon and jade lid, removed from the bottle. 7cm x 4cm x 2.5cm. Dated 1921. The reverse of the bottle (right-hand image) depicts squirrels.

Right: Peking cased (layered) glass snuff bottle. 9cm x 4.5cm x 2.5cm. The red outer layer has been cut away to make the bird, flower and fruit design.

*Far right: **Flowers and Moth** red lacquer Chinese snuff bottle, c.1736-1795. 6.1cm x 3.5cm. The embossed characters on the brass foot (see image between two bottles) read from top to bottom then to the right and then to the left, meaning 'Manufactured in Qianlong period'.*

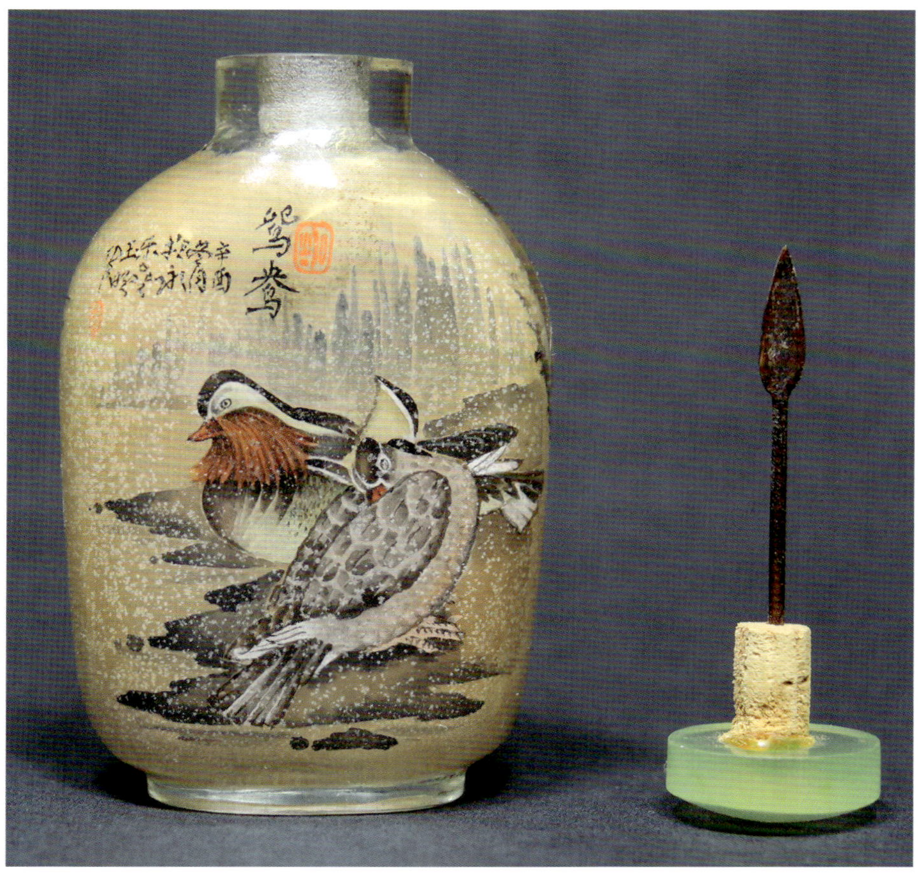

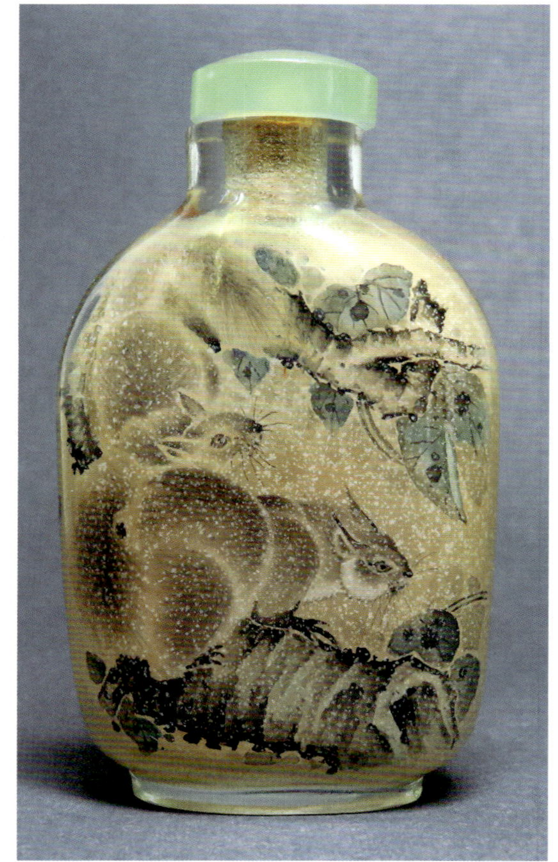

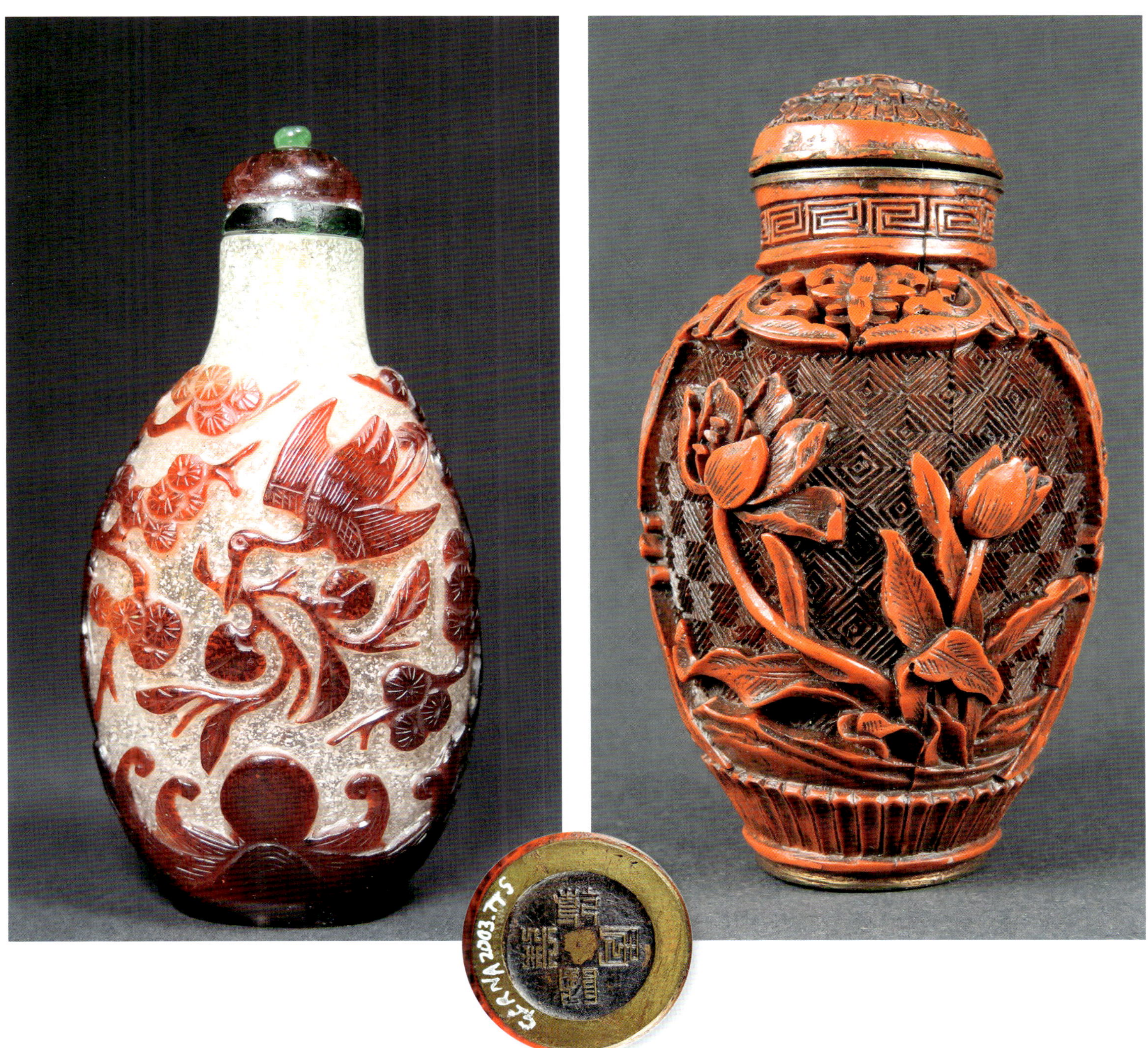

JAPANESE NETSUKE

Netsuke were carved, decorative knobs which prevented, like a button, the cord going through them from slipping from the sash worn around the waist. Such miniature sculptures are popular collector's items.

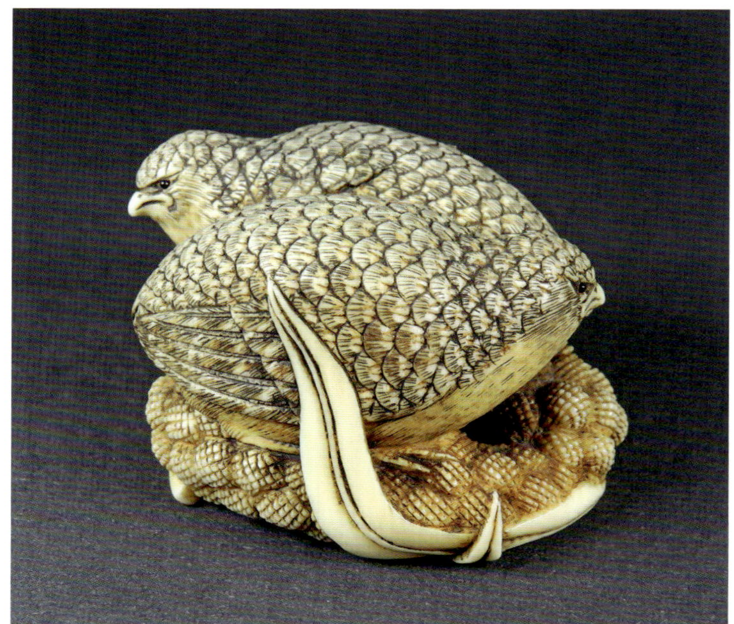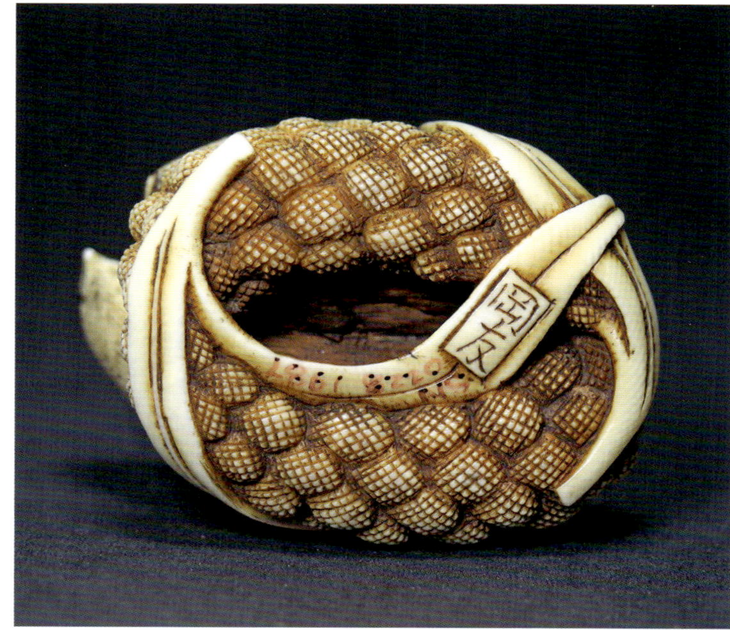

Quail on millet Japanese netsuke, made of ivory with inlaid eyes, late 19th century. 3cm x 3.5cm x 4.3cm.
The underside (above right) shows the maker's name, 'Kanji', carved in Chinese characters.
Netsuke bearing the maker's name are particularly sought after by collectors.

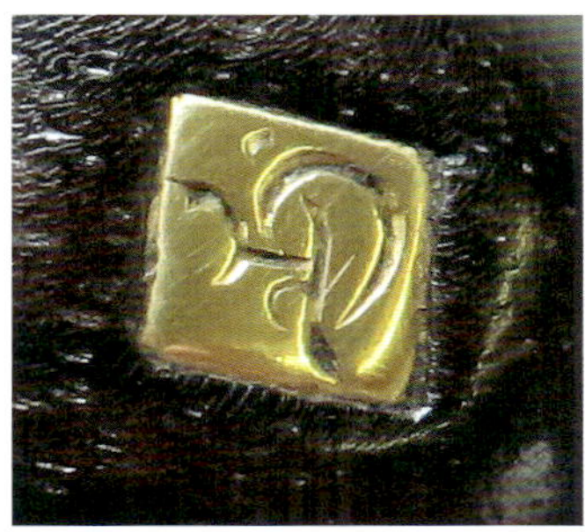

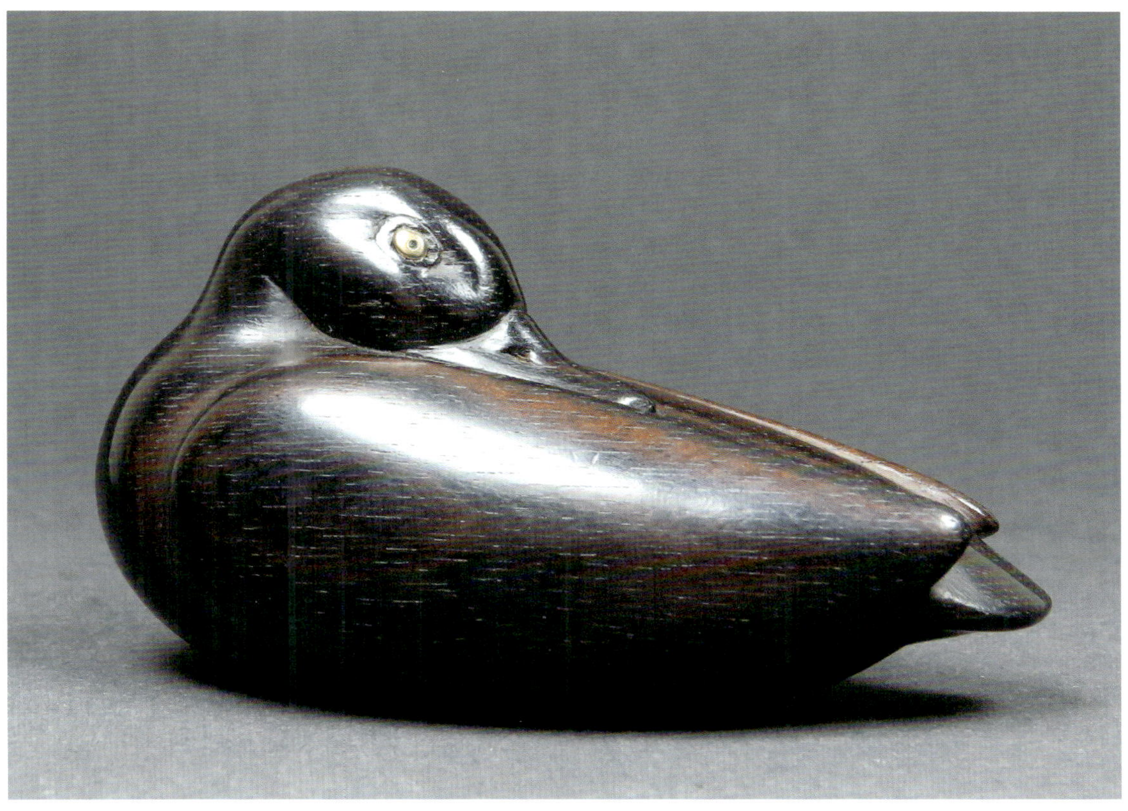

*Duck netsuke made of ebony wood, with inlaid gold eye and maker's signature, 'Kangi',
on a small gold inlay under the tail (top left). 3cm x 3cm x 6cm (as with the images opposite,
shown larger than life size). Very few netsuke were made in ebony.*

JAPANESE CLOISONNÉ

Bottom: Indo Jubei, arguably the most famous Japanese maker.
Goldfish and Carp. *Top-quality cloisonné on silver, late 19th century,*
Japan. 15.6cm x 7.8cm. Signed on the base.

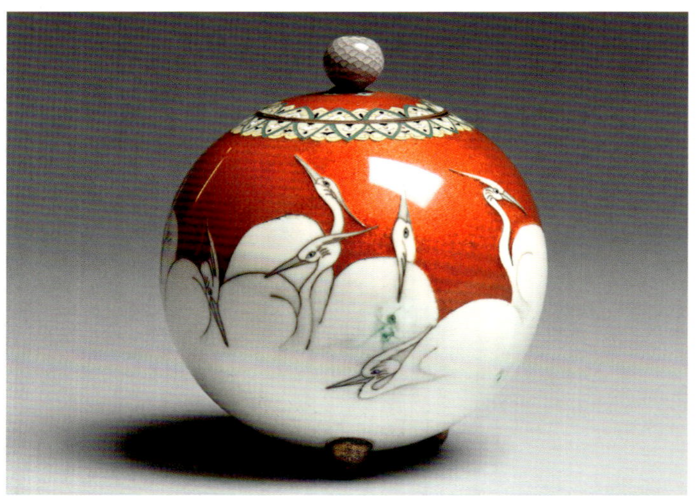

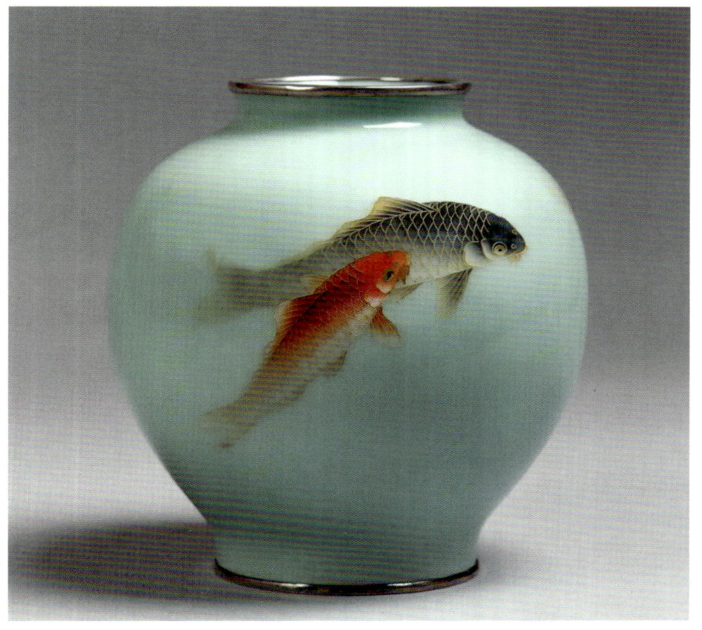

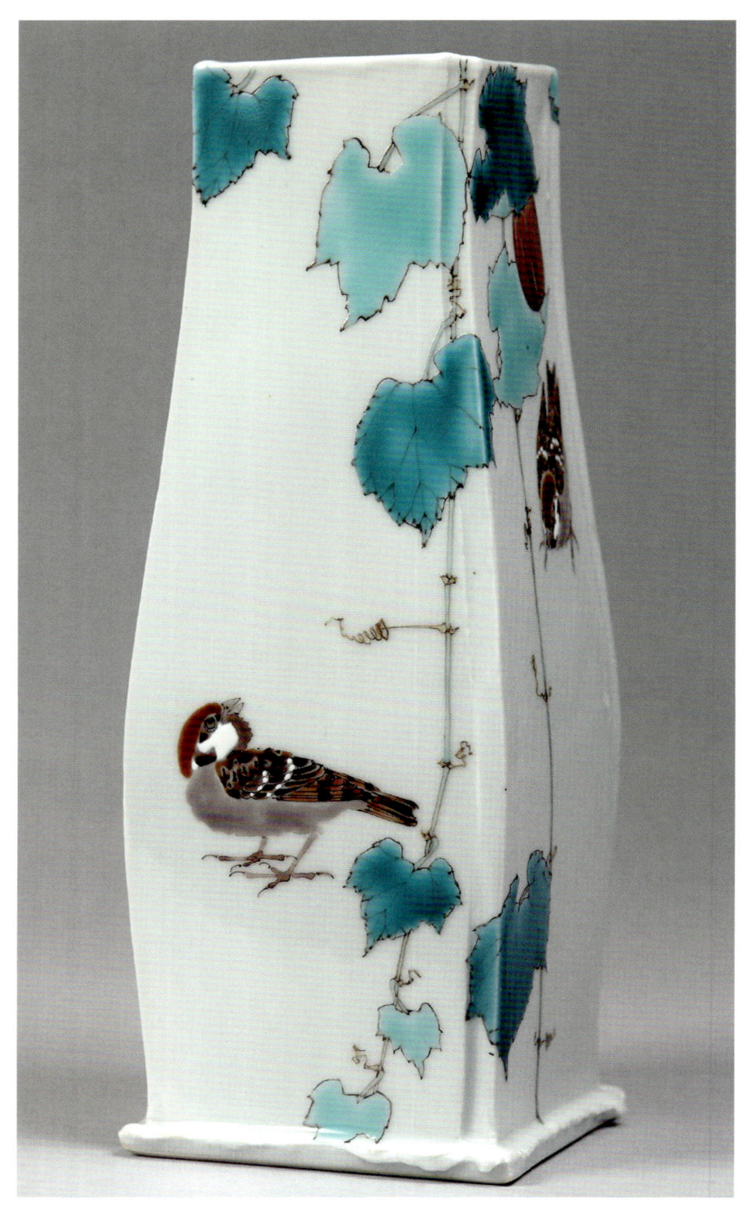

JAPANESE CERAMICS

Above: Jun Takegoshi (1948 –), Japan.
House Sparrows *vase, porcelain.*
26.5cm x 10cm x 10cm.
Purchased with the help of
the MGC/V&A
Purchase Grant Fund.

L'ENVOI – THE SEVEN SEAS (1896)
Rudyard Kipling

When Earth's last picture is painted and the tubes are twisted and dried,
When the oldest colours have faded, and the youngest critic has died,
We shall rest, and faith, we shall need it – lie down for an aeon or two,
Till the Master of All Good Workmen shall put us to work anew.

And those that were good shall be happy; they shall sit in a golden chair;
They shall splash at a ten-league canvas with brushes of comet's hair.
They shall find real saints to draw from – Magdelene, Peter, and Paul;
They shall work for an age at a sitting and never be tired at all!

And only The Master shall praise us, and only The Master shall blame;
And no one shall work for money, and no one shall work for fame,
But each for the joy of the working, and each, in his separate star,
Shall draw the Thing as he sees It for the God of the Things as They are!

ACKNOWLEDGEMENTS

The objects illustrated in this book have been acquired by Nature in Art from many sources over the last thirty years and more. Some were given by the artist. Each represents one or more generous donors. To them all posterity will be very grateful. This book would have been impossible without the huge and conscientious help of Simon Trapnell, Director of Nature in Art. He has provided masses of information, arranged (or taken himself) the digital images and written the short preface. Much of the excellent photography was by The Darkroom UK Ltd and Paul Highnam. Hong Fei Lu has kindly made the translations of Chinese characters. Alan and Marion Marshall of Mascot Media have done an excellent job in designing the book. And, Reader, if you have read thus far, many thanks to you too!

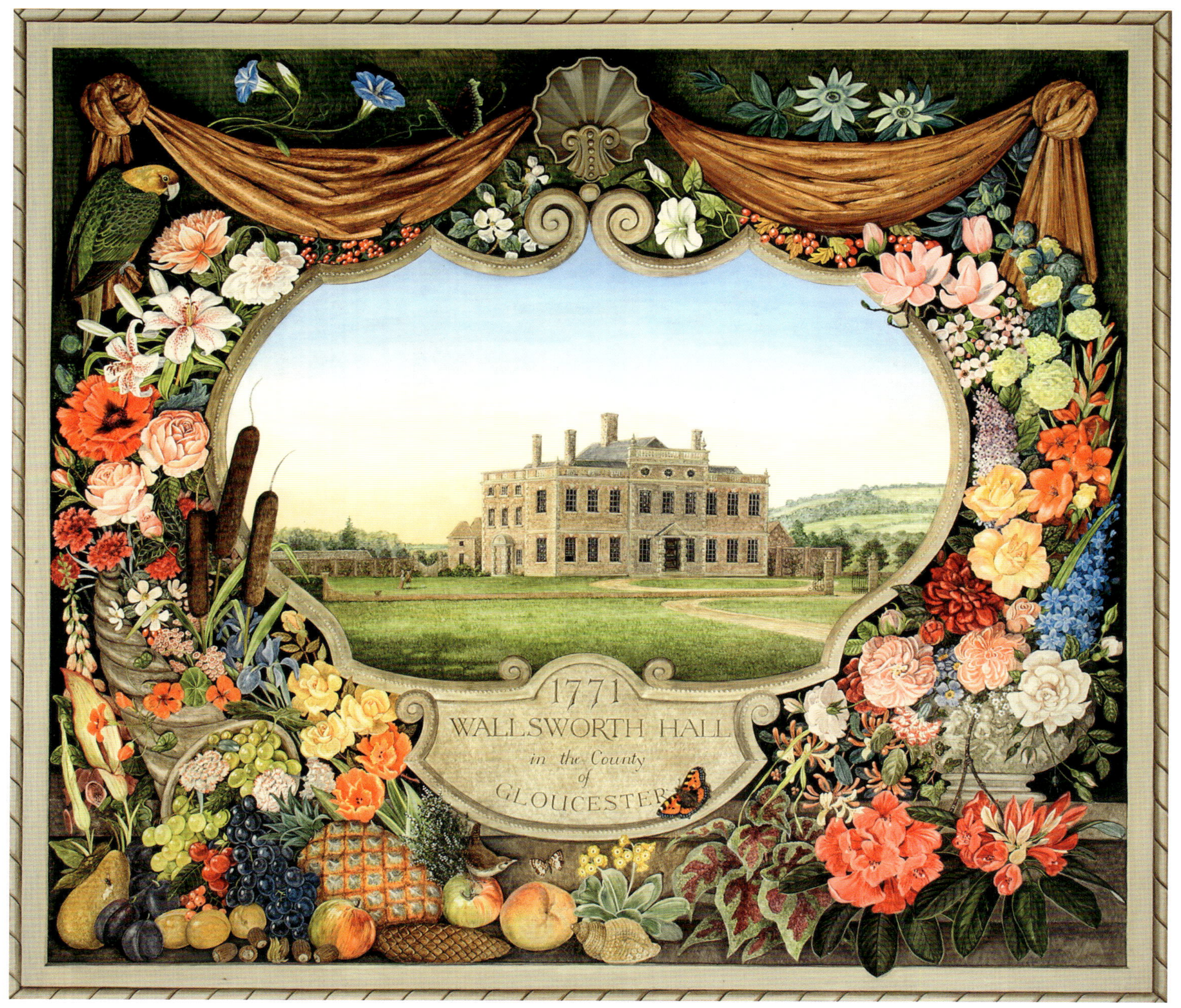

NATURE IN ART

Wallsworth Hall, Twigworth, Gloucester GL2 9PA
www.natureinart.org.uk
Open 10.00–17.00 hours every day except Mondays (other than bank holidays)
Closed 24, 25 and 26 December